ARIZONA TRAILS

NORTHEAST REGION

Cover photos
Clockwise from bottom left: Cinder Hills Loop Trail, The Moggollon Rim Road, Fluted Rock Road

Rear cover photos
Both: Canyon de Chelly Trail

ARIZONA TRAILS

NORTHEAST REGION

PETER MASSEY
JEANNE WILSON
ANGELA TITUS

ADLER
PUBLISHING

Acknowledgements

Many people and organizations have made contributions to the research and production of this book.

Cover Design Concept: **Rudy Ramos**
Text Design and Maps: **Deborah Rust Design**
Copyediting and Proofreading: **Alice Levine, Jody Berman, and Sallie Greenwood**

We would like to thank Kee Long and the staff at the Navajo Film Office; the Navajo Tourist Office; John Largo, Largo Navajoland Tours, Window Rock, Arizona; Carol Ann Ciallella, Staff at many offices of the U.S. Forest Service also provided us with valuable assistance.

The book includes many photos, and we are grateful to the organizations and people who have helped research photographs or allowed us to publish the photographs they have taken

Publisher' s Note: Every effort has been taken to ensure that the information in this book is accurate at press time. Please visit our website to advise us of any changes or corrections you find. We also welcome recommendations for new trails or other suggestions to improve the information in this book.

Adler Publishing Company, Inc.
1601 Pacific Coast Highway, Suite 290
Hermosa Beach, CA 90254
Toll-free: 800-660-5107
Fax: 310-698-0709
4WDbooks.com

Contents

Before You Go

Why a 4WD Does It Better

The design and engineering of 4WD vehicles provide them with many advantages over normal cars when you head off the paved road:

- improved distribution of power to all four wheels;
- a transmission transfer case, which provides low-range gear selection for greater pulling power and for crawling over difficult terrain;
- high ground clearance;
- less overhang of the vehicle's body past the wheels, which provides better front- and rear-clearance when crossing gullies and ridges;
- large-lug, wide-tread tires;
- rugged construction (including underbody skid plates on many models).

If you plan to do off-highway touring, all of these considerations are important whether you are evaluating the capabilities of your current 4WD or are looking to buy one; each is considered in detail in this chapter.

To explore the most difficult trails described in this book, you will need a 4WD vehicle that is well rated in each of the above features. If you own a 2WD sport utility vehicle, a lighter car-type SUV, or a pickup truck, your ability to explore the more difficult trails will depend on conditions and your level of experience.

A word of caution: Whatever type of 4WD vehicle you drive, understand that it is not invincible or indestructible. Nor can it go everywhere. A 4WD has a much higher center of gravity and weighs more than a car, and so has its own consequent limitations.

Experience is the only way to learn what your vehicle can and cannot do. Therefore, if you are inexperienced, we strongly recommend that you start with trails that have lower difficulty ratings. As you develop an understanding of your vehicle and of your own taste for adventure, you can safely tackle the more challenging trails.

One way to beef up your knowledge quickly, while avoiding the costly and sometimes dangerous lessons learned from on-the-road mistakes, is to undertake a 4WD course taught by a professional. Look in the Yellow Pages for courses in your area.

Using This Book

Route Planning

The maps on pages 26 and 27 provide a convenient overview of the trails in the Northeast Region of Arizona. Each 4WD trail is shown, as are major highways and towns, to help you plan various routes by connecting a series of 4WD trails and paved roads.

As you plan your overall route, you will probably want to utilize as many 4WD trails as possible. However, check the difficulty rating and time required for each trail before finalizing your plans. You don't want to be stuck 50 miles from the highway—at sunset and without camping gear, since your trip was supposed to be over hours ago—when you discover that your vehicle can't handle a certain difficult passage.

Difficulty Ratings

We use a point system to rate the difficulty of each trail. Any such system is subjective, and your experience of the trails will vary depending on your skill and the road conditions at the time. Indeed, any amount of rain may make the trails much more difficult, if not completely impassable.

We have rated the 4WD trails on a scale of 1 to 10—1 being passable for a normal passenger vehicle in good conditions and 10 requiring a heavily modified vehicle and an experienced driver who expects to encounter vehicle damage. Because this book is designed for owners of unmodified 4WD vehicles—who we assume do not want to damage their vehicles—most of the trails are rated 5 or lower. A few trails are included that rate as high as 7, while those rated 8 to 10 are beyond the scope of this book.

This is not to say that the moderate-rated trails are easy. We strongly recommend that inexperienced drivers not tackle trails rated at 4 or higher until they have undertaken a number of the lower-rated ones, so that they can gauge their skill level and prepare for the difficulty of the higher-rated trails.

In assessing the trails, we have always assumed good road conditions (dry road surface, good visibility, and so on). The factors influencing our ratings are as follows:

■ obstacles such as rocks, mud, ruts, sand, slickrock, and stream crossings;

■ the stability of the road surface;

■ the width of the road and the vehicle clearance between trees or rocks;

■ the steepness of the road;

■ the margin for driver error (for example, a very high, open shelf road would be rated more difficult even if it was not very steep and had a stable surface).

The following is a guide to the ratings.

Rating 1: The trail is graded dirt but suitable for a normal passenger vehicle. It usually has gentle grades, is fairly wide, and has very shallow water crossings (if any).

Rating 2: High-clearance vehicles are preferred but not necessary. These trails are dirt roads, but they may have rocks, grades, water crossings, or ruts that make clearance a concern in a normal passenger vehicle. The trails are fairly wide, making passing possible at almost any point along the trail. Mud is not a concern under normal weather conditions.

Rating 3: High-clearance 4WDs are preferred, but any high-clearance vehicle is acceptable. Expect a rough road surface; mud and sand are possible but will be easily passable. You may encounter rocks up to 6 inches in diameter, a loose road surface, and shelf roads, though these will be wide enough for passing or will have adequate pull-offs.

Rating 4: High-clearance 4WDs are recommended, though most stock SUVs are acceptable. Expect a rough road surface with rocks larger than 6 inches, but there will be a reasonable driving line available. Patches of mud are possible but can be readily negotiated; sand may be deep and require lower tire pressures. There may be stream crossings up to 12 inches deep, substantial sections of single-lane shelf road, moderate grades, and sections of moderately loose road surface.

Rating 5: High-clearance 4WDs are required. These trails have either a rough, rutted surface, rocks up to 9 inches, mud and deep sand that may be impassable for inexperienced drivers, or stream crossings up to 18 inches deep. Certain sections may be steep enough to cause traction problems, and you may encounter very narrow shelf roads with steep drop-offs and tight clearance between rocks or trees.

Rating 6: These trails are for experienced four-wheel drivers only. They are potentially dangerous, with large rocks, ruts, or terraces that may need to be negotiated. They may also have stream crossings at least 18 inches deep, involve rapid currents, unstable stream bottoms, or difficult access; steep slopes, loose surfaces, and narrow clearances; or very narrow sections of shelf road with steep drop-offs and possibly challenging road surfaces.

Rating 7: Skilled, experienced four-wheel drivers only. These trails include very challenging sections with extremely steep grades, loose surfaces, large rocks, deep ruts, and/or tight clearances. Mud or sand may necessitate winching.

Rating 8 and above: Stock vehicles are likely to be damaged, and drivers may find the trail impassable. Highly skilled, experienced four-wheel drivers only.

Scenic Ratings

If rating the degree of difficulty is subjective, rating scenic beauty is guaranteed to lead to arguments. The Northeast Region of Arizona contains a spectacular variety of scenery. Despite the subjectivity of attempting a comparative rating of diverse scenery, we have tried to provide a guide to the relative scenic quality of the various trails. The ratings are based on a scale of 1 to 10, with 10 being the most attractive.

Remoteness Ratings

Many trails in this region are in remote mountain or desert country; sometimes the trails are seldom traveled, and the likelihood is low that another vehicle will appear within a reasonable time to assist you if you get stuck or break down. We have included a ranking for remoteness of +0 through +2. Extreme summer temperatures can make a breakdown in the more remote areas a life-threatening experience. Prepare carefully before tackling the higher-rated, more remote trails (see Special Preparations for Remote Travel, page 11). For trails with a high remoteness rating, consider traveling with a second vehicle.

Estimated Driving Times

In calculating driving times, we have not allowed for stops. Your actual driving time may be considerably longer depending on the number and duration of the stops you make. Add more time if you prefer to drive more slowly than good conditions allow.

Current Road Information

All the 4WD trails described in this book may become impassable in poor weather conditions. Storms can alter roads, remove tracks, and create impassable washes. Most of the trails described, even easy 2WD trails, can quickly become impassable even to 4WD vehicles after only a small amount of rain. For each trail, we have provided a phone number for obtaining current information about conditions.

Abbreviations

The route directions for the 4WD trails use a series of abbreviations as follows:

SO	CONTINUE STRAIGHT ON
TL	TURN LEFT
TR	TURN RIGHT
BL	BEAR LEFT
BR	BEAR RIGHT
UT	U-TURN

Using Route Directions

For every trail, we describe and pinpoint (by odometer reading) nearly every significant feature along the route—such as intersections, streams, washes, gates, cattle guards, and so on—and provide directions from these landmarks. Odometer readings will vary from vehicle to vehicle, so you should allow for slight variations. Be aware that trails can quickly change in the desert. A new trail may be cut around a washout, a faint trail can be graded by the county, or a well-used trail may fall into disuse. All these factors will affect the accuracy of the given directions.

If you diverge from the route, zero your trip meter upon your return and continue along the route, making the necessary adjustment to the point-to-point odometer readings. In the directions, we regularly reset the odometer readings—at significant landmarks or popular lookouts and spur trails—so that you won't have to recalculate for too long.

Most of the trails can be started from either end, and the route directions include both directions of travel; reverse directions are printed in gold below the main directions. When traveling in reverse, read from the bottom of the table and work up.

Route directions include cross-references whenever two 4WD trails included in this book connect; these cross-references allow for an easy change of route or destination.

Each trail includes periodic latitude and longitude readings to facilitate using a global positioning system (GPS) receiver. These readings may also assist you in finding your location on the maps. The GPS coordinates are given in the format dd°mm.mm'. To save time when loading coordinates into your GPS receiver, you may wish to include only one decimal place, since in Arizona, the first decimal place equals about 165 yards and the second only about 16 yards.

Map References

We recommend that you supplement the information in this book with more-detailed maps. For each trail, we list the sheet maps and road atlases that provide the best detail for the area. Typically, the following references are given:

- Bureau of Land Management Maps
- U.S. Forest Service Maps
- *Arizona Atlas & Gazetteer,* 6th ed. (Freeport, Maine: DeLorme Mapping, 2004)—Scale 1:250,000
- *Arizona Road & Recreation Atlas,* 5th ed. (Medford, Oregon: Benchmark Maps, 2004)—Scale 1:400,000
- Maptech-Terrain Navigator Topo Maps—Scale 1:100,000 and 1:24,000
- *Trails Illustrated* Topo Maps; National Geographic Maps—Various scales, but all contain good detail
- Recreational Map of Arizona (Canon City, Colorado: GRT Mapping, 2006)—Scale: 1 inch=12.5 miles

We recommend the *Trails Illustrated* series of maps as the best for navigating these trails. They are reliable, easy to read, and printed on nearly indestructible plastic paper. However, this series covers only a few of the 4WD trails described in this book.

The DeLorme Atlas has the advantage of providing you with maps of the state at a reasonable price. Although its 4WD trail information doesn't go beyond what we pro-

vide, it is useful if you wish to explore the hundreds of side roads.

The *Arizona Road & Recreation Atlas* provides two types of maps for each part of the state. The landscape maps show changes in terrain and elevation while the public lands maps show what organizations control what lands. Aside from the maps, the atlas also provides a good recreation guide with a number of local contacts for different recreation opportunities.

U.S. Forest Service maps lack the topographic detail of the other sheet maps and, in our experience, are occasionally out of date. They have the advantage of covering a broad area and are useful in identifying land use and travel restrictions. These maps are most useful for the longer trails.

In our opinion, the best single option by far is the Terrain Navigator series of maps published on CD-ROM by Maptech. These CD-ROMs contain an amazing level of detail because they include the entire set of 1,941 U.S. Geological Survey topographical maps of Arizona at the 1:24,000 scale and all 71 maps at the 1:100,000 scale. These maps offer many advantages over normal maps:

- GPS coordinates for any location can be found and loaded into your GPS receiver. Conversely, if you have your GPS coordinates, your location on the map can be pinpointed instantly.
- Towns, rivers, passes, mountains, and many other sites are indexed by name so that they can be located quickly.
- 4WD trails can be marked and profiled for elevation changes and distances from point to point.
- Customized maps can be printed out.

Maptech uses eight CD-ROMs to cover the entire state of Arizona; they can be purchased individually or as part of a two-state package at a heavily discounted price. The CD-ROMs can be used with a laptop computer and a GPS receiver in your vehicle to monitor your location on the map and navigate directly from the display.

All these maps should be available through good map stores. The Maptech

CD-ROMs are available directly from the company (800-627-7236, or on the internet at www.maptech.com).

Backcountry Driving Rules and Permits

Four-wheel driving involves special driving techniques and road rules. This section is an introduction for 4WD beginners.

4WD Road Rules

To help ensure that these trails remain open and available for all four-wheel drivers to enjoy, it is important to minimize your impact on the environment and not be a safety risk to yourself or anyone else. Remember that the 4WD clubs in Arizona fight a constant battle with the government and various lobby groups to retain the access that currently exists.

The fundamental rule when traversing the 4WD trails described in this book is to use common sense. In addition, special road rules for 4WD trails apply:

■ Vehicles traveling uphill have the right of way.

■ If you are moving more slowly than the vehicle behind you, pull over to let the other vehicle by.

■ Park out of the way in a safe place. Blocking a track may restrict access for emergency vehicles as well as for other recreationalists. Set the parking brake—don't rely on leaving the transmission in park. Manual transmissions should be left in the lowest gear.

Tread Lightly!

Remember the rules of the Tread Lightly! program:

■ Be informed. Obtain maps, regulations, and other information from the forest service or from other public land agencies. Learn the rules and follow them.

■ Resist the urge to pioneer a new road or trail or to cut across a switchback. Stay on constructed tracks and avoid running over young trees, shrubs, and grasses, damaging or killing them. Don't drive across alpine tundra; this fragile environment can take years to recover.

■ Stay off soft, wet roads and 4WD trails readily torn up by vehicles. Repairing the damage is expensive, and quite often authorities find it easier to close the road rather than repair it.

■ Avoid meadows, steep hillsides, stream banks, and lake shores that are easily scarred by churning wheels.

■ Stay away from wild animals that are rearing young or suffering from a food shortage. Do not camp close to water sources of domestic or wild animals.

■ Obey gate closures and regulatory signs.

■ Preserve America's heritage by not disturbing old mining camps, ghost towns, or other historical features. Leave historic sites, Native American rock art, ruins, and artifacts in place and untouched.

■ Carry out all your trash, and even that of others.

■ Stay out of designated wilderness areas. They are closed to all vehicles. It is your responsibility to know where the boundaries are.

■ Get permission to cross private land. Leave livestock alone. Respect landowners' rights.

Report violations of these rules to help keep these 4WD trails open and to ensure that others will have the opportunity to visit these backcountry sites. Many groups are actively seeking to close these public lands to vehicles, thereby denying access to those who are unable, or perhaps merely unwilling, to hike long distances. This magnificent countryside is owned by, and should be available to, all Americans.

Special Preparations for Remote Travel

Due to the remoteness of some areas in Arizona and the very high summer temperatures, you should take some special precautions to ensure that you don't end up in a life-threatening situation:

■ When planning a trip into the desert, always inform someone as to where you are going, your route, and when you expect to return. Stick to your plan.

■ Carry and drink at least one gallon of water per person per day of your trip. (Plastic gallon jugs are handy and portable.)

■ Be sure your vehicle is in good condition with a sound battery, good hoses, spare tire, spare fan belts, necessary tools, and reserve gasoline and oil. Other spare parts and extra radiator water are also valuable. If traveling in pairs, share the common spares and carry a greater variety.

■ Keep an eye on the sky. Flash floods can occur in a wash any time you see thunderheads—even when it's not raining a drop where you are.

■ If you are caught in a dust storm while driving, get off the road and turn off your lights. Turn on the emergency flashers and back into the wind to reduce windshield pitting by sand particles.

■ Test trails on foot before driving through washes and sandy areas. One minute of walking may save hours of hard work getting your vehicle unstuck.

■ If your vehicle breaks down, stay near it. Your emergency supplies are there. Your car has many other items useful in an emergency. Raise your hood and trunk lid to denote "help needed." Remember, a vehicle can be seen for miles, but a person on foot is very difficult to spot from a distance.

■ When you're not moving, use available shade or erect shade from tarps, blankets, or seat covers—anything to reduce the direct rays of the sun.

■ Do not sit or lie directly on the ground. It may be 30 degrees hotter than the air.

■ Leave a disabled vehicle only if you are positive of the route and the distance to help. Leave a note for rescuers that gives the time you left and the direction you are taking.

■ If you must walk, rest for at least 10 minutes out of each hour. If you are not normally physically active, rest up to 30 minutes out of each hour. Find shade, sit down, and prop up your feet. Adjust your shoes and socks, but do not remove your shoes—you may not be able to get them back on swollen feet.

■ If you have water, drink it. Do not ration it.

■ If water is limited, keep your mouth closed. Do not talk, eat, smoke, drink alcohol, or take salt.

■ Keep your clothing on despite the heat. It helps to keep your body temperature down and reduces your body's dehydration rate. Cover your head. If you don't have a hat, improvise a head covering.

■ If you are stalled or lost, set signal fires. Set smoky fires in the daytime and bright ones at night. Three fires in a triangle denote "help needed."

■ A roadway is a sign of civilization. If you find a road, stay on it.

■ When hiking in the desert, equip each person, especially children, with a police-type whistle. It makes a distinctive noise with little effort. Three blasts denote "help needed."

■ To avoid poisonous creatures, put your hands or feet only where your eyes can see. One insect to be aware of in Northeast Arizona is the Africanized honeybee. Though indistinguishable from its European counterpart, these bees are far more aggressive and can be a threat. They have been known to give chase of up to a mile and even wait for people who have escaped into the water to come up for air. The best thing to do if attacked is to cover your face and head with clothing and run to the nearest enclosed shelter. Keep an eye on your pet if you notice a number of bees in the area, as many have been killed by Africanized honeybees.

■ Avoid unnecessary contact with wildlife. Some mice in Arizona carry the deadly hantavirus, a pulmonary syndrome fatal in 60 to 70 percent of human cases. Fortunately the disease is very rare—by May 2006, only 46 cases had been reported in Arizona and 438 nationwide—but caution is still advised. Other rodents may transmit bubonic plague, the same epidemic that killed one-third of Europe's population in the 1300s. Be especially wary near sick animals and keep pets, especially cats, away from wildlife and their fleas. Another creature to watch for is the western black-legged tick, the carrier of Lyme disease. Wearing clothing that covers legs and arms, tucking pants into boots, and using insect repellent are good ways to avoid fleas and ticks.

Special Note on Travel Near the Mexican Border

Arizona's long southern border forms part of the international boundary with Mexico. This location can bring with it its own unique set of potential situations that the intrepid traveler may encounter. Every month, thousands of undocumented aliens attempt to gain unauthorized entry into the United States from Mexico. In recent years, the U.S. Border Patrol, which is responsible for monitoring the international boundary, has stepped up surveillance in Texas and California, resulting in more people attempting the more difficult and dangerous crossings into the United States through Arizona.

Apprehensions from the region around the Organ Pipe Cactus National Monument, to give one typical example, have nearly tripled, from 8,000 in 1998 to more than 21,000 in 1999. Apprehensions reported through Wellton, which covers El Camino del Diablo, increased by 142 percent during the first three months of 2000. Other hotspots report similar figures. It is estimated that approximately 70 percent of all border jumpers will be apprehended and returned to Mexico immediately.

What does this mean for you? Any remote area traveler who spends any time at all in the desert of southern Arizona is highly likely to encounter undocumented aliens. First and foremost, it should be stressed that the vast majority of meetings pose absolutely no threat to the traveler at all. You are most likely to meet people just like you who want little more than food and water before they move on, leaving you alone. However, many people find these meetings worrisome and upsetting, and some even feel threatened.

It is suggested that travelers adopt the following guidelines compiled from advice given by the U.S. Border Patrol:

■ If possible, avoid all contact with suspected undocumented alien activity. Do not go out of your way to offer unsolicited assistance.

■ If it is impossible to avoid contact—for example, if you are approached and asked for help—then stop. Remain in your vehicle. Most of the time you will be asked for food and water. Give them what you can safely spare without running your own supplies dangerously low and move on as soon as possible. This is not seen by the border patrol as aiding and abetting; it is humanitarian aid and you may be saving another human being's life. Many people die each year trying to cross the desert.

■ Do not give anyone a lift in your vehicle unless you can see it is a life-threatening situation.

■ As soon as is practical, notify the border patrol or sheriff's department of the location, number, and physical condition of the group so that they can be apprehended as soon as possible. Be as specific as you can; GPS coordinates are extremely useful. Again, by doing this you may be saving someone's life.

■ Do not attempt to engage people in conversation and avoid giving exact distances to the nearest town. Many undocumented aliens arrive in the United States by paying a "coyote" to bring them safely across the border. They are often deliberately misled and woefully unprepared for the desert conditions they encounter and the distances they will have to travel to safety. Giving exact distances, especially if it is many miles away, is putting yourself and your vehicle at risk. Carjackings are *extremely rare,* but the possibility should not be discounted.

■ Be extremely wary of groups traveling in vehicles, as these are the professionals who smuggle both humans and drugs. However, fewer than 5 percent of encounters are with smugglers; most are with individuals or groups after the "coyotes" have dropped them off.

■ If you are traveling exceptionally remote routes in areas of high activity, consider traveling as part of a large group. Individual vehicles and small groups stand a higher chance of being approached.

■ Always lock your vehicle when you leave it, even for a short period of time, and carry as few valuables as possible.

■ The distance from the border is not the determining factor in how likely you are to have an encounter.

■ Finally, do not let this be a deterrent to exploring the wonderful trails to be found in Arizona. Be alert and aware but not paranoid. Many thousands of recreationalists travel these trails every year with very little danger to themselves or their vehicles.

Obtaining Permits

Backcountry permits, which usually cost a fee, are required for certain activities on public lands in Arizona, whether the area is a national park, state park, national monument, Indian reservation, or BLM land.

Restrictions may require a permit for all overnight stays, which can include backpacking and 4WD or bicycle camping. Permits may also be required for day use by vehicles, horses, hikers, or bikes in some areas.

When possible, we include information about fees and permit requirements and where permits may be obtained, but these regulations change constantly. If in doubt, check with the most likely governing agency.

Travel Etiquette on Indian Lands

When traveling on Indian lands, the first and foremost rule is to respect the land and its owners. When driving, obey all road signs. If you leave your vehicle to explore a certain area, first make sure that you are allowed on that land. Be gentle with the land and its artifacts as you walk around, resisting the urge to take a "souvenir;" it is illegal to remove artifacts from federal land.

If you wish to take pictures of Native Americans, make sure to obtain their permission first. The Hopi, for example, will not allow you to photograph or sketch them. If you visit an Indian monument, guides will often allow their pictures to be taken. A small gratuity is customary.

When you approach a village, get permission from the village leader before entering. Remember that hogans (traditional mud-covered dwellings) are someone's home, not a tourist attraction. Do not walk up to the hogan without first being invited.

Firearms and alcoholic beverages are both stricly prohibited in the Navajo Nation.

Finally, if you are lucky enough to see a Hopi or Navajo ceremony, remember to act with the utmost respect. Do not photograph, sketch, record, or take notes of the ceremony. Stand quietly in the back, without applauding, so as to avoid interfering; do not walk around or ask questions while the ceremony is taking place. Finally, make sure that you are dressed appropriately. Men should wear long pants and shirts and women should dress so their bodies are covered; hats are discouraged. If you see a "closed" sign at the entrance to the village, there is most likely a ceremony in progress that cannot be disturbed. Obey the sign and continue on your way.

Assessing Your Vehicle's Off-Road Ability

Many issues come into play when evaluating your 4WD vehicle, although most of the 4WDs on the market are suitable for even the roughest trails described in this book. Engine power will be adequate in even the least-powerful modern vehicle. However, some vehicles are less suited to off-highway driving than others, and some of the newest, carlike sport utility vehicles simply are not designed for off-highway touring. The following information should enable you to identify the good, the bad, and the ugly.

Differing 4WD Systems

All 4WD systems have one thing in common: The engine provides power to all four wheels rather than to only two, as is typical in most standard cars. However, there are a number of differences in the way power is applied to the wheels.

The other feature that distinguishes nearly all 4WDs from normal passenger vehicles is that the gearboxes have high and low ratios that effectively double the number of gears. The high range is comparable to the range on a passenger car. The low range provides lower speed and more power, which is useful when towing heavy loads, driving up steep hills, or crawling over rocks. When driving downhill, the 4WD's low range increases engine braking.

Various makes and models of SUVs offer different drive systems, but these differences center on two issues: the way power is applied to the other wheels if one or more wheels slip, and the ability to select between 2WD and 4WD.

Normal driving requires that all four wheels be able to turn at different speeds; this allows the vehicle to turn without scrubbing its tires. In a 2WD vehicle, the front wheels (or rear wheels in a front-wheel-drive vehicle) are not powered by the engine and thus are free to turn individually at any speed. The rear wheels, powered by the engine, are only able to turn at different speeds because of the differential, which applies power to the faster-turning wheel.

This standard method of applying traction has certain weaknesses. First, when power is applied to only one set of wheels, the other set cannot help the vehicle gain traction. Second, when one powered wheel loses traction, it spins, but the other powered wheel doesn't turn. This happens because the differential applies all the engine power to the faster-turning wheel and no power to the other wheels, which still have traction. All 4WD systems are designed to overcome these two weaknesses. However, different 4WDs address this common objective in different ways.

Full-Time 4WD. For a vehicle to remain in 4WD all the time without scrubbing the tires, all the wheels must be able to rotate at different speeds. A full-time 4WD system allows this to happen by using three differentials. One is located between the rear wheels, as in a normal passenger car, to allow the rear wheels to rotate at different speeds. The second is located between the front wheels in exactly the same way. The third differential is located between the front and rear wheels to allow different rotational speeds between the front and rear sets of wheels. In nearly all vehicles with full-time 4WD, the center differential operates only in high range. In low range, it is completely locked. This is not a disadvantage because when using low range the additional traction is normally desired and the deterioration of steering response will be less noticeable due to the vehicle traveling at a slower speed.

Part-Time 4WD. A part-time 4WD system does not have the center differential located between the front and rear wheels. Consequently, the front and rear drive shafts are both driven at the same speed and with the same power at all times when in 4WD.

This system provides improved traction because when one or both of the front or rear wheels slips, the engine continues to provide power to the other set. However, because such a system doesn't allow a difference in speed between the front and rear sets of wheels, the tires scrub when turning, placing additional strain on the whole drive system. Therefore, such a system can be used only in slippery conditions; otherwise, the ability to steer the vehicle will deteriorate and the tires will quickly wear out.

Some vehicles, such as Jeeps with Selectrac and Mitsubishi Monteros with Active Trac 4WD, offer both full-time and part-time 4WD in high range.

Manual Systems to Switch Between 2WD and 4WD. There are three manual systems for switching between 2WD and 4WD. The most basic requires stopping and getting out of the vehicle to lock the front hubs manually before selecting 4WD. The second requires you to stop, but you change to 4WD by merely throwing a lever inside the vehicle (the hubs lock automatically). The third allows shifting between 2WD and 4WD high range while the vehicle is moving. Any 4WD that does not offer the option of driving in 2WD must have a full-time 4WD system.

Automated Switching Between 2WD and 4WD. Advances in technology are leading to greater automation in the selection of two- or four-wheel drive. When operating in high range, these high-tech systems use sensors to monitor the rotation of each wheel. When any slippage is detected, the vehicle switches the proportion of power from the wheel(s) that is slipping to the wheels that retain grip. The proportion of power supplied to each wheel is therefore infinitely variable as opposed to the original systems where the vehicle was either in two-wheel drive or four-wheel drive.

In recent years, this process has been spurred on by many of the manufacturers of luxury vehicles entering the SUV market—Mercedes, BMW, Cadillac, Lincoln, and Lexus have joined Range Rover in this segment.

Manufacturers of these pricier vehicles have led the way in introducing sophisticated computer-controlled 4WD systems. Although each of the manufacturers has its own approach to this issue, all the systems automatically vary the allocation of power between the wheels within milliseconds of the sensors' detecting wheel slippage.

Limiting Wheel Slippage

All 4WDs employ various systems to limit wheel slippage and transfer power to the wheels that still have traction. These systems may completely lock the differentials or they may allow limited slippage before transferring power back to the wheels that retain traction.

Lockers completely eliminate the operation of one or more differentials. A locker on the center differential switches between full-time and part-time 4WD. Lockers on the front or rear differentials ensure that power remains equally applied to each set of wheels regardless of whether both have traction. Lockers may be controlled manually, by a switch or a lever in the vehicle, or they may be automatic.

The Toyota Land Cruiser offers the option of having manual lockers on all three differentials, while other brands such as the Mitsubishi Montero offer manual lockers on the center and rear differential. Manual lockers are the most controllable and effective devices for ensuring that power is provided to the wheels with traction. However, because they allow absolutely no slippage, they must be used only on slippery surfaces.

An alternative method for getting power to the wheels that have traction is to allow limited wheel slippage. Systems that work this way may be called limited-slip differentials, posi-traction systems, or in the center differential, viscous couplings. The advantage of these systems is that the limited difference they allow in rotational speed between wheels enables such systems to be used when driving on a dry surface. All full-time 4WD systems allow limited slippage in the center differential.

For off-highway use, a manually locking differential is the best of the above systems, but it is the most expensive. Limited-slip differentials are the cheapest but also the least satisfactory, as they require one wheel to be slipping at 2 to 3 mph before power is transferred to the other wheel. For the center differential, the best system combines a locking differential and, to enable full-time use, a viscous coupling.

Tires

The tires that came with your 4WD vehicle may be satisfactory, but many 4WDs are fitted with passenger-car tires. These are unlikely to be the best choice because they are less rugged and more likely to puncture on rocky trails. They are particularly prone to sidewall damage as well. Passenger vehicle tires also have a less aggressive tread pattern than specialized 4WD tires, and provide less traction in mud.

For information on purchasing tires better suited to off-highway conditions, see Special 4WD Equipment, page 20.

Clearance

Road clearances vary considerably among different 4WD vehicles—from less than 7 inches to more than 10 inches. Special vehicles may have far greater clearance. For instance, the Hummer has a 16-inch ground clearance. High ground clearance is particularly advantageous on the rockier or more rutted 4WD trails in this book.

When evaluating the ground clearance of your vehicle, you need to take into account the clearance of the bodywork between the wheels on each side of the vehicle. This is particularly relevant for crawling over larger rocks. Vehicles with sidesteps have significantly lower clearance than those without.

Another factor affecting clearance is the approach and departure angles of your vehicle—that is, the maximum angle the ground can slope without the front of the vehicle hitting the ridge on approach or the rear of the vehicle hitting on departure. Mounting a winch or tow hitch to your vehicle is likely to reduce your angle of approach or departure.

If you do a lot of driving on rocky trails, you will inevitably hit the bottom of the vehicle. When this happens, you will be far less likely to damage vulnerable areas such as the oil pan and gas tank if your vehicle is fitted with skid plates. Most manufacturers offer skid plates as an option. They are worth every penny.

Maneuverability

When you tackle tight switchbacks, you will quickly appreciate that maneuverability is an important criterion when assessing 4WD vehicles. Where a full-size vehicle may be forced to go back and forth a number of times to get around a sharp turn, a small 4WD might go straight around. This is not only easier, it's safer.

If you have a full-size vehicle, all is not lost. We have traveled many of the trails in this book in a Suburban. That is not to say that some of these trails wouldn't have been easier to negotiate in a smaller vehicle! We have noted in the route descriptions if a trail is not suitable for larger vehicles.

In Summary

Using the criteria above, you can evaluate how well your 4WD will handle off-road touring, and if you haven't yet purchased your vehicle, you can use these criteria to help select one. Choosing the best 4WD system is, at least partly, subjective. It is also a matter of your budget. However, for the type of off-highway driving covered in this book, we make the following recommendations:

■ Select a 4WD system that offers low range and, at a minimum, has some form of limited slip differential on the rear axle.

■ Use light truck, all-terrain tires as the standard tires on your vehicle. For sand and slickrock, these will be the ideal choice. If conditions are likely to be muddy, or if traction will be improved by a tread pattern that will give more bite, consider an additional set of mud tires.

■ For maximum clearance, select a vehicle with 16-inch wheels or at least choose the tallest tires that your vehicle can accommodate. Note that if you install tires with a diameter greater than standard, the odometer will under calculate the distance you have traveled. Your engine braking and gear ratios will also be affected.

■ If you are going to try the rockier 4WD trails, don't install a sidestep or low-hanging front bar. If you have the option, have underbody skid plates mounted.

■ Remember that many of the obstacles you encounter on backcountry trails are more difficult to navigate in a full-size vehicle than in a compact 4WD.

Four-Wheel Driving Techniques

Safe four-wheel driving requires that you observe certain golden rules:

■ Size up the situation in advance.

■ Be careful and take your time.

■ Maintain smooth, steady power and momentum.

■ Engage 4WD and low-range gears before you get into a tight situation.

■ Steer toward high spots, trying to put the wheel over large rocks.

■ Straddle ruts.

■ Use gears and not just the brakes to hold the vehicle when driving downhill. On very steep slopes, chock the wheels if you park your vehicle.

■ Watch for logging and mining trucks and smaller recreational vehicles, such as all-terrain vehicles (ATVs).

■ Wear your seat belt and secure all luggage, especially heavy items such as tool boxes or coolers. Heavy items should be secured by ratchet tie-down straps rather than elastic-type straps, which are not strong enough to hold heavy items if the vehicle rolls.

Arizona's 4WD trails have a number of common obstacles, and the following provides an introduction to the techniques required to surmount them.

Rocks. Tire selection is important in negotiating rocks. Select a multiple-ply, tough sidewall, light-truck tire with a large-lug tread.

As you approach a rocky stretch, get into 4WD low range to give yourself maximum slow-speed control. Speed is rarely necessary, since traction on a rocky surface is usually good. Plan ahead and select the line you wish to take. If a rock appears to be larger than the clearance of your vehicle, don't try to straddle it. Check to see that it is not higher than the frame of your vehicle once you get a wheel over it. Put a wheel up on the rock and slowly climb it, then gently drop over the other side using the brake to ensure a smooth landing. Bouncing the car over rocks increases the likelihood of damage, because the body's clearance is reduced by the suspension compressing. Running boards also significantly reduce your clearance in this respect. It is often helpful to use a "spotter" outside the vehicle to assist you with the best wheel placement.

Steep Uphill Grades. Consider walking the trail to ensure that the steep hill before you is passable, especially if it is clear that backtracking is going to be a problem.

Select 4WD low range to ensure that you have adequate power to pull up the hill. If the wheels begin to lose traction, turn the steering wheel gently from side to side to give the wheels a chance to regain traction.

If you lose momentum, but the car is not

in danger of sliding, use the foot brake, switch off the ignition, leave the vehicle in gear (if manual transmission) or park (if automatic), engage the parking brake, and get out to examine the situation. See if you can remove any obstacles, and figure out the line you need to take. Reversing a couple of yards and starting again may allow you to get better traction and momentum.

If halfway up, you decide a stretch of road is impassably steep, back down the trail. Trying to turn the vehicle around on a steep hill is extremely dangerous; you will very likely cause it to roll over.

Steep Downhill Grades. Again, consider walking the trail to ensure that a steep downhill is passable, especially if it is clear that backtracking uphill is going to be a problem.

Select 4WD low range and use first gear to maximize braking assistance from the engine. If the surface is loose and you are losing traction, change up to second or third gear. Do not use the brakes if you can avoid it, but don't let the vehicle's speed get out of control. Feather (lightly pump) the brakes if you slip while braking. For vehicles fitted with an antilock breaking system, apply even pressure if you start to slip; the ABS helps keep vehicles on line.

Travel very slowly over rock ledges or ruts. Attempt to tackle these diagonally, letting one wheel down at a time.

If the back of the vehicle begins to slide around, gently apply the throttle and correct the steering. If the rear of the vehicle starts to slide sideways, do not apply the brakes.

Sand. As with most off-highway situations, your tires are the key to your ability to cross sand. It is difficult to tell how well a particular tire will handle in sand just by looking at it, so be guided by the manufacturer and your dealer.

The key to driving in soft sand is floatation, which is achieved by a combination of low tire pressure and momentum. Before crossing a stretch of sand, reduce your tire pressure to between 15 and 20 pounds. If necessary, you can safely go to as low as 12 pounds. As you cross, maintain momentum so that your vehicle rides on the top of the soft sand without digging in or stalling. This may require plenty of engine power. Avoid using the brakes if possible; removing your foot from the accelerator alone is normally enough to slow or stop. Using the brakes digs the vehicle deep in the sand.

Pump the tires back up as soon as you are out of the sand to avoid damaging the tires and the rims. Pumping the tires back up requires a high-quality air compressor. Even then, it is a slow process.

In the backcountry of Arizona, sandy conditions are commonplace. You will therefore find a good compressor most useful.

Slickrock. When you encounter slickrock, first assess the correct direction of the trail. It is easy to lose sight of the trail on slickrock, because there are seldom any developed edges. Often the way is marked with small cairns, which are simply rocks stacked high enough to make a landmark.

All-terrain tires with tighter tread are more suited to slickrock than the more open, luggier type tires. As with rocks, a multiple-ply sidewall is important. In dry conditions, slickrock offers pavement-type grip. In rain or snow, you will soon learn how it got its name. Even the best tires may not get an adequate grip. Walk steep sections first; if you are slipping on foot, chances are your vehicle will slip, too.

Slickrock is characterized by ledges and long sections of "pavement." Follow the guidelines for travel over rocks. Refrain from speeding over flat-looking sections, because you may hit an unexpected crevice or water pocket, and vehicles bend easier than slickrock! Turns and ledges can be tight, and vehicles with smaller overhangs and better maneuverability are at a distinct advantage—hence the popularity of the compacts in the slickrock mecca of Moab, Utah.

On the steepest sections, engage low range and pick a straight line up or down the slope. Do not attempt to traverse a steep slope sideways.

Mud. Muddy trails are easily damaged, so they should be avoided if possible. But if you must traverse a section of mud, your success will depend heavily on whether you have open-lugged mud tires or chains. Thick mud fills the tighter tread on normal tires, leaving the tire with no more grip than if it were bald. If the muddy stretch is only a few yards long, the momentum of your vehicle may allow you to get through regardless.

If the muddy track is very steep, uphill or downhill, or off camber, do not attempt it. Your vehicle is likely to skid in such conditions, and you may roll or slip off the edge of the road. Also, check to see that the mud has a reasonably firm base. Tackling deep mud is definitely not recommended unless you have a vehicle-mounted winch—and even then—be cautious, because the winch may not get you out. Finally, check to see that no ruts are too deep for the ground clearance of your vehicle.

When you decide you can get through and have selected the best route, use the following techniques to cross through the mud:

■ Avoid making detours off existing tracks to minimize environmental damage.

■ Select 4WD low range and a suitable gear; momentum is the key to success, so use a high enough gear to build up sufficient speed.

■ Avoid accelerating heavily, so as to minimize wheel spinning and to provide maximum traction.

■ Follow existing wheel ruts, unless they are too deep for the clearance of your vehicle.

■ To correct slides, turn the steering wheel in the direction that the rear wheels are skidding, but don't be too aggressive or you'll overcorrect and lose control again.

■ If the vehicle comes to a stop, don't continue to accelerate, as you will only spin your wheels and dig yourself into a rut. Try backing out and having another go.

■ Be prepared to turn back before reaching the point of no return.

Stream Crossings. By crossing a stream that is too deep, drivers risk far more than water flowing in and ruining the interior of their vehicles. Water sucked into the engine's air intake will seriously damage the engine. Likewise, water that seeps into the air vent on the transmission or differential will mix with the lubricant and may lead to serious problems in due course.

Even worse, if the water is deep or fast flowing, it could easily carry your vehicle downstream, endangering the lives of everyone in the vehicle.

Some 4WD manuals tell you what fording depth the vehicle can negotiate safely. If your vehicle's owner's manual does not include this information, your local dealer may be able to assist. If you don't know, then avoid crossing through water that is more than a foot or so deep.

The first rule for crossing a stream is to know what you are getting into. You need to ascertain how deep the water is, whether there are any large rocks or holes, if the bottom is solid enough to avoid bogging down the vehicle, and whether the entry and exit points are negotiable. This may take some time and involve getting wet, but you take a great risk by crossing a stream without first properly assessing the situation.

The secret to water crossings is to keep moving, but not too fast. If you go too fast, you may drown the electrics, causing the vehicle to stall midstream. In shallow water (where the surface of the water is below the bumper), your primary concern is to safely negotiate the bottom of the stream, to avoid any rock damage, and to maintain momentum if there is a danger of getting stuck or of slipping on the exit.

In deeper water (between 18 and 30 inches), the objective is to create a small bow wave in front of the moving vehicle. This requires a speed that is approximately walking pace. The bow wave reduces the depth of the water around the engine compartment. If the water's surface reaches your tailpipe, select a gear that will maintain moderate engine revs to avoid water backing up into the exhaust; and do not change gears midstream.

Crossing water deeper than 25 to 30 inches requires more extensive preparation of the vehicle and should be attempted only by experienced drivers.

Snow. The trails in this book that receive heavy snowfall are closed in winter. Therefore, the snow conditions that you are most likely to encounter are an occasional snowdrift that has not yet melted or fresh snow from an unexpected storm. Getting through such conditions depends on the depth of the snow, its consistency, the stability of the underlying surface, and your vehicle.

If the snow is no deeper than about 9 inches and there is solid ground beneath it, crossing the snow should not be a problem. In deeper snow that seems solid enough to support your vehicle, be extremely cautious: If you break through a drift, you are likely to be stuck, and if conditions are bad, you may have a long wait.

The tires you use for off-highway driving, with a wide tread pattern, are probably suitable for these snow conditions. Nonetheless, it is wise to carry chains (preferably for all four wheels), and if you have a vehicle-mounted winch, even better.

Vehicle Recovery Methods

If you do enough four-wheel driving, you are sure to get stuck sooner or later. The following techniques will help you get back on the go. The most suitable method will depend on the equipment available and the situation you are in—whether you are stuck in sand, mud, or snow, or are high-centered or unable to negotiate a hill.

Towing. Use a nylon yank strap of the type discussed in the Special 4WD Equipment section below. This type of strap will stretch 15 to 25 percent, and the elasticity will assist in extracting the vehicle.

Attach the strap only to a frame-mounted tow point. Ensure that the driver of the stuck vehicle is ready, take up all but about 6 feet of slack, then move the towing vehicle away at a moderate speed (in most circumstances this means using 4WD low range in second gear) so that the elasticity of the strap is employed in the way it is meant to be. Don't take off like a bat out of hell or you risk breaking the strap or damaging a vehicle.

Never join two yank straps together with a shackle. If one strap breaks, the shackle will become a lethal missile aimed at one of the vehicles (and anyone inside). For the same reason, never attach a yank strap to the tow ball on either vehicle.

Jacking. Jacking the vehicle allows you to pack rocks, dirt, or logs under the wheel or to use your shovel to remove an obstacle. However, the standard vehicle jack is unlikely to be of as much assistance as a high-lift jack. We highly recommend purchasing a good high-lift jack as a basic accessory if you decide that you are going to do a lot of serious, off-highway four-wheel driving. Remember a high-lift jack is of limited use if your vehicle does not have an appropriate jacking point. Some brush bars have two built-in forward jacking points.

Tire Chains. Tire chains can be of assistance in both mud and snow. Cable-type chains provide much less grip than link-type chains. There are also dedicated mud chains with larger, heavier links than on normal snow chains. It is best to have chains fitted to all four wheels.

Once you are bogged down is not the best time to try to fit the chains; if at all possible, try to predict their need and have them on the tires before trouble arises. An easy way to affix chains is to place two small cubes of wood under the center of the stretched-out chain. When you drive your tires up on the blocks of wood, it is easier to stretch the chains over the tires because the pressure is off of them.

Winching. Most recreational four-wheel drivers do not have a winch. But if you get serious about four-wheel driving, this is probably the first major accessory you should consider buying.

Under normal circumstances, a winch would be warranted only for the more difficult 4WD trails in this book. Having a winch is certainly comforting when you see a difficult section of road ahead and have to decide whether to risk it or turn back. Also, major obstacles can appear when you least expect them, even on trails that are otherwise easy.

Owning a winch is not a panacea to all your recovery problems. Winching depends on the availability of a good anchor point, and electric winches may not work if they are submerged in a stream. Despite these constraints, no accessory is more useful than a high-quality, powerful winch when you get into a difficult situation.

If you acquire a winch, learn to use it properly; take the time to study your owner's manual. Incorrect operation can be extremely dangerous and may cause damage to the winch or to your anchor points, which are usually trees.

Navigation by the Global Positioning System (GPS)

Although this book is designed so that each trail can be navigated simply by following the detailed directions provided, nothing makes navigation easier than a GPS receiver.

The global positioning system (GPS) consists of a network of 24 satellites, nearly 13,000 miles in space, in six different orbital paths. The satellites are constantly moving at about 8,500 miles per hour and make two complete orbits around the earth every 24 hours.

Each satellite is constantly transmitting data, including its identification number, its operational health, and the date and time. It also transmits its location and the location of every other satellite in the network.

By comparing the time the signal was transmitted to the time it is received, a GPS receiver calculates how far away each satellite is. With a sufficient number of signals, the receiver can then triangulate its location. With three or more satellites, the receiver can determine latitude and longitude coordinates. With four or more, it can calculate elevation. By constantly making these calculations, it can determine speed and direction. To facilitate these calculations, the time data broadcast by GPS is accurate to within 40 billionths of a second.

The U.S. military uses the system to provide positions accurate to within half an inch. When the system was first established, civilian receivers were deliberately fed slightly erroneous information in order to effectively deny military applications to hostile countries or terrorists—a practice called selective availability (SA). However on May 1, 2000, in response to the growing importance of the system for civilian applications, the U.S. government stopped intentionally downgrading GPS data. The military gave its support to this change once new technology made it possible to selectively degrade the system within any defined geographical area on demand. This new feature of the system has made it safe to have higher-quality signals available for civilian use. Now, instead of the civilian-use signal having a margin of error between 20 and 70 yards, it is only about one-tenth of that.

A GPS receiver offers the four-wheeler numerous benefits:

■ You can track to any point for which you know the longitude and latitude coordinates with no chance of heading in the wrong direction or getting lost. Most receivers provide an extremely easy-to-understand graphic display to keep you on track.

■ It works in all weather conditions.

■ It automatically records your route for easy backtracking.

■ You can record and name any location, so that you can relocate it with ease. This may include your campsite, a fishing spot, or even a silver mine you discover!

■ It displays your position, enabling you to pinpoint your location on a map.

■ By interfacing the GPS receiver directly to a portable computer, you can monitor and record your location as you travel (using the appropriate map software) or print the route you took.

However, remember that GPS units can fail, batteries can go flat, and tree cover and tight canyons can block the signals. Never rely entirely on GPS for navigation. Always carry a compass for backup.

Special 4WD Equipment

Tires

When 4WD touring, you will likely encounter a variety of terrain: rocks, mud, talus, slickrock, sand, gravel, dirt, and bitumen. The immense array of tires on the market includes many specifically targeted

at one or another of these types of terrain, as well as tires designed to adequately handle a range of terrain.

Every four-wheel driver seems to have a preference when it comes to tire selection, but most people undertaking the 4WD trails in this book will need tires that can handle all of the above types of terrain adequately.

The first requirement is to select rugged, light-truck tires rather than passenger-vehicle tires. Check the size data on the sidewall: it should have "LT" rather than "P" before the number. Among light-truck tires, you must choose between tires that are designated "all-terrain" and more-aggressive, wider-tread mud tires. Either type will be adequate, especially on rocks, gravel, talus, or dirt. Although mud tires have an advantage in muddy conditions and soft snow, all-terrain tires perform better on slickrock, in sand, and particularly on ice and paved roads.

When selecting tires, remember that they affect not just traction but also cornering ability, braking distances, fuel consumption, and noise levels. It pays to get good advice before making your decision.

Global Positioning System Receivers

GPS receivers have come down in price considerably in the past few years and are rapidly becoming indispensable navigational tools. Many higher-priced cars now offer integrated GPS receivers, and within the next few years, receivers will become available on most models.

Battery-powered, hand-held units that meet the needs of off-highway driving currently range from less than $100 to a little over $300 and continue to come down in price. Some high-end units feature maps that are incorporated in the display, either from a built-in database or from interchangeable memory cards. Currently, only a few of these maps include 4WD trails.

If you are considering purchasing a GPS unit, keep the following in mind:

■ Price. The very cheapest units are likely outdated and very limited in their display features. Expect to pay from $125 to $300.

■ The display. Compare the graphic display of one unit with another. Some are much easier to decipher or offer more alternative displays.

■ The controls. GPS receivers have many functions, and they need to have good, simple controls.

■ Vehicle mounting. To be useful, the unit needs to be placed where it can be read easily by both the driver and the navigator. Check that the unit can be conveniently located in your vehicle. Different units have different shapes and different mounting systems.

■ Map data. More and more units have map data built in. Some have the ability to download maps from a computer. Such maps are normally sold on a CD-ROM. GPS units have a finite storage capacity and having the ability to download maps covering a narrower geographical region means that the amount of data relating to that specific region can be greater.

■ The number of routes and the number of sites (or "waypoints") per route that can be stored in memory. For off-highway use, it is important to be able to store plenty of waypoints so that you do not have to load coordinates into the machine as frequently. Having plenty of memory also ensures that you can automatically store your present location without fear that the memory is full.

■ Waypoint storage. The better units store up to 500 waypoints and 20 reversible routes of up to 30 waypoints each. Also consider the number of characters a GPS receiver allows you to use to name waypoints. When you try to recall a waypoint, you may have difficulty recognizing names restricted to only a few characters.

■ Automatic route storing. Most units automatically store your route as you go along and enable you to display it in reverse to make backtracking easy.

After you have selected a unit, a number of optional extras are also worth considering:

■ A cigarette lighter electrical adapter. Despite GPS units becoming more power efficient, protracted in-vehicle use still makes this accessory a necessity.

■ A vehicle-mounted antenna, which will improve reception under difficult conditions. (The GPS unit can only "see" through the windows of your vehicle; it cannot monitor satellites through a metal roof.) Having a vehicle-mounted antenna also means that you do not have to consider reception when locating the receiver in your vehicle.

■ An in-car mounting system. If you are going to do a lot of touring using the GPS, consider attaching a bracket on the dash rather than relying on a Velcro mount.

■ A computer-link cable and digital maps. Data from your GPS receiver can be downloaded to your PC; maps and waypoints can be downloaded from your PC; or if you have a laptop computer, you can monitor your route as you go along, using one of a number of inexpensive map software products on the market.

Yank Straps

Yank straps are industrial-strength versions of the flimsy tow straps carried by the local discount store. They are 20 to 30 feet long and 2 to 3 inches wide, made of heavy nylon, rated to at least 20,000 pounds, and have looped ends.

Do not use tow straps with metal hooks in the ends (the hooks can become missiles in the event the strap breaks free). Likewise, never join two yank straps together using a shackle.

CB Radios

If you are stuck, injured, or just want to know the conditions up ahead, a citizen's band (CB) radio can be invaluable. CB radios are relatively inexpensive and do not require an Federal Communications Comission license. Their range is limited, especially in very hilly country, as their transmission patterns basically follow lines of sight. Range can be improved using single sideband (SSB) transmission, an option on more expensive units. Range is even better on vehicle-mounted units that have been professionally fitted to ensure that the antenna and cabling are matched appropriately.

Winches

There are three main options when it comes to winches: manual winches, removable electric winches, and vehicle-mounted electric winches.

If you have a full-size 4WD vehicle—which can weigh in excess of 7,000 pounds when loaded—a manual winch is of limited use without a lot of effort and considerable time. However, a manual winch is a very handy and inexpensive accessory if you have a small 4WD. Typically, manual winches are rated to pull about 5,500 pounds.

An electric winch can be mounted to your vehicle's trailer hitch to enable it to be removed, relocated to the front of your vehicle (if you have a hitch installed), or moved to another vehicle. Although this is a very useful feature, a winch is heavy, so relocating one can be a two-person job. Consider that 5,000-pound-rated winches weigh only about 55 pounds, while 12,000-pound-rated models weigh around 140 pounds. Therefore, the larger models are best permanently front-mounted. Unfortunately, this position limits their ability to winch the vehicle backward.

When choosing among electric winches, be aware that they are rated for their maximum capacity on the first wind of the cable around the drum. As layers of cable wind onto the drum, they increase its diameter and thus decrease the maximum load the winch can handle. This decrease is significant: A winch rated to pull 8,000 pounds on a bare drum may only handle 6,500 pounds on the second layer, 5,750 pounds on the third layer, and 5,000 pounds on the fourth. Electric winches also draw a high level of current and may necessitate upgrading the battery in your 4WD or adding a second battery.

There is a wide range of mounting options—from a simple, body-mounted frame that holds the winch to heavy-duty winch bars that replace the original bumper and incorporate brush bars and mounts for auxiliary lights.

If you buy a winch, either electric or manual, you will also need quite a range of additional equipment so that you can operate it correctly:

- at least one choker chain with hooks on each end,
- winch extension straps or cables,
- shackles,
- a receiver shackle,
- a snatch block,
- a tree protector,
- gloves.

Grille/Brush Bars and Winch Bars

Brush bars protect the front of the vehicle from scratches and minor bumps; they also provide a solid mount for auxiliary lights and often high-lift jacking points. The level of protection they provide depends on how solid they are and whether they are securely mounted onto the frame of the vehicle. Lighter models attach in front of the standard bumper, but the more substantial units replace the bumper. Prices range from about $150 to $450.

Winch bars replace the bumper and usually integrate a solid brush bar with a heavy-duty winch mount. Some have the brush bar as an optional extra to the winch bar component. Manufacturers such as Warn, ARB, and TJM offer a wide range of integrated winch bars. These are significantly more expensive, starting at about $650.

Remember that installing heavy equipment on the front of the vehicle may necessitate increasing the front suspension rating to cope with the additional weight.

Portable Air Compressors

Most portable air compressors on the market are flimsy models that plug into the cigarette lighter and are sold at the local discount store. These are of very limited use for four-wheel driving. They are very slow to inflate the large tires of a 4WD vehicle; for instance, to reinflate from 15 to 35 pounds typically takes about 10 minutes for each tire. They are also unlikely to be rated for continuous use, which means that they will overheat and cut off before completing the job. If you're lucky, they will start up again when they have cooled down, but this means that you are unlikely to reinflate your tires in less than an hour.

The easiest way to identify a useful air compressor is by the price—good ones cost $200 or more. Many of the quality units feature a Thomas-brand pump and are built to last. Another good unit is sold by ARB. All these pumps draw between 15 and 20 amps and thus should not be plugged into the cigarette lighter socket but attached to the vehicle's battery with clips. The ARB unit can be permanently mounted under the hood. Quick-Air makes a range of units including a 10-amp compressor that can be plugged into the cigarette lighter socket and performs well.

Auxiliary Driving Lights

There is a vast array of auxiliary lights on the market today and selecting the best lights for your purpose can be a confusing process.

Auxiliary lights greatly improve visibility in adverse weather conditions. Driving lights provide a strong, moderately wide beam to supplement headlamp high beams, giving improved lighting in the distance and to the sides of the main beam. Fog lamps throw a wide-dispersion, flat beam; and spots provide a high-power, narrow beam to improve lighting range directly in front of the vehicle. Rear-mounted auxiliary lights provide greatly improved visibility for backing up.

For off-highway use, you will need quality lights with strong mounting brackets. Some high-powered off-highway lights are not approved by the U.S. Department of Transportation for use on public roads.

Roof Racks

Roof racks can be excellent for storing gear, as well as providing easy access for certain weatherproof items. However, they raise the center of gravity on the vehicle, which can substantially alter the rollover angle. A roof rack is best used for lightweight objects that are well-strapped down. Heavy recovery gear and other bulky items should be packed low in the vehicle's interior to lower the center of gravity and stabilize the vehicle.

Packing Checklist

Before embarking on any 4WD adventure, whether a lazy Sunday drive on an easy trail or a challenging climb over rugged terrain, be prepared. The following checklist will help you gather the items you need.

Essential

❑ Rain gear
❑ Small shovel or multipurpose ax, pick, shovel, and sledgehammer
❑ Heavy-duty yank strap
❑ Spare tire that matches the other tires on the vehicle
❑ Working jack and base plate for soft ground
❑ Maps
❑ Emergency medical kit, including sun protection and insect repellent
❑ Bottled water
❑ Blankets or space blankets
❑ Parka, gloves, and boots
❑ Spare vehicle key
❑ Jumper leads
❑ Heavy-duty flashlight
❑ Multipurpose tool, such as a Leatherman
❑ Emergency food—high-energy bars or similar

Worth Considering

❑ Global Positioning System (GPS) receiver
❑ Cell phone
❑ A set of light-truck, off-highway tires and matching spare
❑ High-lift jack
❑ Additional tool kit
❑ CB radio
❑ Portable air compressor
❑ Tire gauge
❑ Tire-sealing kit
❑ Tire chains
❑ Handsaw and ax
❑ Binoculars
❑ Firearms
❑ Whistle
❑ Flares
❑ Vehicle fire extinguisher
❑ Gasoline, engine oil, and other vehicle fluids
❑ Portable hand winch
❑ Electric cooler

If Your Credit Cards Aren't Maxed Out

❑ Electric, vehicle-mounted winch and associated recovery straps, shackles, and snatch blocks
❑ Auxiliary lights
❑ Locking differential(s)

Trails in the Northeast Region

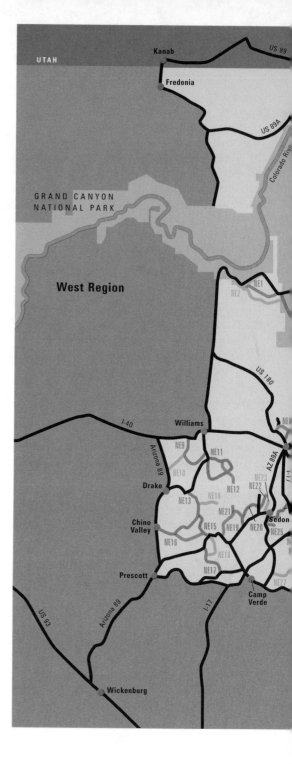

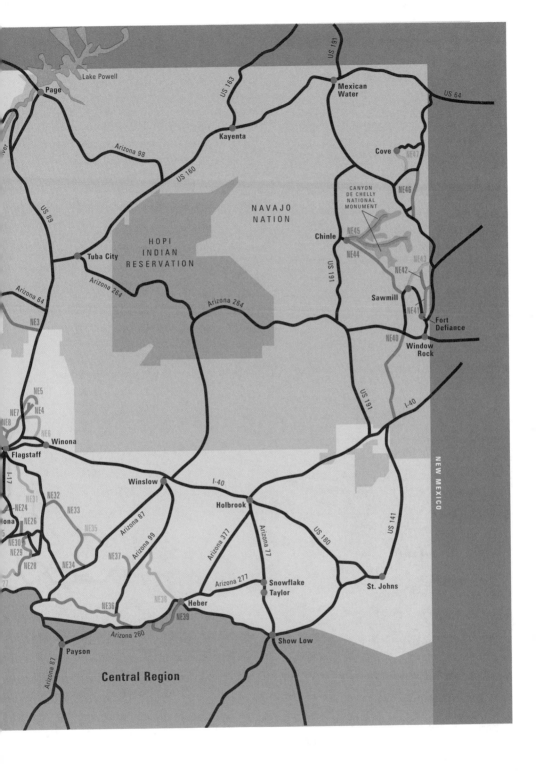

Hull Cabin Trail

STARTING POINT: Northeast #2: Coconino Rim Trail, 1.3 miles south of Arizona 64

FINISHING POINT: Arizona 64, 0.6 miles west of mile marker 276

TOTAL MILEAGE: 13.7 miles

UNPAVED MILEAGE: 13.7 miles

DRIVING TIME: 1 hour

ELEVATION RANGE: 6,300–7,500 feet

USUALLY OPEN: April to December

BEST TIME TO TRAVEL: Dry weather

DIFFICULTY RATING: 2

SCENIC RATING: 8

REMOTENESS RATING: +0

Special Attractions

- Hull Cabin Historic District.
- Trail travels beneath curving Coconino Rim.
- Can be combined with Northeast #2: Coconino Rim Trail to create a loop.

History

The Hull brothers, Phillip and William, established their ranch south of the Grand Canyon in 1884. Initially, they raised cattle but later switched to sheep. When the Atlantic & Pacific Railroad was constructed through northern Arizona, the enterprising brothers started a stage line to carry tourists from the railroad in Flagstaff to the Grand Canyon. Phillip died of a heart attack in 1888, but William continued to run the ranch and tourist business until he started prospecting in the canyon. Another settler, Captain John Hance, set up tent cabins a short distance north of the Hull Cabin to house tourists. He also provided food and guided tours into the Grand Canyon.

The cabins and Hull Tank were constructed in 1888. The cabins are built of round logs, V-notched at the corners—a time-consuming construction technique. The barn is constructed of hand-hewn ponderosa pine logs, dovetailed at the corners.

The U.S. Forest Service, which purchased the site in 1907, used it until 1940 as a summer ranger station. The forest service

Hull Cabin is set in a clearing among ponderosa pines

has recently restored the cabin, using logs, siding, and shingles of the same type as the original construction. Hull Cabin Historic District was listed on the National Register of Historic Places in October 1984.

Description

Northeast #1: Hull Cabin Trail joins Northeast #2: Coconino Rim Road with Arizona 64, exiting onto the highway farther to the east than Northeast #2: Coconino Rim Road does. The trail leaves from beside the Grandview Fire Lookout and travels down the side of the Coconino Rim through ponderosa pine forest. A side trail leads 0.4 miles to the Hull Cabins, actually two cabins and a barn, which are used occasionally as a work center in the summer months by the forest service. The cabins are often photographed in their pretty setting—a clearing in a grove of large ponderosa pines.

Back on the main trail, the soft formed trail continues through the trees. Deep ruts bear evidence to the fact that this trail should only be driven in dry weather. With rain, many sections of the trail become very muddy and are often impassable, even for 4WDs. In dry weather the trail is suitable for a high-clearance 2WD vehicle. The trail may be passable for longer than the travel dates suggest. In low snowfall years it may be open all year.

After 6.1 miles, the trail leaves the pine forest and enters an area of more open lower vegetation as it travels through the Upper Basin below the swooping curve of the Coconino Rim. Many tracks to the right lead to the base of the rim. The trail travels briefly along Lee Canyon before finishing on Arizona 64, 1 mile west of the eastern boundary of the Kaibab National Forest.

Current Road Information

Kaibab National Forest
Tusayan Ranger District
Hwy 64, Administrative Site
PO Box 3088
Grand Canyon, AZ 86023
(928) 638-2443

Map References

BLM   Cameron
USFS   Kaibab National Forest: Tusayan
       Ranger District
USGS   1:24,000   Grandview Point,
       Grandview Point NE, Hellhole Bend
       1:100,000 Cameron
Maptech CD-ROM: Flagstaff/Sedona/Prescott
Arizona Atlas & Gazetteer, p. 32
Arizona Road & Recreation Atlas, pp. 28,
       29, 62, 63
Recreational Map of Arizona

Route Directions

▼ 0.0   From Northeast #2: Coconino Rim
               Trail, immediately east of Grandview
               Fire Lookout, zero trip meter and turn
               northeast on graded dirt road, FR 307,
               at the sign for Hull Cabin.
1.4 ▲   Trail ends on Northeast #2: Coconino
               Rim Trail, immediately east of
               Grandview Fire Lookout. Turn right to
               exit to Arizona 64 and Grand Canyon
               National Park; turn left to travel along
               Northeast #2: Coconino Rim Trail.
               GPS: N35°57.37′ W111°57.23′

▼ 0.2   SO   Arizona Trail on left; then cattle guard;
               then Arizona Trail on right.
1.2 ▲   SO   Arizona Trail on left; then cattle guard;
               then Arizona Trail on right.
▼ 0.7   SO   Trail starts to descend Coconino Rim.
0.7 ▲   SO   Top of the Coconino Rim.
▼ 1.2   SO   Hull Tank on left.
0.2 ▲   SO   Hull Tank on right.
▼ 1.4   SO   Track on left is FR 851, which goes
               through gate, 0.4 miles to Hull Cabin.
               Zero trip meter.
0.0 ▲   Continue to the southwest.
               GPS: N35°58.05′ W111°56.37′

▼ 0.0   Continue to the east.
2.3 ▲   SO   Track on right is FR 851, which goes
               through gate, 0.4 miles to Hull Cabin.
               Zero trip meter.
▼ 0.2   BR   Track on left is FR 2805; bear right,
               remaining on FR 307.
2.1 ▲   BL   Track on right is FR 2805; bear left,
               remaining on FR 307.

▼ 0.8 SO Track on left; then track on right; then cross over wash.

1.5 ▲ SO Cross over wash; then track on left; then track on right.

▼ 1.3 SO Small track on left.

1.0 ▲ SO Small track on right.

▼ 1.8 SO Cross over wash.

0.5 ▲ SO Cross over wash.

▼ 1.9 SO Track on right.

0.4 ▲ SO Track on left.

▼ 2.3 SO Track on left is FR 2805. Zero trip meter.

0.0 ▲ Continue to the northwest on FR 307.

GPS: N35°57.58′ W111°54.12′

▼ 0.0 Continue to the southeast on FR 307.

3.4 ▲ BL Track on right is FR 2805. Zero trip meter.

▼ 0.3 SO Track on left is FR 854; then cross through wash.

3.1 ▲ SO Cross through wash; then track on right is FR 854.

▼ 0.6 SO Cross through wash.

2.8 ▲ SO Cross through wash.

▼ 0.9 SO Closure gate.

2.5 ▲ SO Closure gate.

GPS: N35°57.30′ W111°53.41′

▼ 1.0 BR Track on left is FR 683; bear right, remaining on FR 307.

2.4 ▲ BL Track on right is FR 683; bear left, remaining on FR 307.

GPS: N35°57.33′ W111°53.32′

▼ 1.2 SO Track on left to Trash Dam.

2.2 ▲ SO Track on right to Trash Dam.

▼ 1.3 SO Track on right.

2.1 ▲ SO Track on left.

▼ 1.4 SO Track on right and track on left.

2.0 ▲ SO Track on left and track on right.

▼ 1.8 SO Track on right.

1.6 ▲ SO Track on left.

▼ 2.1 SO Track on right.

1.3 ▲ SO Track on left.

▼ 2.2 SO Track on right.

1.2 ▲ SO Track on left.

▼ 2.4 SO Cattle guard; then track on left and track on right is FR 784.

In Upper Basin, the trail runs parallel to the Coconino Rim and many tracks lead to the base of the rim

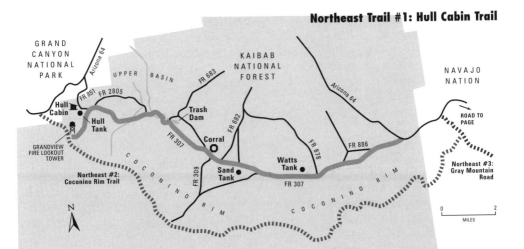

▲ 1.0   SO   Track on left is FR 784 and track on right; then cattle guard.
    GPS: N35º56.34' W111º52.43'

▼ 3.0   SO   Track on left.
▲ 0.4   SO   Track on right.

▼ 3.1   SO   Corral on left; track on right is FR 309.
▲ 0.3   SO   Corral on right; track on left is FR 309.
    GPS: N35º56.01' W111º51.85'

▼ 3.4   SO   Track on left is FR 682. Zero trip meter.
▲ 0.0   Continue to the west.
    GPS: N35º55.81' W111º51.53'

▼ 0.0   Continue to the east.
▲ 3.6   SO   Track on right is FR 682. Zero trip meter.

▼ 0.7   SO   Sand Tank on right and track on left; then cattle guard.
▲ 2.9   SO   Cattle guard; then Sand Tank on left and track on right.

▼ 1.5   SO   Track on left is FR 877.
▲ 2.1   SO   Track on right is FR 877.
    GPS: N35º55.25' W111º50.04'

▼ 1.6   SO   Track on right.
▲ 2.0   SO   Track on left.

▼ 2.1   SO   Two tracks on right.
▲ 1.5   SO   Two tracks on left.

▼ 2.6   SO   Track on right.
▲ 1.0   SO   Track on left.

▼ 3.0   SO   Watts Tank on left.
▲ 0.6   SO   Watts Tank on right.

GPS: N35º54.92' W111º48.43'

▼ 3.6   SO   Track on left is FR 878; also track on right. Zero trip meter.
▲ 0.0   Continue to the southwest.
    GPS: N35º54.82' W111º47.83'

▼ 0.0   Continue to the northeast.
▲ 3.0   SO   Track on right is FR 878; also track on left. Zero trip meter.

▼ 0.5   SO   Small track on left.
▲ 2.5   SO   Small track on right.

▼ 0.8   SO   Track on left.
▲ 2.2   SO   Track on right.

▼ 0.9   SO   Track on left is FR 791.
▲ 2.1   SO   Track on right is FR 791.
    GPS: N35º55.01' W111º46.90'

▼ 1.0   SO   Track on left; then track on right; then cross over wash.
▲ 2.0   SO   Cross over wash; then track on left; then track on right.

▼ 1.4   SO   Cattle guard; then track on left is FR 2815.
▲ 1.6   SO   Track on right is FR 2815; then cattle guard.
    GPS: N35º55.05' W111º46.35'

▼ 1.6   SO   Cattle guard; then track on right.
▲ 1.4   SO   Track on left; then cattle guard.

▼ 1.7   SO   Track on right.
▲ 1.3   SO   Track on left.

▼ 1.9   SO   Track on right.

1.1 ▲	SO	Track on left.
▼ 2.1	SO	Well-used track on left is FR 886.
0.9 ▲	BL	Well-used track on right is FR 886.

GPS: N35°55.28' W111°45.63'

▼ 2.6	SO	Track on right.
0.4 ▲	SO	Track on left.
▼ 2.9	SO	Track on right.
0.1 ▲	SO	Track on left.
▼ 3.0		Track on right; then cattle guard and closure gate. Trail ends at the T-intersection with Arizona 64. Turn right for Page and Flagstaff; turn left for the Grand Canyon National Park.
0.0 ▲		Trail commences on Arizona 64, 0.6 miles west of mile marker 276, 1 mile from the eastern boundary of the Kaibab National Forest. Zero trip meter and turn east on graded dirt road marked FR 307. Cattle guard and closure gate; then immediately track on left.

GPS: N35°55.37' W111°44.64'

NORTHEAST REGION TRAIL #2

Coconino Rim Trail

STARTING POINT: Northeast #3: Gray Mountain Road, 1.7 miles from Arizona 64

FINISHING POINT: Arizona 64 (East Rim Drive, Grand Canyon National Park), 0.4 miles east of mile marker 252

TOTAL MILEAGE: 21 miles

UNPAVED MILEAGE: 21 miles

DRIVING TIME: 2.5 hours

ELEVATION RANGE: 7,000–7,500 feet

USUALLY OPEN: April to December

BEST TIME TO TRAVEL: Dry weather

DIFFICULTY RATING: 3

SCENIC RATING: 7

REMOTENESS RATING: +0

Special Attractions

- Grandview Fire Lookout and views into Grand Canyon National Park.
- Wildlife viewing—deer, elk, wild turkeys, javelina, antelope.
- Cross-country ski area in winter.

Description

This trail explores the Kaibab National Forest along the edge of the Coconino Rim. In this region, the rim is lightly vegetated with pinyons and junipers, and is very different from the more open section that Northeast #3: Gray Mountain Road passes through. Initially, the trail leaves Northeast #3: Gray Mountain Road, and for the first 2 miles it follows small tracks within the Navajo Nation. Navigation can be tricky; there are many small trails very close together. Some of them rejoin the main trail after a short distance, but most go to dwellings. Should you find yourself on one of these, turn around and retrace your steps. The trail does not directly pass by any dwellings.

The national forest boundary is marked by a sign and a cattle guard; past this point, the trail is slightly wider and smoother. The trail is very rutted in places and in wet weather can be impassable. It is often open longer than the dates given and is closed naturally as a result of snowfall.

Near the western end of the trail is the intersection with Northeast #1: Hull Cabin Trail, which can be driven in conjunction with this one to create a loop. The Grandview Fire Lookout Tower is rarely manned. The number of tourist joy flights over the Grand Canyon and surrounding area has made it redundant—pilots normally report the fires. You are welcome to climb the tower to see the view, but the cabin at the top is usually locked. The climb up the tower is worthwhile. There are views over the tree tops to the rim of the Grand Canyon and the Coconino Rim. To the south are the San Francisco Peaks. The 80-foot-tall steel tower was erected in 1936 to replace an older, wooden tower. At its base is a two-room bungalow, which was the living quarters for the lookouts. Both the Vishnu Hiking Trail and the Tusayan Mountain Bike Trail commence from the tower.

The final section of the trail enters Grand Canyon National Park before finishing on the East Rim.

Arizona Trail access and Grandview Fire Lookout

Current Road Information

Kaibab National Forest
Tusayan Ranger District
PO Box 3088
Grand Canyon, AZ 86023
(928) 638-2443

Map References

BLM   Cameron
USFS Kaibab National Forest: Tusayan
      Ranger District
USGS 1:24,000   Hellhole Bend, Grandview
      Point NE, Grandview Point
      1:100,000 Cameron
Maptech CD-ROM: Flagstaff/Sedona/Prescott
Arizona Atlas & Gazetteer, pp. 32, 31
Arizona Road & Recreation Atlas, pp. 28,
      34, 35, 62, 68, 69
Recreational Map of Arizona

Route Directions

▼ 0.0   From Northeast #3: Gray Mountain
          Road, 1.7 miles south of Arizona 64,
          zero trip meter and turn southwest on
          well-used, unmarked trail.

2.5 ▲   Trail ends at the intersection with
         Northeast #3: Gray Mountain Road,
         1.7 miles south of Arizona 64. Turn left
         to exit to Arizona 64; turn right to con-
         tinue along Northeast #3: Gray
         Mountain Road to US 89.
         GPS: N35°55.31′ W111°41.86′

▼ 0.1 BR Two tracks on left; then track on right.
2.4 ▲ BL Track on left; then two tracks on right.
▼ 0.3 BL Trail forks; keep left.
2.2 ▲ SO Track on left.
         GPS: N35°55.13′ W111°42.07′

▼ 0.5 BL/BR Track on right into private property;
         then immediately bear right, leaving
         the second track on your left.
2.0 ▲SO/BR Track on right; then immediately bear
         right; track on left into private property.
▼ 0.6 SO Track on right and track on left.
1.9 ▲ SO Track on right and track on left.
▼ 0.7 TR Track on left and track straight on;
         then track on right.
1.8 ▲ TL Track on left; then crossroads; track on
         right and track straight on.
         GPS: N35°54.85′ W111°42.32′

The rim of the Grand Canyon from the Grandview Fire Lookout

Northeast Trail #2: Coconino Rim Trail

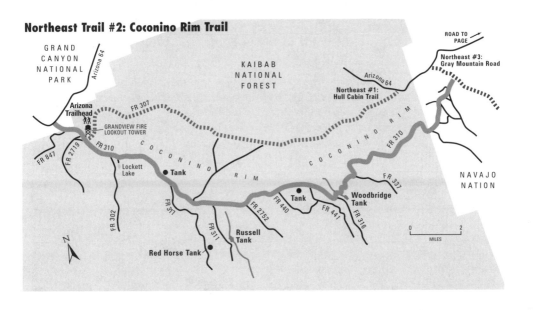

▼ 0.9   BR   Track on right; then trail forks; bear right at fork.

1.6 ▲   SO   Track on right; then track on left.

GPS: N35°54.86' W111°42.57'

▼ 1.0   BR   Track on left.

1.5 ▲   BR   Track on right.

▼ 1.1   SO   Track on right; then track on left.

1.4 ▲   SO   Track on right; then track on left.

GPS: N35°54.74' W111°42.71'

▼ 1.3   SO   Track on left.

1.2 ▲   BL   Track on right.

GPS: N35°54.58' W111°42.77'

▼ 1.6   SO   Trail forks.

0.9 ▲   SO   Trail rejoins.

▼ 1.7   SO   Trail rejoins.

0.8 ▲   SO   Trail forks.

▼ 1.8   SO   Track on left.

0.7 ▲   SO   Track on right.

▼ 1.9   SO   Well-used track on left.

0.6 ▲   BL   Well-used track on right.

GPS: N35°54.14' W111°43.02'

▼ 2.0   SO   Track on left.

0.5 ▲   SO   Track on right.

▼ 2.4   BR   Track on left.

0.1 ▲   BL   Track on right.

GPS: N35°53.83' W111°43.44'

▼ 2.5   SO   Cattle guard; entering Kaibab National Forest. Zero trip meter.

0.0 ▲   Continue to the southeast into the Navajo Nation.

GPS: N35°53.85' W111°43.52'

▼ 0.0   Continue to the northwest; trail is now marked FR 310.

4.7 ▲   SO   Cattle guard; leaving Kaibab National Forest. Zero trip meter.

▼ 0.5   SO   Track on left.

4.2 ▲   SO   Track on right.

▼ 1.1   SO   Track on left.

3.6 ▲   SO   Track on right.

▼ 1.3   SO   Track on left.

3.4 ▲   SO   Track on right.

▼ 1.5   SO   Faint track on right.

3.2 ▲   SO   Faint track on left.

▼ 1.7   SO   Track on left.

3.0 ▲   SO   Track on right.

▼ 1.9   SO   Faint track on left.

2.8 ▲   SO   Faint track on right.

▼ 3.1   SO   Track on right.

1.6 ▲   SO   Track on left.

GPS: N35°53.77' W111°46.06'

▼ 3.4   SO   Track on left.

1.3 ▲   SO   Track on right.

▼ 4.1   BL   Track straight on.

0.6 ▲   BR   Track on left.

THE GRAND CANYON

Of all Arizona's geological treasures, the most widely renowned is the Grand Canyon. Water, wind, and ice carved away the land to form the majestic canyon walls. About 60 to 70 million years ago, the area of the Grand Canyon was actually level and covered by an ancient sea. The sea deposited sand, which hardened into rock. As more and more sand was deposited, layering took place. As today's Grand Canyon gets deeper, older stone is revealed. As the ancient sea receded, rivers drained from mountain peaks and formed the

The Grand Canyon

ancestral Colorado River, which poured into Marble Canyon. As the Colorado Plateau began to lift, the river continued to cut its way through the landscape. About 5 million years ago, the river changed course to that of the present-day Colorado River. It is uncertain why this happened, but it is probable that the Colorado joined with another river. By that time, the canyon had already started to form and the erosive force of the Colorado hastened the canyon's creation. Today, Glen Canyon Dam has slowed the erosive force on the Grand Canyon. Also, the river now rolls over solid rockbed, which will take more time to erode. But even now the awe-inspiring Grand Canyon continues to be shaped by forces of nature.

GPS: N35°53.74′ W111°47.02′

▼ 4.7 TR T-intersection. Turn right, remaining on FR 310. Track on left is FR 337. Zero trip meter.

0.0 ▲ Continue to the northeast.

GPS: N35°53.22′ W111°47.06′

▼ 0.0 Continue to the west.

1.3 ▲ TL Turn left, remaining on FR 310. Track straight ahead is FR 337. Zero trip meter.

▼ 0.2 SO Wire gate; then track on left.

1.1 ▲ SO Track on right; then wire gate.

▼ 0.3 SO Track on left.

1.0 ▲	SO	Track on right.
▼ 0.5	SO	Track on right.
0.8 ▲	SO	Track on left.
▼ 0.8	SO	Track on right.
0.5 ▲	SO	Track on left.
▼ 1.1	SO	Cross through wash; then Woodbridge Tank on left.
0.2 ▲	SO	Woodbridge Tank on right; then cross through wash.

GPS: N35°52.82′ W111°48.00′

▼ 1.3	TR	T-intersection. Turn right, remaining on FR 310. Road on left is FR 316. Zero trip meter.
0.0 ▲		Continue to the northeast.

GPS: N35°52.71′ W111°48.04′

▼ 0.0		Continue to the west; trail is now smoother and roughly graded.
5.1 ▲	TL	Turn left, remaining on FR 310. Track ahead is FR 316. Zero trip meter.
▼ 1.1	SO	Track on left is FR 441; also track on right.
4.0 ▲	SO	Track on right is FR 441; also track on left.

GPS: N35°53.32′ W111°48.89′

▼ 1.6	SO	Game tank on left.
3.5 ▲	SO	Game tank on right.
▼ 2.4	SO	Track on left is FR 440.
2.7 ▲	SO	Track on right is FR 440.

GPS: N35°53.55′ W111°50.27′

▼ 3.7	SO	Track on left.
1.4 ▲	SO	Track on right.
▼ 3.9	SO	Track on left is FR 2752.
1.2 ▲	BL	Track on right is FR 2752.

GPS: N35°53.46′ W111°51.78′

▼ 4.5	SO	Track on left.
0.6 ▲	SO	Track on right.
▼ 4.7	SO	Russell Wash section of the Arizona Trail crosses the main trail.
0.4 ▲	SO	Russell Wash section of the Arizona Trail crosses the main trail.

GPS: N35°53.67′ W111°52.58′

▼ 5.0	SO	Cattle guard.
0.1 ▲	SO	Cattle guard.
▼ 5.1	SO	Graded road on left is FR 311 to

		Russell Tank. Zero trip meter. There is no sign in this direction.
0.0 ▲		Continue to the east, following the sign to Woodbridge.

GPS: N35°53.79′ W111°52.97′

▼ 0.0		Continue to the west.
4.8 ▲	SO	Graded road on right is FR 311 to Russell Tank. Zero trip meter.
▼ 0.8	SO	Track on right.
4.0 ▲	SO	Track on left.
▼ 1.3	SO	Track on right.
3.5 ▲	SO	Track on left.
▼ 2.0	SO	Track on left is FR 317 to Red Horse Tank. Continue straight on, following the sign to Grandview and cross cattle guard; closure gate at cattle guard.
2.8 ▲	SO	Closure gate and cattle guard; then track on right is FR 317 to Red Horse Tank. Continue straight on, following the sign to Russell Tank.

GPS: N35°54.90′ W111°54.37′

▼ 2.4	SO	Game tank on right.
2.4 ▲	SO	Game tank on left.

GPS: N35°55.25′ W111°54.66′

▼ 2.6	SO	Track on left is FR 729.
2.2 ▲	SO	Track on right is FR 729.
▼ 3.2	SO	Track on left is FR 735.
1.6 ▲	SO	Track on right is FR 735.

GPS: N35°55.86′ W111°54.92′

▼ 3.5	SO	Cattle guard.
1.3 ▲	SO	Cattle guard.
▼ 3.6	SO	Track on left is FR 728.
1.2 ▲	SO	Track on right is FR 728.
▼ 4.1	SO	Track on left is FR 712.
0.7 ▲	SO	Track on right is FR 712.

GPS: N35°56.24′ W111°55.71′

▼ 4.6	SO	Track on left is FR 301 to Lockett Lake. No sign in this direction.
0.2 ▲	SO	Track on right is FR 301 to Lockett Lake.

GPS: N35°56.43′ W111°56.25′

▼ 4.8	SO	Track on left is FR 302 to Bucklar and Camp 36 Tank. Zero trip meter.
0.0 ▲		Continue to the east, following the sign to Russell Tank.

▼ 0.0   Continue to the west, following sign to Grandview Fire Lookout.

1.3 ▲   SO   Track on right is FR 302 to Bucklar and Camp 36 Tank. Zero trip meter.

▼ 0.6   SO   Track on right.

0.7 ▲   SO   Track on left.

▼ 0.8   SO   Track on left.

0.5 ▲   SO   Track on right.

▼ 1.0   SO   Track on left; then cattle guard.

0.3 ▲   SO   Cattle guard; then track on right.

▼ 1.3   SO   Graded road on right is FR 307, Northeast #1: Hull Cabin Trail. Graded dirt road on left is FR 2719. Zero trip meter.

0.0 ▲   Continue to the southeast on FR 310, following the sign to Russell Tank.

GPS: N35°57.37' W111°57.23'

▼ 0.0   Continue to the northwest on FR 310, following the sign to Grand Canyon National Park.

1.3 ▲   SO   Graded dirt road on left is FR 307, Northeast #1: Hull Cabin Trail. Graded dirt road on right is FR 2719. Zero trip meter.

▼ 0.1   SO   Grandview Fire Lookout on right and Arizona Trail on right.

1.2 ▲   SO   Grandview Fire Lookout on left and Arizona Trail on left.

GPS: N35°57.44' W111°57.28'

▼ 0.6   SO   Track on left.

0.7 ▲   SO   Track on right.

▼ 0.7   SO   Track on left is FR 847. Leaving Kaibab National Forest.

0.6 ▲   SO   Entering Kaibab National Forest. Track on right is FR 847.

GPS: N35°57.75' W111°57.83'

▼ 0.8   SO   Cattle guard; entering Grand Canyon National Park.

0.5 ▲   SO   Cattle guard; leaving Grand Canyon National Park.

▼ 1.3   Trail ends on Arizona 64, East Rim Drive in Grand Canyon National Park. Turn right for Page; turn left for Grand Canyon south rim.

0.0 ▲   Trail commences on Arizona 64, East

Rim Drive in Grand Canyon National Park, 2.1 miles southeast of the turn to Grandview Point. Zero trip meter and turn south on graded dirt road. The turn is signed for the Arizona Trail. Turn is 0.4 mile east of mile marker 252.

GPS: N35°58.09' W111°58.29'

NORTHEAST REGION TRAIL #3

Gray Mountain Road

STARTING POINT: US 89 at Gray Mountain

FINISHING POINT: Arizona 64 (Navahopi Road), 1.8 miles east of the Kaibab National Forest boundary

TOTAL MILEAGE: 22.2 miles

UNPAVED MILEAGE: 20.3 miles

DRIVING TIME: 2.25 hours

ELEVATION RANGE: 4,900–7,100 feet

USUALLY OPEN: Year-round

BEST TIME TO TRAVEL: Dry weather

DIFFICULTY RATING: 2

SCENIC RATING: 9

REMOTENESS RATING: +1

Special Attractions

■ Remote, lightly traveled trail through the Navajo Nation.

■ Spectacular, deep Burro Canyon.

■ Views of the San Francisco Volcanic Field.

Description

This lightly traveled trail follows Indian Road 6150 as it travels up onto the plateau of Gray Mountain. The road is also marked on some maps as the Gray Mountain Truck Trail. It leaves US 89 at the settlement of Gray Mountain and follows a paved road to the west. This is the only road leaving to the west, so although it is not marked, it is easy to find. After a couple of miles, the route turns onto a graded dirt road, suitable for high-clearance vehicles. It travels across an open plain covered with sagebrush toward the rise of the Coconino Rim. One pretty point along the trail is the crossing of Tappan Wash, which is a moderately deep, rocky canyon at this point.

The road climbs onto the Coconino Rim, crossing a narrow saddle with deep drops into Burro Canyon to the north and Tappan Wash to the south. This is the best view along the trail. Once up on the rim the road runs across the plateau of Gray Mountain, a sparsely vegetated, wind-blown plateau, dissected with deep canyons and light-colored gullies.

The road is graded all the way but is subject to ruts and bulldust, a fine dust that settles in potholes and ruts that can make the road look flat. It is impassable after rain. The road is mostly unmarked, but it follows the main graded road for most of the way, so it is easy to navigate. The final section of the trail descends the Coconino Rim to Arizona 64. As it descends, the Little Colorado River Gorge can be seen to the north.

Remember that all land within the Navajo Nation is privately owned. Remain on the main route as you pass through. The side trails noted in the route directions are included for navigational purposes and are not necessarily open for travel; most of them lead to dwellings. Hiking and camping require specific permits. Please check requirements and restrictions before traveling. Refer to the section on travel etiquette in the Navajo Nation for more details. The area is used by the Navajo people for grazing and you are likely to encounter flocks of sheep and goats. Be sure you drive slowly to avoid startling them.

Current Road Information

Navajo Nation Parks and Recreation
PO Box 2520
Window Rock, AZ 86515
(928) 871-6647

Map References

BLM   Cameron
USGS 1:24,000   Gray Mtn., Cameron
      South, Coconino Point SE, Willows
      Camp, Hellhole Bend
      1:100,000 Cameron
Maptech CD-ROM: Flagstaff/Sedona/
      Prescott
Arizona Atlas & Gazetteer, p. 32
Arizona Road & Recreation Atlas, pp. 35, 69

Navajo hogan (private property—please view only from the trail)

Route Directions

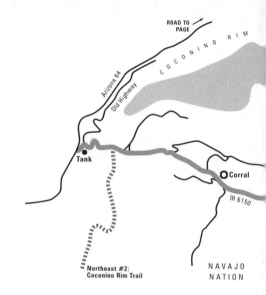

▼ 0.0   From US 89 at the settlement of Gray Mountain, zero trip meter and turn west on the paved road in the middle of Gray Mountain. The road is unmarked, but it is the only road leading out to the west. Immediately cross cattle guard. Remain on the paved road, ignoring tracks on right and left.

1.9 ▲   Trail ends at the T-intersection with US 89 in Gray Mountain. Turn left for Page; turn right for Flagstaff.

    GPS: N35°44.72′ W111°28.40′

▼ 1.9 TL On a right-hand bend, turn left opposite mile marker 2 onto graded dirt road marked Navajo Highway 6150. Zero trip meter.

0.0 ▲   Continue to the east.

    GPS: N35°46.00′ W111°29.90′

▼ 0.0   Continue to the west.

6.0 ▲ TR T-intersection with paved road; zero trip meter and turn right. Remain on the paved road into Gray Mountain, ignoring tracks on left and right.

▼ 0.3 SO Track on left and track on right.

5.7 ▲ SO Track on left and track on right.

▼ 0.5 SO Track on left; then track on right.

5.5 ▲ SO Track on left; then track on right.

▼ 0.6 SO Track on right.

5.4 ▲ SO Track on left.

▼ 1.0 SO Pass under power lines.

5.0 ▲ SO Pass under power lines.

▼ 1.2 BL Cross over Cedar Wash; then track on right.

4.8 ▲ BR Track on left; then cross over Cedar Wash.

    GPS: N35°46.52′ W111°31.15′

▼ 1.4 SO Track on left under power lines.

4.6 ▲ SO Track on right under power lines.

▼ 1.8 SO Track on right.

4.2 ▲ SO Track on left.

▼ 2.0 SO Track on left.

4.0 ▲ SO Track on right.

▼ 2.1 SO Cross through Needmore Wash.

3.9 ▲ SO Cross through Needmore Wash.

▼ 2.4 SO Track on left.

3.6 ▲ SO Track on right.

Northeast Trail #3: Gray Mountain Road

▼ 2.5 SO Track on left.

3.5 ▲ SO Track on right.

▼ 2.6 SO Track on right.

3.4 ▲ SO Track on left.

▼ 2.8 SO Graded road on left and track on right.

3.2 ▲ SO Graded road on right and track on left.

    GPS: N35°46.90′ W111°32.51′

▼ 3.3 SO Track on left; then road descends to cross through Tappan Wash.

2.7 ▲ SO Track on right as road climbs away from wash.

▼ 3.5 SO Cross through Tappan Wash.

2.5 ▲ SO Cross through Tappan Wash.

    GPS: N35°46.97′ W111°33.15′

▼ 3.8 SO Track on left.

2.2 ▲ SO Track on right.

▼ 4.1 SO Track on right.

1.9 ▲ SO Track on left.

▼ 5.1 SO Track on left and track on right.

0.9 ▲ BR Track on left; bear right, remaining on main dirt road; then track on right.

    GPS: N35°47.55′ W111°34.46′

▼ 5.2 SO Track on left.

0.8 ▲ SO Track on right.

▼ 5.3 SO Cross through wash.

0.7 ▲ SO Cross through wash.

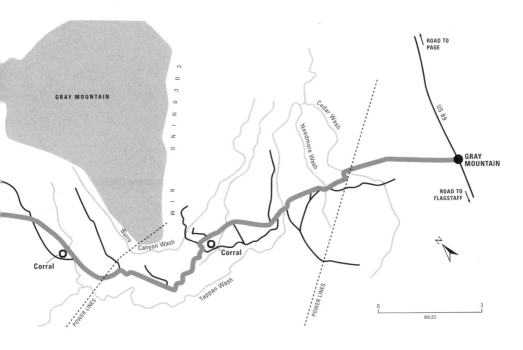

▼ 5.8   SO   Small track on right.

0.2 ▲   SO   Small track on left.

▼ 6.0   BL   Graded road on right. There is a stone corral on the left. Zero trip meter.

0.0 ▲   Continue to the east.

GPS: N35°47.78′ W111°35.39′

▼ 0.0   Continue to the west.

9.2 ▲   SO   Graded road on left. There is a stone corral on the right. Zero trip meter.

▼ 0.3   SO   Track on right; then cross through wash.

8.9 ▲   BR   Cross through wash; then track on left.

▼ 0.4   SO   Track on left.

8.8 ▲   SO   Track on right.

▼ 1.9   SO   Saddle between two canyons. Burro Canyon on the right and Tappan Wash on the left.

7.3 ▲   SO   Saddle between two canyons. Burro Canyon on the left and Tappan Wash on the right.

GPS: N35°47.48′ W111°36.99′

▼ 2.4   SO   Top of Gray Mountain.

6.8 ▲   SO   Top of Gray Mountain.

▼ 3.1   SO   Track on right.

6.1 ▲   SO   Track on left.

▼ 3.5   SO   Track on right.

5.7 ▲   SO   Track on left.

▼ 3.7   SO   Track on right.

5.5 ▲   SO   Track on left.

▼ 4.0   SO   Track on right.

5.2 ▲   SO   Track on left.

▼ 4.2   SO   Small track on left.

5.0 ▲   SO   Small track on right.

▼ 4.6   SO   Pass under power lines; small track on right.

4.6 ▲   SO   Pass under power lines; small track on left.

GPS: N35°48.92′ W111°38.60′

▼ 5.5   SO   Cross through wash; track on left.

3.7 ▲   SO   Track on right; cross through wash.

▼ 5.7   SO   Track on left to corral; then cross through wash.

3.5 ▲   SO   Cross through wash; then track on right to corral.

▼ 5.9   SO   Track on left.

3.3 ▲   SO   Track on right.

▼ 6.3   SO   Track on left.

2.9 ▲   SO   Track on right.

▼ 6.7   SO   Two tracks on right; track on left.

2.5 ▲   SO   Track on right; two tracks on left.

▼ 6.9   SO   Track on right.

2.3 ▲   SO   Track on left.

▼ 7.0   SO   Small track on left.

2.2 ▲   SO   Small track on right.

▼ 7.2   SO   Track on right and track on left.

2.0 ▲   SO   Track on left and track on right.

▼ 8.1   SO   Track on right.

View of Burro Canyon from the trail

1.1 ▲	SO	Track on left.
▼ 8.3	SO	Track on right.
0.9 ▲	SO	Track on left.
		GPS: N35°52.04' W111°39.66'

▼ 8.6	SO	Track on left.
0.6 ▲	SO	Track on right.
		GPS: N35°52.30' W111°39.86'

▼ 9.1	SO	Well-used track on left.
0.1 ▲	SO	Well-used track on right.
		GPS: N35°52.69' W111°40.06'

▼ 9.2	SO	Track on left; then dam on left; then corral on right. Zero trip meter.
0.0 ▲		Continue to the south.
		GPS: N35°52.83' W111°40.10'

▼ 0.0		Continue to the north.
3.4 ▲	SO	Corral on left; then dam on right; then track on right. Zero trip meter.
▼ 0.1	SO	Track on left; then small track on right.
3.3 ▲	SO	Small track on left; then track on right.
▼ 0.4	SO	Two tracks on right.
3.0 ▲	SO	Two tracks on left.
▼ 1.5	SO	Two tracks on right.

1.9 ▲	SO	Two tracks on left.
▼ 1.9	SO	Track on left.
1.5 ▲	SO	Track on right.
▼ 2.0	SO	Track on left.
1.4 ▲	SO	Track on right.
▼ 2.2	SO	Track on right; then track on left.
1.2 ▲	SO	Track on right; then track on left.
▼ 2.4	SO	Track on right.
1.0 ▲	SO	Track on left.
▼ 2.6	SO	Well-used track on left.
0.8 ▲	SO	Well-used track on right.
		GPS: N35°54.76' W111°41.32'

▼ 2.9	SO	Track on left.
0.5 ▲	SO	Track on right.
▼ 3.0	SO	Track on right; then track on left.
0.4 ▲	SO	Track on right; then track on left.
		GPS: N35°54.99' W111°41.63'

▼ 3.1	SO	Track on right.
0.3 ▲	SO	Track on left.
▼ 3.4	SO	Track on left is Northeast #2: Coconino Rim Trail; track on right. Zero trip meter.
0.0 ▲		Continue to the northwest.
		GPS: N35°55.31' W111°41.85'

▼ 0.0		Continue toward Arizona 64.
1.7 ▲	SO	Track on left; track on right is Northeast #2: Coconino Rim Trail. Zero trip meter.
▼ 0.3	SO	Track on right; then track on left.
1.4 ▲	SO	Track on right; then track on left.
▼ 1.3	SO	Tank on left.
0.4 ▲	SO	Tank on right.
▼ 1.4	TL	T-intersection with paved Old Highway.
0.3 ▲	TR	Turn right onto graded dirt road.
		GPS: N35°55.90′ W111°42.41′

▼ 1.7	TR	Turn right and cross cattle guard; then trail ends at the T-intersection with Arizona 64.
0.0 ▲	TL	From Arizona 64, 18 miles west of the intersection with US 89, zero trip meter and turn southeast on small road across a cattle guard and then immediately turn left at the T-intersection onto the paved Old Highway. Turn is immediately west of roadside trading stands, but intersection is unmarked.
		GPS: N35°55.86′ W111°42.76′

O'Leary Peak Trail

STARTING POINT: US 89, 6 miles north of Flagstaff, 0.1 miles south of mile marker 427

FINISHING POINT: Gate of O'Leary Peak Fire Lookout

TOTAL MILEAGE: 8.7 miles

UNPAVED MILEAGE: 8.1 miles

DRIVING TIME: 1 hour (one-way)

ELEVATION RANGE: 6,900–8,200 feet

USUALLY OPEN: Year-round

BEST TIME TO TRAVEL: Year-round

DIFFICULTY RATING: 2

SCENIC RATING: 10

REMOTENESS RATING: +0

Special Attractions

■ Twisting black cinder trail.

■ Sunset Crater National Monument.

■ Trail passes beside Bonito Lava Flow and offers views over it.

History

Sunset Crater Volcano is the youngest of all the volcanoes included within the San Francisco Volcano Field, a group of volcanic features located north of Flagstaff. This trail passes alongside the Bonito Lava Flow, a jagged black stream of cooled lava that flowed out of the base of Sunset Crater more than a hundred years after its initial eruption in 1064. The flow hardened and covered nearly 2 square miles of the landscape. The flow of black basalt, the most common volcanic rock to be found on the earth's surface, is composed mainly of silica but also contains many tiny mineral grains, mainly iron- and magnesium-rich minerals that give it its dark color. The quick cooling of the flow prevented the minerals from forming larger structures. The texture of the flow, with its uneven surface, comes from the bubbles of gas trapped within the cooling lava. The geological term for these cavities created by bubbles is vesicles.

O'Leary Peak and O'Leary Basin are named after Dan O'Leary, a guide and interpreter for 19th century Indian fighter, General George Crook.

Description

This trail travels through the edge of the Cinder Hills OHV Area and Sunset Crater National Monument to climb O'Leary Peak, one of the volcanic peaks contained within the San Francisco Volcano Field.

The trail leaves US 89 north of Flagstaff at the same point as Northeast #6: Cinder Hills Loop Trail but diverges from this trail after 0.5 miles. Initially, the trail follows a well-graded road through ponderosa pines that cover the black cinder hills. It crosses the paved road to Sunset Crater National Monument just inside the western edge of the monument boundary. You will have to pass through the entrance booth to continue along the trail, but normally there is no fee required if you just wish to pass through.

The route turns away from the paved road almost immediately, following the rougher trail to O'Leary Peak. It passes directly alongside the Bonito Lava Flow, characterized by hardened waves of black basalt. The flow is clearly defined as it rises above the trail.

Once away from the lava flow, the trail ascends O'Leary Peak. It is not possible to drive all the way to the fire lookout because there is a locked gate 1.3 miles from the top. You can park and hike the final section to the tower. The shelf road to the gate is wide and gives a spectacular view over the lava flow to pink-tipped Sunset Crater.

A second short spur, a much smaller, 3-rated trail, travels over the ridge top of Robinson Mountain to end at a viewpoint over Bonito Park and the San Francisco Peaks.

Current Road Information
Coconino National Forest
Peaks Ranger District
5075 North Hwy 89
Flagstaff, AZ 86004
(928) 526-0866

Sunset Crater Volcano National Monument
6400 N. Hwy 89
Flagstaff, AZ 86004
(928) 526-0502

Map References
BLM   Flagstaff
USFS Coconino National Forest: Peaks
      Ranger District
USGS 1:24,000   Sunset Crater West,
      O'Leary Peak
      1:100,000 Flagstaff
Maptech CD-ROM: Flagstaff/Sedona/Prescott
Arizona Atlas & Gazetteer, pp. 42, 32

Route Directions

▼ 0.0   From US 89, 6 miles north of Flagstaff,
         zero trip meter and turn northeast on
         FR 776 sign-posted to the Cinder Hills
         OHV Area. Road is graded dirt. Turn is
         0.1 miles south of mile marker 427.
0.5 ▲   Trail ends on US 89 north of Flagstaff.
         Turn left for Flagstaff.
         GPS: N35°19.70' W111°32.68'

One of the contorted mounds created by the Bonito Lava Flow

Northeast Trail #4: O'Leary Peak Trail

COCONINO NATIONAL FOREST

BONITO PARK

US 89

Viewpoint

Viewpoint

Robinson Mountain

LOOKOUT TOWER

O'Leary Peak

FR 545A

Bonito Campground

FR 545E

LENOX CRATER

BONITO LAVA FLOW

FR 414

FR 545

FR 776

ROAD TO FLAGSTAFF

0   1
MILES

Northeast #6: Cinder Hills Loop Trail

SUNSET CRATER NATIONAL MONUMENT

SUNSET CRATER

▼ 0.5   TL   Turn left onto the graded road, FR 414. Northeast #6: Cinder Hills Loop Trail continues ahead. Zero trip meter.

0.0 ▲   Continue to the west.

GPS: N35°19.93' W111°32.22'

▼ 0.0   Continue to the northwest.

2.5 ▲   TR   Turn right onto graded road, FR 776. Track on left is Northeast #6: Cinder Hills Loop Trail. Zero trip meter.

Sunset Crater viewed from the spur trail

THE SAN FRANCISCO VOLCANO FIELD AND SUNSET CRATER

On the southern edge of the Colorado Plateau lies the San Francisco Volcano Field. This 2,000-square-mile patch of northeastern Arizona is the result of several million years of volcanic activity. The most recent activity, however, led to the formation of Sunset Crater in A.D. 1064–1065, when a massive eruption sprayed molten rock, which solidified in the air and rained down in small cylinders. A large lava flow, the Kana-A flow, spewed out from the fissure, killing all within its deadly path. As the years passed, debris from further eruptions accumulated around the volcanic vent and the crater was slowly born. In 1180, the Bonito Lava Flow spewed from the fissure. Around 1250, sulfur and iron were vented and collected on the sides of the crater. The sulfur, combined with the oxidized iron, created an eerie glow that inspired John Wesley Powell to name the fissure Sunset Crater in 1869. Cinder cones of the San Francisco Volcano Field are spread across the region of the Sunset Crater area. These cinder cones are actually tiny volcanoes that formed around volcanic vents. Many of these cones contain crater lakes.

Looming above Sunset Crater and the volcanic field is San Francisco Mountain (or San Francisco Peaks). San Francisco Mountain is a very old volcano that takes after the notorious Mount St. Helens, Mount Hood, and Mount Fujiyama. The northeast face is said to have exploded, just as Mount St. Helens did, creating a roughly hewn valley. The valley was later smoothed by glacial activity. The explosion also caused the mountain to collapse in upon itself and fall into the emptied magma chamber. The highest point in the state can be found on one of this mountain's four lonesome peaks; Humphreys Peak rises to 12,670 feet.

Sunset Crater was nearly obliterated in 1928. A movie company had plans to dynamite the slopes of the cone to create a landslide effect for a film. Local citizens stepped in to halt the move, and as a result, President Herbert Hoover created the Sunset Crater Volcano National Monument in 1930.

▼ 0.1   SO   Track on right.

2.4 ▲   SO   Track on left.

▼ 0.2   SO   Graded road on right is FR 9143C.

2.3 ▲   SO   Graded road on left is FR 9143C.

GPS: N35°20.14' W111°32.11'

▼ 0.4   SO   Track on left.

2.1 ▲   SO   Track on right.

▼ 0.5   SO   Track on left.

2.0 ▲   SO   Track on right.

▼ 0.6   SO   Track on right.

1.9 ▲   BR   Track on left.

▼ 0.7   SO   Track on right.

1.8 ▲   SO   Track on left.

▼ 0.8   SO   Track on left is FR 9141U (no vehicles), and track on right goes into OHV area (ATVs only).

1.7 ▲   SO   Track on right is FR 9141U (no vehicles), and track on left goes into OHV area (ATVs only).

GPS: N35°20.54' W111°31.84'

▼ 1.5   BL   Well-used track on right. Bear left, remaining on FR 414.

1.0 ▲   SO   Well-used track on left. Continue straight on, remaining on FR 414.

GPS: N35°21.18' W111°31.80'

▼ 2.5   TL   Join paved road to Sunset Crater and turn left. Zero trip meter.

0.0 ▲   Continue to the southeast.

GPS: N35°21.96' W111°32.14'

▼ 0.0   Continue to the northwest.

0.6 ▲   TR   Leave paved road turning right onto small, formed unmarked trail, which is 0.1 miles beyond the trail marked FR 414. Zero trip meter.

▼ 0.5   SO   Exit Sunset Crater National Monument; then track on right is FR 545E into Bonito USFS Campground.

0.1 ▲ SO Track on left is FR 545E into Bonito
          USFS Campground. Enter Sunset
          Crater National Monument.
          GPS: N35°22.22' W111°32.66'

▼ 0.6 TR Turn right at Bonito Park onto graded
          dirt road, FR 545A.
0.0 ▲   Continue to the southeast along paved
          road toward the entrance to Sunset
          Crater National Monument.
          GPS: N35°22.29' W111°32.75'

▼ 0.0   Continue to the east. Camping and
          campfires are prohibited from this
          point.
▼ 0.6 SO Edge of the Bonito Lava Flow on the right.
▼ 1.2 SO Track on left.
▼ 2.3 SO Start of wide shelf road up O'Leary Peak.
▼ 2.6 BR Track on left is spur to viewpoint on
          right-hand switchback. Remain on
          main trail.
          GPS: N35°23.47' W111°32.30'

▼ 3.7 UT Trail ends at the locked gate to the
          lookout tower. Turn around at the gate.
          From here it is a 1.3-mile hike to the
          fire lookout.
          GPS: N35°23.84' W111°31.28'

Spur to Viewpoint

▼ 0.0   Turn west on small unmarked trail on
          the right-hand switchback.
          GPS: N35°23.47' W111°32.30'

▼ 0.3 BL Track on right on left-hand bend.
          GPS: N35°23.45' W111°32.53'

▼ 0.5 SO Viewpoint at top of steep hill; track
          on right.
          GPS: N35°23.34' W111°32.71'

▼ 0.8 SO Track on right.
          GPS: N35°23.14' W111°32.83'

▼ 1.4   Trail ends at second viewpoint.
          GPS: N35°22.90' W111°32.91'

O'Leary Basin Trail

STARTING POINT: FR 545 on the eastern edge
of Sunset Crater National Monument
FINISHING POINT: Sunset Crater Road, FR
545, 0.1 miles east of US 89, 15 miles
north of Flagstaff
TOTAL MILEAGE: 13.6 miles
UNPAVED MILEAGE: 13.6 miles
DRIVING TIME: 1.5 hours
ELEVATION RANGE: 6,300–7,500
USUALLY OPEN: Year-round
BEST TIME TO TRAVEL: Year-round
DIFFICULTY RATING: 3
SCENIC RATING: 10
REMOTENESS RATING: +0

Special Attractions
■ Views of Sunset Crater.
■ Trail travels on the black lava dunes of the
San Francisco Volcano Field.
■ One of the less traveled trails within this
region.

Description
This trail travels through the black lava dunes
that surround Sunset Crater National Monument but outside of the popular OHV area. If
anything, this trail has the most impressive
scenery of all those that pass through this
unique region, and the trail is infinitely quieter
than the busy trails within the OHV area.

The trail leaves paved FR 545 at the eastern edge of Sunset Crater National Monument and travels as a formed single-track trail
across the black cinder "dunes" on the edge of
the monument. The surface, similar to loose
sand, is very smooth and soft in places.

This undulating trail winds in a large loop
around the north face of the jutting volcanic
cones of O'Leary Peak, passing along the
edge of O'Leary Basin through ponderosa
pines that grow out of the black cinders.

Around the west side of O'Leary Peak the
trail becomes rougher and more eroded. It follows a smaller track, FR 9124C, descending to
rejoin FR 545 near the intersection with US 89.

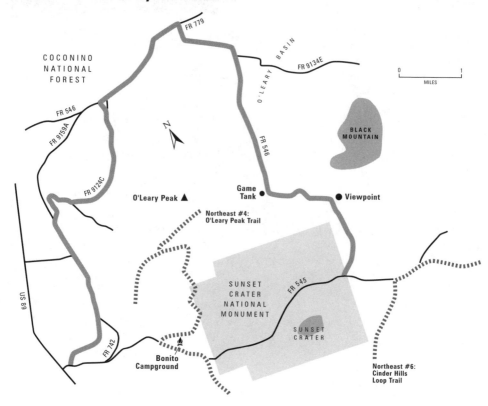

There are exceptional views all along the trail of the San Francisco Peaks, Sunset Crater, O'Leary Peak, and over O'Leary Basin. There are some good campsites as well, especially those on beds of black cinders. Light snow, which can make the trail temporarily impassable, is possible during the winter months.

Current Road Information

Coconino National Forest
Peaks Ranger District
5075 North Hwy 89
Flagstaff, AZ 86004
(928) 526-0866

Sunset Crater Volcano National Monument
6400 N. Hwy 89
Flagstaff, AZ 86004
(928) 526-0502

Map References

BLM   Flagstaff
USFS   Coconino National Forest: Peaks
       Ranger District
USGS   1:24,000   Sunset Crater East,
       Strawberry Crater, O'Leary Peak
       1:100,000 Flagstaff
Maptech CD-ROM: Flagstaff/Sedona/Prescott
Arizona Atlas & Gazetteer, p. 32
Arizona Road & Recreation Atlas, pp. 35, 69

Route Directions

▼ 0.0   From FR 545 at the eastern edge of
           Sunset Crater National Monument,
           zero trip meter and turn northeast on
           small dirt road marked FR 546.

4.6 ▲   Trail ends at the intersection with
           paved FR 545 at the eastern edge of
           Sunset Crater National Monument.
           Turn left for Wupatki National

Sunset Crater ahead

The trail winds along the side of the black volcanic O'Leary Peak

Monument; turn right for Flagstaff.
GPS: N35°22.36' W111°29.33'

▼ 0.6   SO   Trail crosses open black lava dune.
4.0 ▲   SO   Trail crosses open black lava dune.
▼ 1.3   BL   Track on right is viewpoint over Black Mountain.
3.3 ▲   BR   Track on left is viewpoint over Black Mountain.
GPS: N35°23.40' W111°29.10'

▼ 2.5   SO   Game tank on left.
2.1 ▲   SO   Game tank on right.
GPS: N35°23.81' W111°30.11'

▼ 3.0   SO   Track on left.
1.6 ▲   SO   Track on right.
▼ 4.6   SO   Track on right is FR 9134E. Zero trip meter.
0.0 ▲   Continue to the south.
GPS: N35°25.71' W111°29.92'

▼ 0.0   Continue to the north.
2.9 ▲   SO   Track on left is FR 9134E. Zero trip meter.
▼ 1.1   TL   T-intersection; FR 546 continues to the left; track on right is FR 779.
1.8 ▲   TR   Turn right, remaining on FR 546. Track ahead is FR 779.
GPS: N35°26.37' W111°30.71'

▼ 1.4   SO   Track on left.
1.5 ▲   SO   Track on right.
▼ 2.0   SO   Cattle guard.
0.9 ▲   SO   Cattle guard.
▼ 2.2   SO   Track on left.
0.7 ▲   SO   Track on right.
▼ 2.8   SO   Track on left.
0.1 ▲   SO   Track on right.
GPS: N35°25.69' W111°32.31'

▼ 2.9   TL   Turn left onto smaller trail, FR 9124C. FR 546 continues ahead. Zero trip meter.
0.0 ▲   Continue to the east.

Cinder Hills Loop Trail

▼ 0.0		Continue to the south.
4.4 ▲	TR	T-intersection with FR 546. Turn right onto the slightly larger trail. Zero trip meter.
▼ 0.1	SO	Small track on right.
4.3 ▲	SO	Small track on left.
▼ 0.5	SO	Track on left.
3.9 ▲	SO	Track on right.
▼ 1.2	SO	Track on left.
3.2 ▲	SO	Track on right.
▼ 2.0	SO	Track on right; then track on left.
2.4 ▲	SO	Track on right; then track on left.

GPS: N35°24.51' W111°33.47'

▼ 2.1	SO	Start to descend shelf road.
2.3 ▲	SO	End of climb.
▼ 2.6	SO	End of descent.
1.8 ▲	SO	Start to climb shelf road.
▼ 2.8	BL	Trail forks; bear left on unmarked trail. Track on right is FR 9159A. Both tracks are equally used.
1.6 ▲	SO	Track on left is FR 9159A; continue straight on FR 9124C.

GPS: N35°24.29' W111°33.81'

▼ 3.7	SO	Track on right.
0.7 ▲	SO	Track on left.
▼ 4.4	TR	T-intersection with graded dirt road, FR 742. Turn right and zero trip meter.
0.0 ▲		Continue to the west.

GPS: N35°22.92' W111°33.58'

▼ 0.0		Continue to the south toward US 89.
1.7 ▲	TL	Turn left at the marker for FR 545B onto smaller formed trail. Zero trip meter.
▼ 0.4	SO	Track on left.
1.3 ▲	SO	Track on right.
▼ 1.7		Trail ends at the T-intersection with the paved road to Sunset Crater, FR 545, immediately east of US 89.
0.0 ▲		Trail commences on the Sunset Crater Road, FR 545, immediately east of US 89, 15 miles north of Flagstaff. Turn north on wide graded dirt road. Turn is opposite an information board.

GPS: N35°22.36' W111°34.42'

STARTING POINT: US 89, 6 miles north of Flagstaff, 0.1 miles south of mile marker 427

FINISHING POINT: Townsend–Winona Road, 5.5 miles east of US 89

TOTAL MILEAGE: 18.9 miles

UNPAVED MILEAGE: 18.5 miles

DRIVING TIME: 2 hours

ELEVATION RANGE: 6,500–7,300 feet

USUALLY OPEN: Year-round

BEST TIME TO TRAVEL: Year-round

DIFFICULTY RATING: 3

SCENIC RATING: 9

REMOTENESS RATING: +0

Special Attractions

■ Very unusual and spectacular black cinder hills.

■ Popular ATV and dirt bike area.

■ Excellent backcountry camping.

Description

Cinder Hills OHV Area lies within the Coconino National Forest and is specifically managed for vehicle recreation. Thirteen thousand five hundred acres have been designated for use by dirt bikes, ATVs, and 4WD vehicles. The area has a dense network of designated routes as well as open areas of unrestricted use where there is little vegetation. Surrounding the main vehicle-use area is a larger resource area of 53,000 acres in which vehicle use is limited to a lesser number of designated routes.

This trail passes through both regions and gives an excellent introduction to the scenically unique area of the Cinder Hills, part of the San Francisco Volcano Field. The region is a study in contrasts; the black volcanic cinders provide a driving surface that is similar to sand. The green of the vegetation contrasts with the black ground to give an almost surreal effect. Photographers will appreciate the opportunity to obtain some unusual photos of a unique landscape.

Initially, the trail follows the main graded route through the OHV area. There are many side trails on the right and left, particularly past the first main staging and camping area on the edge of Cinder Lake. The dry, black volcanic expanse of Cinder Lake is a major play area for those with dirt bikes, ATVs, and sand rails. The graded road follows the edge and has a firm surface suitable for passenger vehicles when it is dry. The area is extremely popular at all times of the year and especially on weekends, so be on the lookout for fast-moving vehicles. Only the major trails suitable for vehicles have been mentioned in the route directions; it is not possible to list the many trails made by ATVs and dirt bikes.

The route briefly joins the paved road through Sunset Crater National Monument before turning off onto a designated forest route outside the main OHV area. Here the trail is narrower, less frequently used, and has a softer surface. There are fewer, more secluded campsites along this section of the trail. The trail continues to meander along the edge of the OHV area before dropping south to finish on the Townsend-Winona Road.

Note that no glass containers are allowed in the OHV area.

Current Road Information

Coconino National Forest
Peaks Ranger District
5075 North Hwy 89
Flagstaff, AZ 86004
(928) 526-0866

Sunset Crater Volcano National Monument
6400 N. Hwy 89
Flagstaff, AZ 86004
(928) 526-0502

Map References

BLM   Flagstaff
USFS   Coconino National Forest: Peaks
       Ranger District
USGS   1:24,000   Sunset Crater West, Sunset
       Crater East, Winona
       1:100,000 Flagstaff
Maptech CD-ROM: Flagstaff/Sedona/Prescott

Arizona Atlas & Gazetteer, p. 42
Arizona Road & Recreation Atlas, pp. 35, 69
Other: Cinder Hills OHV Area—free map
        put out by Coconino National Forest

Route Directions

▼ 0.0   From US 89, 6 miles north of Flagstaff, zero trip meter and turn northeast on FR 776 signposted to the Cinder Hills OHV Area. Road is graded dirt. Turn is 0.1 miles south of mile marker 427.

4.9 ▲   Trail ends on US 89 north of Flagstaff. Turn left for Flagstaff.
         GPS: N35°19.70' W111°32.68'

▼ 0.5   BR Track on left is Northeast #4: O'Leary Peak Trail, FR 414. Many small tracks for ATV and dirt bike use on left and right for next 4.9 miles.

4.4 ▲   SO Track on right is Northeast #4: O'Leary Peak Trail, FR 414.
         GPS: N35°19.93' W111°32.22'

▼ 1.3   SO Cinders Hill OHV Area. Major staging and camping area on right and left.

3.6 ▲   SO Cinders Hill OHV Area. Major staging and camping area on right and left.
         GPS: N35°19.71' W111°31.45'

▼ 1.4   SO Cinder Lake on right.
3.5 ▲   SO Cinder Lake on left.
▼ 1.9   SO Graded road on right is FR 777 to Little Cinder Basin.

3.0 ▲   SO Graded road on left is FR 777 to Little Cinder Basin.
         GPS: N35°20.03' W111°30.85'

▼ 3.0   SO Information sign on left.
1.9 ▲   SO Information sign on right.
▼ 4.7   SO Track on right is FR 9140X.
0.2 ▲   SO Track on left is FR 9140X.
         GPS: N35°21.49' W111°29.14'

▼ 4.9   SO Track on right is FR 777 to Little Cinder Basin. Sign on left of trail for FR 545 ahead and US 89 back. Zero trip meter.

0.0 ▲   Continue to the south.
         GPS: N35°21.60' W111°28.93'

Northeast Trail #6: Cinder Hills Loop Trail

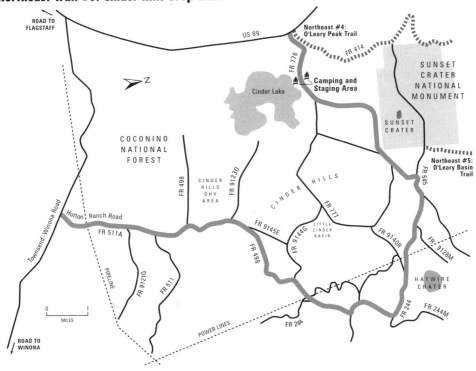

▼ 0.0   Continue to the north.

0.7 ▲   SO   Track on left is FR 777 to Little Cinder Basin. Sign on right of trail for US 89 ahead. Zero trip meter.

▼ 0.3   SO   Unloading area on right.

0.4 ▲   SO   Unloading area on left.

▼ 0.5   SO   Enter no-camping area.

0.2 ▲   SO   Camping permitted past this point.

▼ 0.7   TR   T-intersection with paved FR 545. Turn right and zero trip meter.

0.0 ▲   Continue to the south. Many small tracks on right and left for next 4.9 miles.
       GPS: N35°22.12' W111°28.51'

▼ 0.0   Continue to the east.

0.4 ▲   TL   Turn left onto graded dirt road FR 776, entering the Cinder Hills OHV Area. Turn is immediately before a national parks entrance fee sign for Sunset Crater. Zero trip meter.

▼ 0.4   TR   Turn right onto small trail marked FR 244. Zero trip meter.

0.0 ▲   Continue to the southwest.
       GPS: N35°22.20' W111°28.07'

▼ 0.0   Continue to the east.

2.0 ▲   TL   T-intersection with paved FR 545. Turn left onto paved road. Zero trip meter.

▼ 0.2   SO   Track on left.

1.8 ▲   SO   Track on right.

▼ 0.7   SO   Track on left is FR 9128M.

1.3 ▲   SO   Track on right is FR 9128M.
       GPS: N35°21.97' W111°27.30'

▼ 1.5   SO   Track on left under power lines.

0.5 ▲   SO   Track on right under power lines.

▼ 1.6   SO   Track on right.

0.4 ▲   BR   Track on left.
       GPS: N35°21.71' W111°26.43'

▼ 1.9   SO   Track on right.

0.1 ▲   SO   Track on left.

▼ 2.0   SO   Track on right is FR 9140R to Little Cinder Basin and FR 777. The blue arrows mark this trail. Zero trip meter. Haywire Crater is on the left.

0.0 ▲   Continue to the northwest.
       GPS: N35°21.68' W111°25.98'

▼ 0.0   Continue to the southeast.

3.2 ▲   SO   Track on left is FR 9140R to Little Cinder Basin and FR 777. Zero trip meter. Haywire Crater is on the right.

▼ 1.0   BR   Track on left is FR 244M. Bear right, remaining on FR 244.

2.2 ▲   BL   Track on right is FR 244M. Bear left, remaining on FR 244.

GPS: N35°21.33′ W111°25.02′

▼ 1.9   SO   Track on right.

1.3 ▲   SO   Track on left.

GPS: N35°20.59′ W111°25.44′

▼ 2.3   BR   Track on left.

0.9 ▲   BL   Track on right.

▼ 3.2   BR   FR 244 continues to the left. Bear right onto well-used unmarked trail and zero trip meter.

0.0 ▲   Continue to the north.

GPS: N35°19.61′ W111°25.63′

▼ 0.0   Continue to the southwest; trail is marked with white arrows on blue posts.

4.4 ▲   SO   FR 244 on right; continue straight on and join FR 244. Zero trip meter.

▼ 0.1   SO   Pass under power lines; then track on left and track on right. Road is now marked FR 498.

4.3 ▲   SO   Track on left and track on right; then pass under power lines.

▼ 0.7   SO   Track on left through gate and track on right is FR 9144G. Continue straight on, remaining on FR 498.

3.7 ▲   SO   Track on right through gate and track on left is FR 9144G. Continue straight on, remaining on FR 498.

GPS: N35°19.22′ W111°26.23′

▼ 1.1   SO   Track on left.

3.3 ▲   SO   Track on right.

▼ 1.8   SO   Track on left is FR 9144X.

2.6 ▲   BL   Track on right is FR 9144X. Remain on FR 498.

GPS: N35°18.61′ W111°28.83′

▼ 2.7   SO   Track on left is FR 9145E; then almost immediately track on right is FR 9145E.

▼ 1.7 ▲   BL   Track on left is FR 9145E; then almost immediately track on right is FR 9145E.

GPS: N35°18.27′ W111°27.71′

▼ 2.8   SO   Track on right is marked with blue arrow.

1.6 ▲   BR   Bear right, remaining on FR 498; track on left is marked with blue arrow.

GPS: N35°18.26′ W111°27.73′

▼ 2.9   BL   Track on right is FR 9143T.

1.5 ▲   SO   Track on left is FR 9143T.

GPS: N35°18.20′ W111°27.84′

▼ 3.1   BL   Fork; both unmarked. Track on right is FR 9123O. Bear left across open cinder area; there is a blue arrow after the junction.

1.3 ▲   BR   Fork; both unmarked. Track on left is FR 9123O. Bear right into the trees.

GPS: N35°17.97′ W111°27.96′

▼ 3.4   SO   Track on right and track on left along gas pipeline.

1.0 ▲   SO   Track on right and track on left along gas pipeline.

GPS: N35°17.81′ W111°27.93′

▼ 3.6   SO   Track on left.

0.8 ▲   BL   Track on right.

▼ 4.0   SO   Track on left.

0.4 ▲   SO   Track on right.

▼ 4.1   BL   Trail forks.

0.3 ▲   SO   Track on left rejoins.

GPS: N35°17.15′ W111°27.87′

▼ 4.3   TL   Trail rejoins; then turn left onto well-used unmarked track. Ahead is FR 498.

0.1 ▲   TR   Turn right; then trail forks; bear right (tracks rejoin shortly).

GPS: N35°17.03′ W111°27.95′

▼ 4.4   TL   Track on right is FR 498. Turn left onto unmarked trail, which is FR 511A, and zero trip meter.

0.0 ▲   Continue to the northwest.

GPS: N35°16.97′ W111°27.89′

▼ 0.0   Continue to the southeast. Many tracks and campsites on right and left; remain on main trail for next 0.8 miles.

A black cinder trail travels through the ponderosa pine trees

The black cinder surface of Cinder Lake provides a favorite location for off-road vehicles

3.3 ▲   BR Bear right onto FR 498 at well-used, unmarked intersection and zero trip meter.

▼ 0.5   SO Enclosure contains aspens damaged by fire and being encouraged to regrow.

2.8 ▲   SO Enclosure contains aspens damaged by fire and being encouraged to regrow.

▼ 0.8   SO Track on left is FR 511 at edge of private property. Continue straight on, joining FR 511. Road is now graded.

2.5 ▲   BL At edge of private property bear left, leaving FR 511 and joining the well-used FR 511A. Road is now formed trail. Many tracks and campsites on right and left; remain on main trail for next 0.8 miles.

GPS: N35°16.24' W111°27.82'

▼ 1.6   SO Cattle guard; then track on left is FR 9121Q; track on right.

1.7 ▲   SO Track on right is FR 9121Q; track on left; then cattle guard.

GPS: N35°15.62' W111°28.08'

▼ 1.8   SO Track on right.

1.5 ▲   SO Track on left.

▼ 2.1   SO Track on left.

1.2 ▲   SO Track on right.

▼ 2.3   SO Graded road on right and left.

1.0 ▲   SO Graded road on left and right.

▼ 3.3   Cattle guard; then trail ends at the T-intersection with the Townsend–Winona Road. Turn right for Flagstaff; turn left for Winona.

0.0 ▲   Trail commences on the Townsend—Winona Road, 5.5 miles east of the intersection with US 89 (north of Flagstaff), 0.2 miles east of mile marker 426. Zero trip meter and turn northeast onto the graded dirt Hutton Ranch Road across a cattle guard.

GPS: N35°14.21' W111°28.56'

Schultz Pass Trail

STARTING POINT: US 89, 1.3 miles south of the Sunset Crater National Monument turn-off
FINISHING POINT: US 180, 3 miles north of Flagstaff
TOTAL MILEAGE: 11.4 miles
UNPAVED MILEAGE: 10.7 miles
DRIVING TIME: 45 minutes
ELEVATION RANGE: 7,200–8,200 feet
USUALLY OPEN: March to November
BEST TIME TO TRAVEL: March to November
DIFFICULTY RATING: 2
SCENIC RATING: 8
REMOTENESS RATING: +0

Special Attractions
- Pleasant backcountry trail over the south side of the San Francisco Peaks.
- Views of the cinder hills that form part of the San Francisco Volcanic Field.
- Many backcountry campsites and access to hiking trails.

Description
Schultz Pass is a well-known backcountry drive, which is often combined with a visit to Sunset Crater and can be combined with one or two of the trails within the Cinder Hills OHV Area to make a full-day's tour. The graded road winds over the southern flanks of the San Francisco Peaks through some pretty alpine scenery along the south side of the Kachina Peaks Wilderness. In spring and early summer, there are fields of colorful wildflowers, and in the fall, scattered yellow aspens contrast with pines. The northern end of the road has views over the Cinder Hills area to the east where the undulating black hills can be seen. This area is also part of the San Francisco Volcanic Field.

The road climbs steadily to the top of Schultz Pass (named for Charley H. Schultz, a sheepherder) before descending alongside Schultz Creek toward Flagstaff. Originally, the route served as a shortcut from outlying settlements to Flagstaff. Northeast #8: Freidlein Prairie Trail leads from the top of the pass and offers a smaller, rougher alternate route down the south side of the mountain. The Schultz Creek Trail, a single-track trail for hikers, horses, and mountain bikes, parallels the road for much of the way, running closer to the creek below the road. Because the final few miles of the trail run through watershed, no camping is allowed. There are a couple of places to pitch a tent near the north end of the trail, but better camping can be found in the Cinder Hills OHV Area on the east side of US 89.

Current Road Information
Coconino National Forest
Peaks Ranger District
5075 North Hwy 89
Flagstaff, AZ 86004
(928) 526-0866

Map References
BLM   Flagstaff
USFS   Coconino National Forest: Peaks Ranger District
USGS   1:24,000   Sunset Crater West, Humphreys Peak, Flagstaff West
1:100,000   Flagstaff
Maptech CD-ROM: Flagstaff/Sedona/Prescott
Arizona Atlas & Gazetteer, p. 42
Arizona Road & Recreation Atlas, pp. 35, 69
Recreational Map of Arizona

Route Directions

▼ 0.0   From US 89, 1.3 miles south of the turn to Sunset Crater National Monument and 14 miles north of Flagstaff, zero trip meter and turn west on the graded dirt road at the sign for Schultz Pass (FR 420). Immediately, there is a track on right, FR 553. Continue straight on, following the sign for Schultz Pass. Seasonal closure gate.

6.6 ▲   Track on left is FR 553; then trail ends at the T-intersection with US 89. Turn right for Flagstaff; turn left for the Grand Canyon.

Bike trail that parallels Schultz Creek

GPS: N35º21.22' W111º34.13'

▼ 0.1 SO Track on right; then track on left and second track on right.

6.5 ▲ SO Track on left; then track on right and second track on left.

▼ 0.3 SO Track on left.

6.3 ▲ SO Track on right.

▼ 0.7 SO Track on left; then trailhead for Deer Hill Trail for pack animals, hikers, and mountain bikes.

5.9 ▲ SO Trailhead for Deer Hill Trail for pack animals, hikers, and mountain bikes; then track on right.

GPS: N35º20.72' W111º34.46'

▼ 1.2 SO Track on left and track on right.

5.4 ▲ SO Track on right and track on left.

▼ 1.7 SO Track on right.

4.9 ▲ SO Track on left.

▼ 1.9 SO Track on left.

4.7 ▲ SO Track on right.

▼ 2.3 SO Track on right.

4.3 ▲ SO Track on left.

▼ 2.4 SO Track on right.

4.2 ▲ SO Track on left.

▼ 2.5 SO Cross over creek.

4.1 ▲ SO Cross over creek.

GPS: N35º19.32' W111º35.29'

▼ 2.6 SO Track on right.

4.0 ▲ SO Track on left.

▼ 3.0 SO Track on left is FR 420D.

3.6 ▲ SO Track on right is FR 420D.

GPS: N35º18.88' W111º35.35'

▼ 3.1 SO Two tracks on right; then track on left.

3.5 ▲ SO Track on right; then two tracks on left.

▼ 3.5 SO Track on right.

3.1 ▲ SO Track on left.

▼ 3.7 SO Track on left.

2.9 ▲ SO Track on right.

▼ 3.8 SO Track on right; then track on left.

2.8 ▲ SO Track on right; then track on left.

▼ 4.2 SO Well-used track on right.

2.4 ▲ SO Well-used track on left.

GPS: N35º17.87' W111º35.71'

▼ 4.4 SO Track on right.

2.2 ▲ SO Track on left.

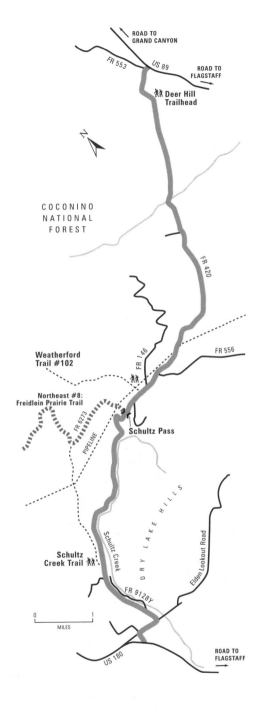

Black cinder hills are visible above the trail

▼ 5.2   SO   Cross over gas pipeline; tracks on right and left along pipeline.

1.4 ▲   SO   Cross over gas pipeline; tracks on left and right along pipeline.

GPS: N35°17.46′ W111°36.61′

▼ 5.5   SO   Track on left.

1.1 ▲   SO   Track on right.

▼ 5.8   SO   Graded road on left is FR 556.

0.8 ▲   SO   Graded road on right is FR 556.

GPS: N35°17.31′ W111°37.16′

▼ 5.9   SO   Cattle guard.

0.7 ▲   SO   Cattle guard.

▼ 6.0   SO   Graded road on right is FR 146.

0.6 ▲   SO   Graded road on left is FR 146.

GPS: N35°17.24′ W111°37.42′

▼ 6.1   SO   Weatherford Trail #102 for hikers, horses, and mountain bikes on right. Trailhead parking on left.

0.5 ▲   SO   Weatherford Trail #102 for hikers, horses, and mountain bikes on left. Trailhead parking on right.

GPS: N35°17.21′ W111°37.54′

▼ 6.4   SO   Schultz Pass. Track on left goes to Sunset Trail #23.

0.2 ▲   SO   Schultz Pass. Track on right goes to Sunset Trail #23.

GPS: N35°17.15′ W111°37.86′

▼ 6.6   SO   Track on right is Northeast #8: Freidlein Prairie Trail, FR 6273. Zero trip meter.

0.0 ▲   Continue to the northeast.

GPS: N35°17.12′ W111°38.00′

▼ 0.0   Continue to the southwest.

4.8 ▲   SO   Track on left is Northeast #8: Freidlein Prairie Trail, FR 6273. Zero trip meter.

▼ 0.2   BL   Well-used track on right.

4.6 ▲   BR   Well-used track on left.

▼ 2.8   SO   Track on right. Trail leaves Schultz Creek.

2.0 ▲   SO   Track on left. Trail follows alongside Schultz Creek.

GPS: N35°15.57′ W111°39.75′

▼ 3.0   SO   Well-used track on right; then cattle guard. Entering watershed area, camping and campfires prohibited. Schultz Creek Trail on left for hikers, horses, and mountain bikes.

1.8 ▲   SO   Schultz Creek Trail on right for hikers, horses, and mountain bikes. Leaving watershed area, camping and campfires permitted. Cattle guard; then well-used track on left.

GPS: N35°15.44′ W111°39.84′

▼ 3.2   SO   Track on right through fence line.

1.6 ▲   SO   Track on left through fence line.

▼ 3.4   SO   Track on right.

1.4 ▲   SO   Track on left.

▼ 3.5   SO   Track on right.

1.3 ▲   SO   Track on left.

▼ 3.6   SO   Track on right.

1.2 ▲   SO   Track on left.

▼ 3.7   SO   Track on right.

1.1 ▲   SO   Track on left.

▼ 3.8   SO   Two tracks on right.

1.0 ▲   SO   Two tracks on left.

▼ 4.0   SO   Track on left is FR 9128Y; then closure gates, leaving Coconino National Forest.

0.8 ▲   SO   Closure gates, entering Coconino National Forest; then track on right is FR 9128Y.

GPS: N35°14.62′ W111°39.66′

▼ 4.1   SO   Road is paved.

0.7 ▲   SO   Road is now graded dirt.

▼ 4.3   BR   Paved road on left is Elden Lookout Road.

0.5 ▲   BL   Paved road on right is Elden Lookout Road.

▼ 4.6   BL   Weatherford Road on right.

0.2 ▲   BR   Weatherford Road on left. Remain on main paved road.

▼ 4.8   Trail ends at the intersection with US 180. Turn left for Flagstaff.

0.0 ▲   Trail starts at the intersection of US 180, 0.6 miles north of mile marker 218, 3 miles north of Flagstaff. Zero trip meter and turn north on the paved Schultz Pass Road.

GPS: N35°14.22′ W111°39.98′

Freidlein Prairie Trail

STARTING POINT: Snowbowl Road, 2.3 miles north of the intersection with US 180
FINISHING POINT: Northeast #7: Schultz Pass Trail
TOTAL MILEAGE: 6.4 miles
UNPAVED MILEAGE: 6.4 miles
DRIVING TIME: 45 minutes
ELEVATION RANGE: 8,000–8,700 feet
USUALLY OPEN: March to late November
BEST TIME TO TRAVEL: March to late November
DIFFICULTY RATING: 3
SCENIC RATING: 8
REMOTENESS RATING: +0

Special Attractions

- Small trail that winds around the flanks of the San Francisco Peaks.
- Spring wildflowers and splashes of golden aspens in the fall.

Description

This short trail is one of only a few smaller trails that travel the southern side of the San Francisco Peaks, which at 12,643 feet are the highest mountains in Arizona and part of the San Francisco Volcanic Field. The towering San Francisco Mountains are sacred to many Indian tribes and are known by several names. To the Navajo, they are Dok'o'sliid, "the sacred mountain of the west." The Hopi name is Nuvateekia-ovi, "the place of snow on the very top." The Hopi believe that their gods (kachinas) live on the peaks for part of each year and that they bring rain to the mesa area where the Hopi live.

This trail runs around the southern end of the Kachina Peaks Wilderness, which encompasses the peaks area, and through pine forests interspersed with stands of aspens, which typically change color around late November and early December. In spring, the area has patches of wildflowers, mainly irises.

The route chosen does not show up on all maps; it diverts to exit onto Northeast #7: Schultz Pass Trail on top of the pass. It is

rough and rutted enough to make 4WD preferable, but it should not cause any problems in dry weather.

Current Road Information

Coconino National Forest
Peaks Ranger District
5075 North Hwy 89
Flagstaff, AZ 86004
(928) 526-0866

Map References

BLM   Flagstaff
USFS   Coconino National Forest: Peaks Ranger District
USGS   1:24,000   Humphreys Peak
1:100,000   Flagstaff
Maptech CD-ROM: Flagstaff/Sedona/Prescott
Arizona Atlas & Gazetteer, p. 42

Route Directions

▼ 0.0		From the Arizona Snowbowl Road, 2.3 miles north of the intersection with US 180, zero trip meter and turn east on FR 522 onto the well-used formed dirt trail. Seasonal closure gate at intersection.
3.7 ▲		Trail ends on the Arizona Snowbowl Road, 2.3 miles north of US 180. Turn left to exit to the highway and Flagstaff; turn right to continue to the Arizona Snowbowl.
		GPS: N35°17.48' W111°42.35'

▼ 0.1	BL	Track on right.
3.6 ▲	SO	Track on left.
▼ 0.8	SO	Track on left to corral.
2.9 ▲	SO	Track on right to corral.
▼ 0.9	SO	Track on right.
2.8 ▲	SO	Track on left.
▼ 1.4	SO	Track on right.
2.3 ▲	SO	Track on left.
▼ 1.7	SO	Track on right.
2.0 ▲	SO	Track on left.
▼ 2.5	SO	Track on right to campsite.
1.2 ▲	SO	Track on left to campsite.
▼ 3.6	SO	Pass through fence line.
0.1 ▲	SO	Pass through fence line.
		GPS: N35°17.77' W111°39.07'

The San Francisco Peaks rise above the aspen

Northeast Trail #8: Freidlein Prairie Trail

▼ 3.7   TR   Well-used track ahead is closed to vehicles 0.1 miles farther on. Turn sharp right onto FR 6273 (unmarked). Zero trip meter.

0.0 ▲   Continue to the southwest.
GPS: N35°17.80' W111°39.04'

▼ 0.0   Continue to the south.

2.7 ▲   TL   Well-used track ahead is closed to vehicles 0.1 miles farther on; turn sharp left and continue on FR 522. Zero trip meter.

▼ 0.8   BL   Hiking trail on right.

1.9 ▲   BR   Hiking trail on left.
GPS: N35°17.15' W111°39.11'

▼ 2.0   BR   Track on left.

0.7 ▲   BL   Track on right.
GPS: N35°17.43' W111°38.22'

▼ 2.6   SO   Cross over gas pipeline. Tracks on left and right along pipeline.

0.1 ▲   SO   Cross over gas pipeline. Tracks on left and right along pipeline.

Passing through the pines below Schultz Peak (at over 8,000 feet)

▼ 2.7   Trail ends at the T-intersection with Northeast #7: Schultz Pass Trail. Turn right to return to Flagstaff; turn left to exit to US 89.

0.0 ▲   Trail commences on Northeast #7: Schultz Pass Trail, 6.6 miles southwest of US 89, 0.1 miles north of the entrance to the Museum of Northern Arizona. Zero trip meter and turn northwest on formed dirt trail, FR 6273.
         GPS: N35°17.12' W111°38.00'

NORTHEAST REGION TRAIL #9

Bill Williams Mountain Loop Road

STARTING POINT: CR 73, 0.2 miles south of mile marker 179
FINISHING POINT: I-40 at exit 157, Devil Dog Road
TOTAL MILEAGE: 17.4 miles
UNPAVED MILEAGE: 17.4 miles
DRIVING TIME: 1.5 hours
ELEVATION RANGE: 6,400–7,200 feet
USUALLY OPEN: Early April to December
BEST TIME TO TRAVEL: Early April to December
DIFFICULTY RATING: 1
SCENIC RATING: 8
REMOTENESS RATING: +0

Special Attractions
■ Views of Bill Williams Mountain.
■ Fall colors and views of wildlife along an easy loop road.
■ Waterfowl watching at Coleman Lake.

Description
This well-graded road makes a wide loop around Bill Williams Mountain, which, like the town of Williams, was named after the infamous and reclusive mountain man. The cinder-surfaced road is suitable for passenger vehicles in dry weather and is a popular drive from spring through fall. The road may be open past the dates listed if there is little or no snow. It is not gated shut—just allowed to close naturally when it snows.

There are some very good campsites along the first part of the road under the pine trees on the edge of the meadows.

Coleman Lake, passed within the first few miles of the trail, is often more marshy than completely full, but it is a good place for bird-watching. The presence of duck nesting mounds created by waterfowl habitat projects attract a wide variety of ducks. The best time for birding is April and May when migrating and nesting birds are present. Observers may see eared grebes, ring-necked ducks, coots, mallards, cinnamon teals, ruddy ducks, buf-fleheads, pintails, and others.

The road travels through a mix of forest and open prairie and crosses through some private property as it nears I-40. Please respect the landowners' property and remain on the road. There are good views of Bill Williams Mountain all along the trail.

The Stage Station Mountain Bike Loop, an 8-mile loop through rolling terrain, starts and finishes from this road. An old cabin, a stage stop on the route between Williams and Prescott, gives the loop its name.

Current Road Information
Kaibab National Forest
Williams Ranger District
742 South Clover Rd.
Williams, AZ 86046
(928) 635-5600

Map References
BLM   Williams
USFS   Kaibab National Forest: Williams Ranger District
USGS   1:24,000   Williams South, May Tank Pocket, Matterhorn, McLellan Reservoir
         1:100,000   Williams
Maptech CD-ROM: Flagstaff/Sedona/Prescott
Arizona Atlas & Gazetteer, p. 41
Arizona Road & Recreation Atlas, pp. 34, 68
Recreational Map of Arizona

Route Directions

▼ 0.0   From CR 73 (Perkinsville Road), 0.2 miles south of mile marker 179, 6.3 miles south of Williams, zero trip meter and turn southwest onto graded dirt road, FR 108, signed to Coleman Lake and I-40.

5.9 ▲   Trail ends on CR 73. Turn left for Williams.

     GPS: N35°09.85′ W112°09.39′

▼ 0.1   SO   Cattle guard and closure gate; then track on left.

5.8 ▲   SO   Track on right; then cattle guard and closure gate.

▼ 0.6   SO   Track on right is FR 401.

5.3 ▲   SO   Track on left is FR 401.

     GPS: N35°09.67′ W112°09.97′

▼ 1.2   SO   Track on left is FR 593.

4.7 ▲   SO   Track on right is FR 593.

     GPS: N35°09.18′ W112°10.16′

▼ 1.5   SO   Cattle guard; then track on left is FR 590; then Coleman Lake on right.

4.4 ▲   SO   Track on right is FR 590; then cattle guard.

     GPS: N35°08.94′ W112°10.24′

▼ 2.1   SO   Track on right through gate. Road leaves Coleman Lake.

3.8 ▲   SO   Coleman Lake on left; then track on left through gate.

▼ 2.8   SO   Small track on right.

3.1 ▲   SO   Small track on left.

▼ 3.1   SO   Track on right.

2.8 ▲   SO   Track on left.

▼ 3.8   SO   Track on right.

2.1 ▲   SO   Track on left.

▼ 4.4   SO   Track on left.

1.5 ▲   SO   Track on right.

▼ 4.5   SO   Cross over wash.

1.4 ▲   SO   Cross over wash.

▼ 4.9   SO   Track on left.

1.0 ▲   SO   Track on right.

▼ 5.5   SO   M.C. Tank on left.

0.4 ▲   SO   M.C. Tank on right.

     GPS: N35°06.94′ W112°12.99′

▼ 5.9   SO   Track on left is FR 186 to D.T. Tank. Zero trip meter.

Bill Williams Mountain viewed from meadows along the trail

Northeast Trail #9: Bill Williams Mountain Loop Road

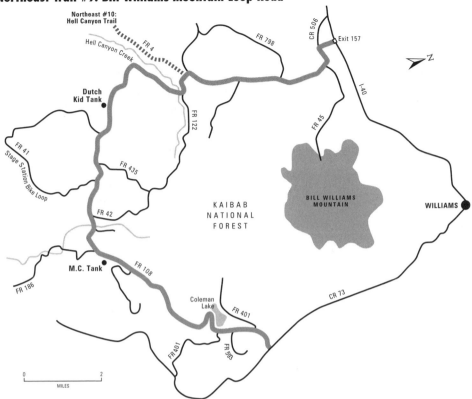

0.0 ▲		Continue to the northeast on FR 108, following the sign to Perkinsville Road. **GPS: N35°06.71′ W112°13.28′**

▼ 0.0		Continue to the southwest, following the sign to Dutch Kid Tank and I-40.
6.9 ▲	SO	Track on right is FR 186 to D.T. Tank. Zero trip meter.
▼ 0.6	SO	Track on right; then cross over creek.
6.3 ▲	SO	Cross over creek; then track on left.
▼ 0.9	SO	Track on right is FR 42.
6.0 ▲	SO	Track on left is FR 42. **GPS: N35°06.83′ W112°14.11′**

▼ 1.9	SO	Track on left is FR 41.
5.0 ▲	SO	Track on right is FR 41. **GPS: N35°07.20′ W112°15.04′**

▼ 2.3	SO	Cattle guard; then track on right is FR 435.
4.6 ▲	SO	Track on left is FR 435; then cattle guard. **GPS: N35°07.27′ W112°15.44′**

▼ 3.1	SO	Cross over creek; then track on left is FR 41, also marked as the Stage Station Bike Loop.
3.8 ▲	SO	Track on right is FR 41, also marked as the Stage Station Bike Loop; then cross over creek. **GPS: N35°07.57′ W112°16.13′**

▼ 3.8	SO	Track on right and track on left; then Dutch Kid Tank on left.
3.1 ▲	SO	Dutch Kid Tank on right; then track on right and track on left. **GPS: N35°07.86′ W112°16.77′**

▼ 4.0	SO	Cross through creek; then track on right is FR 532; then track on left.
2.9 ▲	SO	Track on right; then track on left is FR 532; then cross through creek.
▼ 4.5	SO	Track on left.
2.4 ▲	SO	Track on right.
▼ 5.2	SO	Track on right is FR 446.
1.7 ▲	SO	Track on left is FR 446.

The trail crosses a small meadow enclosed by ponderosa pines

GPS: N35°08.80′ W112°17.42′

▼ 5.7 SO Cross over wash.
1.2 ▲ SO Cross over wash.
▼ 6.3 SO Track on right.
0.6 ▲ SO Track on left.
▼ 6.4 SO Cross through Hell Canyon Creek.
0.5 ▲ SO Cross through Hell Canyon Creek.
GPS: N35°09.52′ W112°16.53′

▼ 6.5 BL Track on right is FR 122; then track on left.
0.4 ▲ BR Track on right; then track on left is FR 122.
▼ 6.6 SO Cattle guard.
0.3 ▲ SO Cattle guard.
▼ 6.9 SO Track on left is Northeast #10: Hell Canyon Trail, FR 4. Zero trip meter.
0.0 ▲ Continue to the southeast and descend to cross through Hell Canyon.
GPS: N35°09.68′ W112°16.89′

▼ 0.0 Continue to the northwest.
4.6 ▲ SO Track on right is Northeast #10: Hell Canyon Trail, FR 4. Zero trip meter.
▼ 0.1 SO Track on left; then cross through creek.

4.5 ▲ SO Cross through creek; then track on right.
▼ 0.6 SO Cattle guard.
4.0 ▲ SO Cattle guard.
▼ 1.0 SO Cross through wash.
3.6 ▲ SO Cross through wash.
▼ 1.5 SO Graded road on right goes into Hat Ranch. Follow sign to Williams.
3.1 ▲ BR Graded road on left goes into Hat Ranch.
GPS: N35°10.89′ W112°16.38′

▼ 1.6 SO Cross through wash.
3.0 ▲ SO Cross through wash.
▼ 2.1 SO Cross over wash.
2.5 ▲ SO Cross over wash.
▼ 2.5 SO Track on left is FR 798.
2.1 ▲ SO Track on right is FR 798.
GPS: N35°11.75′ W112°16.05′
▼ 2.8 SO Track on right is FR 455; then cattle guard.
1.8 ▲ SO Cattle guard; then track on left is FR 455.
GPS: N35°11.94′ W112°15.92′

▼ 3.2 SO Track on left; then track on right.
1.4 ▲ SO Track on left; then track on right.
▼ 3.5 SO Track on right.

1.1 ▲	SO	Track on left.
▼ 3.7	SO	Cross over creek on bridge; then track on right is FR 45. No camping past this point.
0.9 ▲	SO	Track on left is FR 45; then cross over creek on bridge. Camping permitted past this point.

GPS: N35°12.82′ W112°16.08′

▼ 3.9	BL	Track on right; remain on main graded road.
0.7 ▲	BR	Track on left; remain on main graded road.
▼ 4.2	TR	Turn right, remaining on FR 108; follow sign to I-40. Paved road ahead is CR 506.
0.4 ▲	TL	T-intersection; paved road on right is CR 506. Turn left, remaining on graded dirt road FR 108.

GPS: N35°12.78′ W112°16.56′

▼ 4.6	Trail ends at the intersection with I-40, exit 157.
0.0 ▲	Trail commences on I-40, exit 157, Devil Dog Road. Proceed to the south side of the freeway and zero trip meter at cattle guard, and proceed south on graded dirt road. No camping for the first mile.

GPS: N35°13.12′ W112°16.57′

NORTHEAST REGION TRAIL #10

Hell Canyon Trail

STARTING POINT: Northeast #9: Bill Williams Mountain Loop Road, 4.6 miles south of I-40

FINISHING POINT: Arizona 89, 8.9 miles south of Ash Fork, 0.2 miles south of mile marker 355

TOTAL MILEAGE: 9.9 miles

UNPAVED MILEAGE: 9.9 miles

DRIVING TIME: 1 hour

ELEVATION RANGE: 5,100–6,500 feet

USUALLY OPEN: Year-round

BEST TIME TO TRAVEL: Dry weather

DIFFICULTY RATING: 3

SCENIC RATING: 7

REMOTENESS RATING: +0

Northeast Trail #10: Hell Canyon Trail

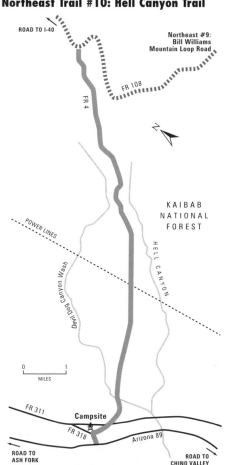

Special Attractions

- Alternative exit from Kaibab National Forest to the west.
- Trail running near the edge of Hell Canyon.

Description

This rough trail is suitable for most high-clearance 4WDs in dry weather. In wet weather it is best avoided, as many sections become extremely greasy and difficult to negotiate. The trail travels down a gentle decline between Northeast #9: Bill Williams Mountain Loop Road and Arizona 89, following the edge of Hell Canyon. Most of the time, the trail is within the juniper vegetation, so views of Hell Canyon are limited. By following a couple of the side trails out to the rim, or leaving your vehicle and walking through the trees, it is possible to view the rugged, dark gray-black depths of Hell Canyon. The canyon is composed of the dark lava predominant in this region, which is probably how it got its name.

Navigation is very easy, although the trail is narrow at times and lightly used. There are few side trails to confuse the navigator. For the most part the trail heads straight in a southwesterly direction. As it descends, there are views ahead to Big Black Mesa and Prescott National Forest.

There are a few suitable campsites, mainly at the top and bottom of the trail, and at the edge of Hell Canyon.

Current Road Information
Kaibab National Forest
Williams Ranger District
742 South Clover Rd.
Williams, AZ 86046
(928) 635-5600

Map References
BLM   Williams
USFS   Kaibab National Forest: Williams
         Ranger District

USGS 1:24,000   McLellan Reservoir,
         Matterhorn, Meath Spring
         1:100,000 Williams
Maptech CD-ROM: Flagstaff/Sedona/Prescott
Arizona Atlas & Gazetteer, p. 41
Arizona Road & Recreation Atlas, pp. 34, 68

Route Directions

▼ 0.0		From Northeast #9: Bill Williams Mountain Loop Road, 4.6 miles south of I-40, zero trip meter and turn southwest on small formed trail, FR 4.
2.7 ▲		Trail ends at the intersection with Northeast #9: Bill Williams Mountain Loop Road. Turn left for I-40; turn right to continue around the loop to CR 73.
		GPS: N35°09.68′ W112°16.89′

▼ 0.8	SO	Cattle guard and closure gate.
1.9 ▲	SO	Cattle guard and closure gate.
▼ 1.1	SO	Track on right.
1.6 ▲	SO	Track on left.
▼ 1.6	SO	Track on left. Trail drops toward Hell Canyon.
1.1 ▲	SO	Track on right.

Views of Bill Williams Mountain as you crest the last rise before intersecting with Northeast #9: Bill Williams Mountain Loop Road

A bumpy section of trail through juniper trees, typical characteristics of the trail

▼ 2.4   SO   Track on left.
0.3 ▲   SO   Track on right.
▼ 2.7   SO   Cattle guard. Zero trip meter.
0.0 ▲   Continue to the northeast.

GPS: N35°08.12′ W112°18.92′

▼ 0.0   Continue to the southwest.
4.3 ▲   SO   Cattle guard. Zero trip meter.
▼ 0.3   SO   Track on left.
4.0 ▲   SO   Track on right.
▼ 2.7   SO   Track on left.
1.6 ▲   SO   Track on right.

GPS: N35°06.74′ W112°21.15′

▼ 3.0   SO   Pass under power lines; track on left and track on right under power lines.
1.3 ▲   SO   Pass under power lines; track on left and track on right under power lines.
▼ 4.3   SO   Track on left is FR 322. Zero trip meter.
0.0 ▲   Continue to the northeast.

GPS: N35°06.40′ W112°22.62′

▼ 0.0   Continue to the southwest; track on right.
2.9 ▲   SO   Track on left; then track on right is FR 322. Zero trip meter.
▼ 1.0   SO   Track on left.
1.9 ▲   SO   Track on right.

GPS: N35°06.12′ W112°23.54′

▼ 1.5   SO   Cross through Devil Dog Canyon Wash.
1.4 ▲   SO   Cross through Devil Dog Canyon Wash.

GPS: N35°05.92′ W112°24.06′

▼ 1.8   SO   Cross through wash.
1.1 ▲   SO   Cross through wash.
▼ 2.1   BR   Track on left, FR 311, follows pipeline.
0.8 ▲   BL   Track on right, FR 311, follows pipeline.

GPS: N35°05.80′ W112°24.70′

▼ 2.2   BL   Track on right follows pipeline.
0.7 ▲   BR   Track on left follows pipeline.
▼ 2.4   SO   Track on right.
0.5 ▲   SO   Track on left.
▼ 2.6   TL   Campsite and cinder pit on right; track ahead is FR 318. Turn left, remaining on FR 4 toward highway.
0.3 ▲   TR   Campsite ahead and cinder pit. Track

on left is FR 318. Turn right, remaining on FR 4.

GPS: N35°06.09′ W112°25.07′

▼ 2.9   Cattle guard; then trail ends at the intersection with Arizona 89. Turn right for Ash Fork; turn left for Chino Valley.
0.0 ▲   Trail commences on Arizona 89, 8.9 miles south of Ash Fork, 0.2 miles south of mile marker 355. Zero trip meter and turn east across cattle guard onto small formed trail marked FR 4. There is no sign on the highway.

GPS: N35°05.87′ W112°25.28′

NORTHEAST REGION TRAIL #11

White Horse Lake Loop Trail

STARTING POINT: CR 73 at mile marker 178
FINISHING POINT: CR 73, 0.1 miles north of mile marker 176
TOTAL MILEAGE: 28 miles
UNPAVED MILEAGE: 28 miles
DRIVING TIME: 2.75 hours
ELEVATION RANGE: 6,300–7,300 feet
USUALLY OPEN: April to December
BEST TIME TO TRAVEL: Dry weather
DIFFICULTY RATING: 2
SCENIC RATING: 8
REMOTENESS RATING: +0

Special Attractions

- Fishing and camping at White Horse Lake and fishing at J. D. Dam Lake.
- J. D. cabins and grave.
- Long trail traveling through the Kaibab National Forest.

History

White Horse Lake was constructed in 1934–1935 as a community lake for the people of Williams. Runoff from snowmelt nearly breached the dam, but it was saved by a quick and concerted effort by the people of Williams. In 1951 the dam was enlarged to

Tule Tank Wash crossing

Picturesque J.D. Dam Lake

double its original size.

J. D. Dam Lake is the older of the two along this trail. It was constructed by local rancher J. D. Douglas, who is buried a short distance from the trail near the remains of three log cabins that he built. He died in 1884 at the age of 64. The site also has a later cabin constructed of railroad sleepers, which is still used by the forest service. Visitors are welcome but are asked to respect the privacy of the occupants.

Description

This trail passes by two popular fishing spots within the Kaibab National Forest. From the start of the trail on CR 73 to White Horse Lake, the trail is an easy 1-rated gravel road. There are many side trails leading off from this road, including the start of Northeast #12: Sycamore Point Trail.

White Horse Lake is set in a shallow dish among ponderosa pines. Along the lake shore, there is a developed campground operated by the forest service. Near the lake, camping is restricted to these developed sites, but there are many options for backcountry camping nearby. There is a boat launch and

the lake is stocked with trout, bluegill, and catfish.

From CR 73 to White Horse Lake the road can be busy. Once past the lake the road becomes more suitable for high-clearance vehicles and sees a lot less traffic as it travels through pine forest as a narrower, single-track road. The road bisects Northeast #12: Sycamore Point Trail again at J. D. Dam Lake, a slightly smaller but very pretty lake that offers excellent blue-ribbon trout fishing. Reeds and water lilies in the water and the surrounding pine forest make an attractive scene. There is abundant bird life and the area is noisy with bird calls. The land immediately surrounding the lake is for day use only, but camping is permitted outside of a fence line a short distance from the lakeshore. There is also a boat-launching point.

Past J. D. Dam, the trail drops in standard again to become a formed single-track trail. The next couple of miles are recommended for dry weather travel only; they become extremely muddy when wet.

Once you are past Tule Tank, the worst of the mud is over and the trail continues to gently climb its way back to CR 73. It crosses open Pine Flat and the start of several hiking trails before finishing back on CR 73, less than 2 miles south of its starting point. There is excellent camping to be found along the southern section of the trail.

Current Road Information
Kaibab National Forest
Williams Ranger District
742 South Clover Rd.
Williams, AZ 86046
(928) 635-5600

Map References
BLM Williams, Flagstaff
USFS Kaibab National Forest: Williams and Chalender Ranger Districts
USGS 1:24,000 Williams South, Davenport Hill, White Horse Lake, Sycamore Point, May Tank Pocket 1:100,000 Williams, Flagstaff
Maptech CD-ROM: Flagstaff/Sedona/Prescott
Arizona Atlas & Gazetteer, p. 41
Arizona Road & Recreation Atlas, pp. 34, 68
Recreational Map of Arizona

Route Directions

▼ 0.0   From CR 73, 8 miles south of Williams at mile marker 178, zero trip meter and turn east on graded dirt road, FR 110, at the sign for White Horse Lake.

7.0 ▲   Trail ends back on CR 73, 8 miles south of Williams. Turn right for Williams.

GPS: N35°08.53' W112°08.86'

▼ 0.4   SO   Cattle guard.
6.6 ▲   SO   Cattle guard.
▼ 1.0   SO   Track on right is FR 165.
6.0 ▲   SO   Track on left is FR 165.

GPS: N35°08.46' W112°07.90'

▼ 1.9   SO   Track on right is FR 706 to Summit Mountain Trailhead.
5.1 ▲   SO   Track on left is FR 706 to Summit Mountain Trailhead.

GPS: N35°08.12' W112°07.11'

▼ 2.2   SO   Track on right is FR 147.

▼ 4.8 ▲   SO   Track on left is FR 147.

GPS: N35°07.88' W112°06.87'

▼ 2.3   SO   Track on left is FR 747.
4.7 ▲   SO   Track on right is FR 747.
▼ 3.7   SO   Cattle guard.
3.3 ▲   SO   Cattle guard.
▼ 4.0   SO   Track on right is FR 730.
3.0 ▲   SO   Track on left is FR 730.
▼ 4.3   SO   Track on right is FR 736.
2.7 ▲   SO   Track on left is FR 736.

GPS: N35°07.55' W112°04.95'

▼ 4.5   SO   Graded road on right is FR 740.
2.5 ▲   SO   Graded road on left is FR 740.

GPS: N35°07.57' W112°04.69'

▼ 4.7   SO   Track on left is FR 747. Take this trail and then turn right onto FR 14 to reach J. D. cabins and grave.
2.3 ▲   SO   Track on right is FR 747. Take this trail and then turn right onto FR 14 to reach J. D. cabins and grave.
▼ 4.8   SO   Small track on right.
2.2 ▲   SO   Small track on left.
▼ 5.1   SO   Track on left is FR 422.
1.9 ▲   SO   Track on right is FR 422.

GPS: N35°07.60' W112°04.06'

▼ 5.2   SO   Corral on left.
1.8 ▲   SO   Corral on right.
▼ 5.5   SO   Track on right is FR 742.
1.5 ▲   SO   Track on left is FR 742.

GPS: N35°07.35' W112°03.78'

▼ 5.6   SO   Track on left.
1.4 ▲   SO   Track on right.
▼ 6.4   SO   Track on right is FR 11.
0.6 ▲   SO   Track on left is FR 11.
▼ 7.0   TL   Turn left onto FR 109, following the sign for White Horse Lake and J. D. Dam. Ahead is Northeast #12: Sycamore Point Trail, FR 110. Zero trip meter.
0.0 ▲   Continue to the northwest.

GPS: N35°06.29' W112°02.89'

▼ 0.0   Continue to the northeast and cross cattle guard.
1.6 ▲   TR   Cattle guard; then T-intersection; turn right onto FR 110, following the sign to

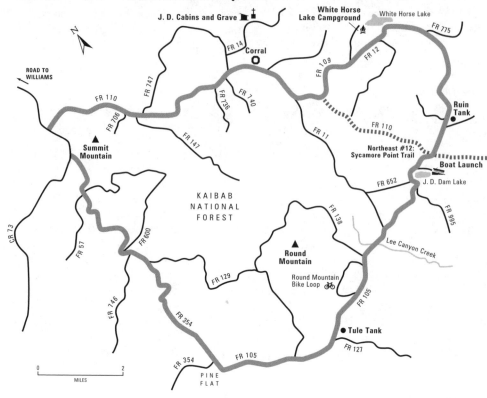

Williams. Zero trip meter. Track on left
is Northeast #12: Sycamore Point
Trail, FR 110.

▼ 1.0   SO   Small track on right.
0.6 ▲   SO   Small track on left.
▼ 1.6   TR   Turn right onto graded road FR 12, following the sign to J. D. Dam and
Sycamore Point. Zero trip meter. White
Horse Lake Campground is straight
ahead, 0.6 miles.
0.0 ▲   Continue to the southeast.
        GPS: N35°06.67' W112°01.51'

▼ 0.0   Continue to the east.
4.7 ▲   TL   T-intersection; turn left onto graded
road FR 109, following the sign to
Williams. Graded road on right goes
0.6 miles to White Horse Lake
Campground.
▼ 0.4   SO   Track on right is FR 765.
4.3 ▲   SO   Track on left is FR 765.
        GPS: N35°06.68' W112°01.09'

▼ 1.0   SO   Track on left.
3.7 ▲   SO   Track on right.
▼ 1.4   SO   Track on left is FR 771.
3.3 ▲   SO   Track on right is FR 771.
        GPS: N35°06.49' W112°00.16'

▼ 1.5   SO   Track on left is FR 775.
3.2 ▲   SO   Track on right is FR 775.
▼ 1.6   SO   Track on right.
3.1 ▲   SO   Track on left.
▼ 2.2   SO   Track on right is FR 786.
2.5 ▲   SO   Track on left is FR 786.
        GPS: N35°05.80' W111°59.78'

▼ 2.5   SO   Cattle guard; then track on left.
2.2 ▲   SO   Track on right; then cattle guard.
▼ 3.0   SO   Track on left.
1.7 ▲   SO   Track on right.
▼ 3.8   SO   Track on right.
0.9 ▲   SO   Track on left.
▼ 3.9   SO   Ruin Tank on left.

0.8 ▲   SO Ruin Tank on right.
       GPS: N35°04.61' W112°00.58'

▼ 4.0   SO Track on left.
0.7 ▲   SO Track on right.
▼ 4.7   TR T-intersection. Turn right onto FR 105, following the sign to J. D. Dam. Track on left is Northeast #12: Sycamore Point Trail, FR 110. Zero trip meter.
0.0 ▲   Continue to the southeast.
       GPS: N35°04.21' W112°01.27'

▼ 0.0   Continue to the west.
0.5 ▲   TL Turn left on FR 12, following the sign to White Horse Lake. Ahead is Northeast #12: Sycamore Point Trail, FR 110. Zero trip meter.
▼ 0.1   SO Track on right is FR 110 and the continuation of Northeast #12: Sycamore Point Trail.
0.4 ▲   SO Track on left is FR 110 and the continuation of Northeast #12: Sycamore Point Trail.
▼ 0.3   SO Cattle guard.
0.2 ▲   SO Cattle guard.
▼ 0.5   SO Graded road on left over cattle guard to J. D. Dam boat launch. Zero trip meter.
0.0 ▲   Continue to the northeast.
       GPS: N35°04.17' W112°01.75'

▼ 0.0   Continue to the west. Track on right is FR 720.
7.4 ▲   SO Track on left is FR 720; then graded road on right over cattle guard to J. D. Dam boat launch. Zero trip meter.
▼ 0.2   SO Cross through wash.
7.2 ▲   SO Cross through wash.
▼ 0.3   BL Track on right is FR 652.
7.1 ▲   BR Track on left is FR 652.
       GPS: N35°04.02' W112°01.96'

▼ 0.4   SO Parking area on left; trail is now small formed trail.
7.0 ▲   SO Parking area on right; trail is now roughly graded.
▼ 0.5   SO Track on left is FR 995.
6.9 ▲   SO Track on right is FR 995.
▼ 1.6   SO Track on left is FR 990.
5.8 ▲   SO Track on right is FR 990.
       GPS: N35°03.46' W112°02.95'

▼ 1.8   SO Track on right is FR 11. Continue on FR 105 and cross through wash.
5.6 ▲   BR Cross through wash; then track on left is FR 11. Continue on FR 105.
       GPS: N35°03.42' W112°03.14'

▼ 2.1   SO Cross through Lee Canyon Creek.
5.3 ▲   SO Cross through Lee Canyon Creek.
       GPS: N35°03.33' W112°03.41'

▼ 2.4   SO Track on left is FR 986; then track on right is FR 646.
5.0 ▲   SO Track on left is FR 646; then track on right is FR 986.
▼ 2.5   SO Cattle guard; then track on right is FR 138. Round Mountain Bike Loop starts from the intersection. Continue on FR 105 and cross through creek.
4.9 ▲   SO Cross through creek; then track on left is FR 138. Round Mountain Bike Loop starts from the intersection. Continue on FR 105 and cross cattle guard.
       GPS: N35°03.24' W112°03.80'

▼ 2.7   SO Track on right is FR 642.
4.7 ▲   SO Track on left is FR 642.
▼ 3.2   SO Cross through creek.
4.2 ▲   SO Cross through creek.
▼ 3.4   SO Track on right is FR 640; then cross through creek.
4.0 ▲   SO Cross through creek; then track on left is FR 640.
       GPS: N35°02.69' W112°04.39'

▼ 4.3   SO Tule Tank on left.
3.1 ▲   SO Tule Tank on right.
       GPS: N35°02.27' W112°05.27'

▼ 4.5   SO Track on left is FR 127.
2.9 ▲   BL Track on right is FR 127. Bear left, remaining on FR 105.
       GPS: N35°02.14' W112°05.45'

▼ 5.5   SO Track on right is FR 138.
1.9 ▲   SO Track on left is FR 138.
       GPS: N35°02.23' W112°06.46'

▼ 5.9   SO Track on left is FR 125. Continue on FR 105.

A patch of water lilies near the trail

1.5 ▲	SO	Track on right is FR 125. Continue on FR 105.	

GPS: N35°02.37′ W112°06.94′

▼ 6.6 SO Track on left through fence line; then cross through creek.
0.8 ▲ SO Cross through creek; then track on right through fence line.

▼ 7.1 BR Cattle guard; then bear right. Track on left is FR 936.
0.3 ▲ BL Track on right is FR 936; bear left over cattle guard.

▼ 7.4 SO Track on left is FR 354. Zero trip meter.
0.0 ▲ Continue to the southeast. Road is now FR 105.

GPS: N35°03.03′ W112°08.12′

▼ 0.0 Continue to the northwest. Road is now FR 354.
3.5 ▲ BL Track on right is FR 354. Zero trip meter.

▼ 0.4 SO Two tracks on right.
3.1 ▲ SO Two tracks on left.

▼ 0.7 SO Track on right is FR 620.
2.8 ▲ SO Track on left is FR 620.

GPS: N35°03.66′ W112°08.25′

▼ 0.8 SO Cross through creek.
2.7 ▲ SO Cross through creek.

▼ 1.1 SO Track on left.
2.4 ▲ SO Track on right.

▼ 1.2 SO Cross through creek.
2.3 ▲ SO Cross through creek.

▼ 1.3 SO Cross through creek.
2.2 ▲ SO Cross through creek.

▼ 1.7 SO Cross over creek on bridge.
1.8 ▲ SO Cross over creek on bridge.

GPS: N35°04.43′ W112°08.45′

▼ 3.1 SO Graded road on right is FR 129 to Round Mountain.
0.4 ▲ BR Graded road on left is FR 129 to Round Mountain.

GPS: N35°05.30′ W112°08.35′

▼ 3.5 SO Graded road on left is FR 746. Zero trip meter.
0.0 ▲ Continue to the southeast.

GPS: N35°05.66′ W112°08.60′

▼ 0.0 Continue to the northwest.
3.3 ▲ SO Graded road on right is FR 746. Zero trip meter.

▼ 0.2	SO	Track on right is FR 600.
3.1 ▲	SO	Track on left is FR 600.

GPS: N35°05.72′ W112°08.72′

▼ 0.7	SO	Cross through wash.
2.6 ▲	SO	Cross through wash.
▼ 0.9	SO	Track on left is FR 904.
2.4 ▲	SO	Track on right is FR 904.

GPS: N35°06.17′ W112°08.61′

▼ 1.3	BR	Track on left is FR 902.
2.0 ▲	BL	Track on right is FR 902.

GPS: N35°06.28′ W112°08.95′

▼ 1.9	SO	Track on left.
1.4 ▲	SO	Track on right.
▼ 2.1	SO	Cattle guard.
1.2 ▲	SO	Cattle guard.
▼ 2.2	SO	Cattle guard.
1.1 ▲	SO	Cattle guard.
▼ 2.4	SO	Track on right is FR 600. Track on left is FR 57, the Overland Trail to Davenport.
0.9 ▲	SO	Track on right is FR 57, the Overland Trail to Davenport. Track on left is FR 600.

GPS: N35°07.19′ W112°08.91′

▼ 2.8	SO	Closure gate.
0.5 ▲	SO	Closure gate.
▼ 3.1	SO	Track on right is FR 195.
0.2 ▲	SO	Track on left is FR 195.

GPS: N35°07.67′ W112°08.69′

▼ 3.3		Trail ends back on CR 73. Turn right for Williams.
0.0 ▲		From CR 73, 0.1 miles north of mile marker 176, zero trip meter and turn north on graded dirt road, FR 354, sign-posted to Pine Flat.

GPS: N35°07.83′ W112°08.72′

Sycamore Point Trail

STARTING POINT: Northeast #11: White Horse Lake Loop Trail, 7 miles from CR 73 along the north end
FINISHING POINT: Sycamore Point
TOTAL MILEAGE: 7.5 miles
UNPAVED MILEAGE: 7.5 miles
DRIVING TIME: 1 hour
ELEVATION RANGE: 6,000–7,000 feet
USUALLY OPEN: April to December
BEST TIME TO TRAVEL: Dry weather
DIFFICULTY RATING: 2
SCENIC RATING: 10
REMOTENESS RATING: +0

Special Attractions

- Exceptional views of Sycamore Canyon from Sycamore Point.
- Can be used to shorten Northeast #11: White Horse Lake Loop Trail.
- Shady campsites under ponderosa pines.

Description

Sycamore Point is an easily accessible, not-to-be-missed viewpoint with stunning vistas more than 1,000 feet down a sheer drop into beautiful Sycamore Canyon, part of the Sycamore Canyon Wilderness Area. The view of the folded red Coconino sandstone cliffs that form Sycamore Canyon is one that will never be forgotten.

The access trail to the point leaves Northeast #11: White Horse Lake Loop Trail 7 miles from the northern exit onto CR 73 and cuts across the loop, bypassing White Horse Lake to intersect with it again at J. D. Dam Lake. This first part of the trail travels in the cool shade of a ponderosa pine forest. There is an excellent chance of seeing elk as well as mule deer and many smaller forest creatures.

Past the second intersection with Northeast #11: White Horse Lake Loop Trail, the road is one-way only as it travels through open forest out to the point. The trail ends in a small loop on Sycamore Point.

Sycamore Point has some shade at the

turnaround point, and there is room to camp and picnic near the edge of the canyon.

Current Road Information
Kaibab National Forest
Williams Ranger District
742 South Clover Rd.
Williams, AZ 86046
(928) 635-5600

Map References
BLM   Williams
USFS   Kaibab National Forest: Williams
      Ranger District
USGS   1:24,000   White Horse Lake,
      Sycamore Point
      1:100,000   Williams
Maptech CD-ROM: Flagstaff/Sedona/Prescott
Arizona Atlas & Gazetteer, p. 41
Arizona Road & Recreation Atlas, p. 34 & p. 68
Recreational Map of Arizona

Route Directions

▼ 0.0   Trail commences on Northeast #11: White Horse Lake Loop Trail, 7 miles from the northern end of the trail. Zero trip meter and turn southeast on small roughly graded trail marked FR 110. There is a sign at the intersection for White Horse Lake Campground 3 miles to the north.

2.9 ▲   Trail ends at the intersection with Northeast #11: White Horse Lake Loop Trail. Turn right for White Horse Lake; turn left to exit to Williams.
           GPS: N35°06.29' W112°02.89'

▼ 0.1 SO Closure gate.
2.8 ▲ SO Closure gate.
▼ 1.1 SO Track on right is FR 660.
1.8 ▲ SO Track on left is FR 660.
           GPS: N35°05.42' W112°02.52'

▼ 1.5 SO Cattle guard.
1.4 ▲ SO Cattle guard.
▼ 2.1 SO Track on right is FR 653.
0.8 ▲ SO Track on left is FR 653.
           GPS: N35°04.74' W112°01.72'

Northeast Trail #12: Sycamore Point Trail

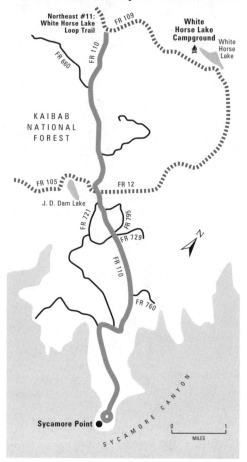

▼ 2.2 SO Track on left.
0.7 ▲ SO Track on right.
▼ 2.5 SO Track on left.
0.4 ▲ SO Track on right.
▼ 2.8 TL Turn left at T-intersection onto graded road FR 105, which is part of Northeast #11: White Horse Lake Loop Trail.
0.1 ▲ TR Turn right onto small roughly graded road FR 110, leaving Northeast #11: White Horse Lake Loop Trail.
           GPS: N35°04.25' W112°01.37'

▼ 2.9 SO Track on left is FR 12, continuation of Northeast #11: White Horse Lake Loop Trail. Zero trip meter and continue on FR 110, following the sign to Sycamore Point.

The view from Sycamore Point into Sycamore Canyon

The trail winds through forest, heading toward Sycamore Point

0.0 ▲		Track on right is FR 12, continuation of Northeast #11: White Horse Lake Loop Trail. Continue to the west on FR 110.
		GPS: N35°04.21' W112°01.27'

▼ 0.0		Continue to the southeast on FR 110.
▼ 0.2	SO	Track on right is FR 721.
		GPS: N35°04.06' W112°01.08'

▼ 0.4	SO	Track on left is FR 795.
▼ 0.8	SO	Track on left is FR 795; then second track on left is FR 729 and track on right.
		GPS: N35°03.83' W112°00.55'

▼ 1.8	SO	Track on left is FR 760; then cross through wash.
		GPS: N35°03.24' W111°59.65'

▼ 2.6	SO	Track on right.
▼ 2.9	SO	Small track on right.
▼ 4.5	BR	Start of final loop.
		GPS: N35°01.50' W111°58.69'

▼ 4.6		Trail ends at Sycamore Point.
		GPS: N35°01.43' W111°58.65'

NORTHEAST REGION TRAIL #13

Perkinsville Road

STARTING POINT: Arizona 89 in Chino Valley
FINISHING POINT: Intersection of CR 71 with
   FR 173, 25 miles south of Williams
TOTAL MILEAGE: 29.8 miles
UNPAVED MILEAGE: 28.2 miles
DRIVING TIME: 1.5 hours
ELEVATION RANGE: 4,000–5,400 feet
USUALLY OPEN: Year-round
BEST TIME TO TRAVEL: Year-round
DIFFICULTY RATING: 1
SCENIC RATING: 8
REMOTENESS RATING: +0

Special Attractions

■ Historic town of Perkinsville and the
   United Verde & Pacific Railroad.
■ Views of the Sycamore Canyon Wilderness.
■ Campsites along the Verde River.

History

Perkinsville is a small ranching community along the Verde River. It is named after Marion Perkins, a rancher from Texas, who purchased the existing property at the site owned by James Baker and John Campbell. Perkins purchased the ranch in 1899 and then returned to New Mexico for his cattle, which had been driven from Texas. He finally settled at his new ranch in November 1900.

In 1912, the Santa Fe Railroad extended a branch from Drake to Clarkdale, which crossed Perkins's ranch. A station was built and named Perkinsville. It is still standing and can be glimpsed from the road, but it is located on private property. Perkinsville had a post office between 1925 and 1939.

The single-lane steel bridge at Perkinsville was originally constructed in another location. Built in 1913, it crossed the Gila River some 200 miles to the southwest, but the bridge was washed out in a flood in 1915. It was brought to its current location and erected across the Verde River by a forest service work team. The bridge is classified by the Historic American Buildings Survey as "technologically noteworthy," being an early example of the most common truss-type bridges built in America.

Description

The long Perkinsville Road is a highly scenic route that offers some impressive panoramas as it travels through the Prescott National Forest in mainly open country. The trail leaves Chino Valley north of Prescott and initially follows a paved road as it runs east across open ranchland to the forest boundary. To the south is Woodchute Mountain. The trail enters Prescott National Forest and runs along a ridge top, which drops off to expose the red rocks of the Sycamore Canyon Wilderness to the northeast. Bill Williams Mountain is to the west, and the San Francisco Peaks can be seen on the horizon to the north.

A short series of switchbacks drops the trail swiftly down to join the Jerome–Perkinsville Road a short distance south of the old settlement of Perkinsville.

At Perkinsville—situated on the Verde River—the railroad, river, and road come together. The Verde Canyon Railroad, which takes tourists on a scenic trip from Clarkdale through Verde Canyon, winds along the river at this point to finish its outbound trip at Perkinsville; it then retraces its route to Clarkdale. There is a single-lane steel bridge over the river, and tracks on the right and the left lead to a small number of campsites set in the riparian area.

From Perkinsville, the trail climbs gradually again, passing the start of Northeast #14: Henderson Flat Trail to finish at the intersection of CR 71 and FR 173, 25 miles south of Williams, at the start of the paved road.

Current Road Information

Prescott National Forest
Chino Valley Ranger District
735 North Hwy 89
Chino Valley, AZ 86323
(928) 777-2200

Map References

BLM   Prescott
USFS   Prescott National Forest: Chino
       Valley Ranger District
USGS   1:24,000   Chino Valley North,
       King Canyon, Munds Draw,
       Perkinsville, Hell Point
       1:100,000 Prescott
Maptech CD-ROM: Flagstaff/Sedona/Prescott
Arizona Atlas & Gazetteer, p. 41
Arizona Road & Recreation Atlas, pp. 34, 68
Recreational Map of Arizona

Route Directions

▼ 0.0   From Arizona 89 in Chino Valley, zero trip
           meter and turn east on the paved road
           signed Perkinsville Road, CR 70. The turn
           is immediately south of mile marker 329.
           Remain on main paved road.
6.2 ▲   Trail ends at the T-intersection with
           Arizona 89 in Chino Valley. Turn left for
           Prescott; turn right for Ash Fork.
           GPS: N34°46.26′ W112°27.13′

▼ 1.4   SO Road on left and right; then cattle

guard. Road turns to graded dirt and
initially crosses private property;
remain on county road.

4.8 ▲   SO Cattle guard; then road is paved. Road
             on right and left after cattle guard;
             remain on main paved road into Chino
             Valley.
             GPS: N34°46.34′ W112°25.61′

▼ 2.3   SO Graded road on right is M. A. Perkins
             Trailway; road on left to ranch.
3.9 ▲   SO Graded road on left is M. A. Perkins
             Trailway; road on right to ranch.
▼ 3.2   SO Graded road on right.
3.0 ▲   SO Graded road on left.
▼ 5.2   SO Cattle guard.
1.0 ▲   SO Cattle guard.
▼ 6.2   SO Graded road right is Northeast #16:
             United Verde & Pacific Railroad Grade
             Trail, FR 318A. Zero trip meter.
0.0 ▲   Continue to the west.
             GPS: N34°45.83′ W112°20.45′

▼ 0.0   Continue to the northeast.
4.0 ▲   SO Graded road on left is Northeast #16:
             United Verde & Pacific Railroad Grade
             Trail, FR 318A. Zero trip meter.
▼ 1.1   SO Cattle guard. Entering state land.
2.9 ▲   SO Cattle guard. Leaving state land.
▼ 1.3   BR Graded road on left. Bear right and
             cross over creek on bridge.
2.7 ▲   BL Cross over creek on bridge; then bear
             left; graded road on right.
             GPS: N34°46.56′ W112°19.36′

▼ 1.8   BL Graded road on right.
2.2 ▲   BR Graded road on left.
▼ 2.5   SO Track on left; then cattle guard; then
             ranch road on right.
1.5 ▲   SO Ranch road on left; then cattle guard;
             then track on right.
             GPS: N34°46.97′ W112°18.36′

▼ 2.6   SO Track on right to ranch.
1.4 ▲   SO Track on left to ranch.
▼ 3.8   SO Track on left is FR 163.
0.2 ▲   SO Track on right is FR 163.
             GPS: N34°47.93′ W112°17.59′

▼ 4.0   SO Entering Prescott National Forest over

Government Wash

cattle guard. Zero trip meter.

0.0 ▲ Continue to the southwest.
GPS: N34°48.04' W112°17.33'

▼ 0.0 Continue to the northeast; track on left.
7.3 ▲ SO Track on right; then leaving Prescott National Forest over cattle guard. Zero trip meter.
▼ 0.7 SO Track on right.
6.6 ▲ SO Track on left.
▼ 1.0 SO Track on left.
6.3 ▲ SO Track on right.
▼ 1.6 SO Track on right is FR 9005U.
5.7 ▲ SO Track on left is FR 9005U.
GPS: N34°47.91' W112°16.28'

▼ 1.8 SO Track on left.
5.5 ▲ SO Track on right.
▼ 2.2 SO Track on left.
5.1 ▲ SO Track on right.
▼ 2.6 SO Cattle guard.
4.7 ▲ SO Cattle guard.
▼ 2.9 SO Cross through two washes.
4.4 ▲ SO Cross through two washes.
▼ 3.0 SO Cross through wash.
4.3 ▲ SO Cross through wash.
▼ 3.3 SO Track on left is FR 164.
4.0 ▲ SO Track on right is FR 164.
GPS: N34°48.83' W112°15.03'

▼ 3.4 SO Pass under power lines.
3.9 ▲ SO Pass under power lines.
▼ 4.1 SO Cattle guard.
3.2 ▲ SO Cattle guard.
▼ 4.3 SO Track on left is FR 9001J.
3.0 ▲ SO Track on right is FR 9001J.
GPS: N34°49.09' W112°14.01'

▼ 4.5 SO Cattle guard.
2.8 ▲ SO Cattle guard.
▼ 4.8 SO Two tracks on left to corral.
2.5 ▲ SO Two tracks on right to corral.
▼ 7.3 SO Viewpoint on left toward Sycamore Canyon Wilderness. Zero trip meter.
0.0 ▲ Continue to the south.
GPS: N34°51.45' W112°13.29'

▼ 0.0 Continue to the north and descend switchback.
3.5 ▲ SO Top of switchback; then viewpoint

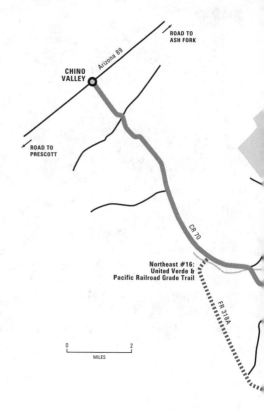

Northeast Trail #13: Perkinsville Road

on right toward Sycamore Canyon Wilderness. Zero trip meter at view point.
▼ 0.3 SO Cross through wash.
3.2 ▲ SO Cross through wash.
▼ 1.1 SO Cross through wash; then track on right. Cattle guard; then track on left.
2.4 ▲ SO Track on right; then cattle guard. Track on left; then cross through wash.
▼ 2.0 SO Cross through Munds Draw.
1.5 ▲ SO Cross through Munds Draw.
GPS: N34°52.06' W112°12.26'

▼ 2.2 SO Track on right is FR 9899D.
1.3 ▲ SO Track on left is FR 9899D.
GPS: N34°52.20' W112°12.28'

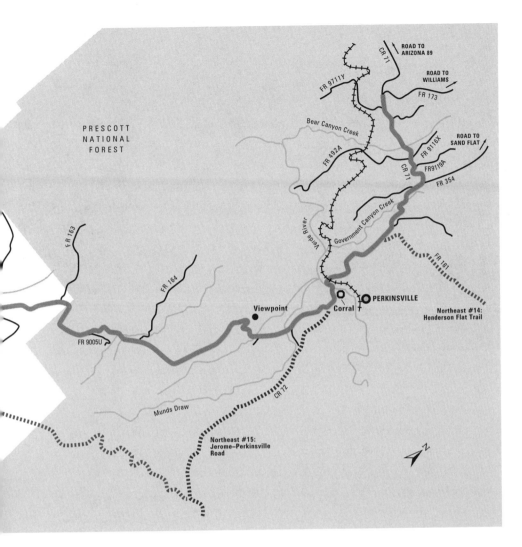

▼ 2.5 SO Track on left.
1.0 ▲ SO Track on right.
▼ 3.0 SO Cross through wash.
0.5 ▲ SO Cross through wash.
▼ 3.4 SO Cross over wash.
0.1 ▲ SO Cross over wash.
▼ 3.5 TL T-intersection. Northeast #15:
           Jerome–Perkinsville Road, CR 72, to
           Jerome on right. Turn left, remaining
           on CR 70. Zero trip meter. There is no
           signpost in this direction.
0.0 ▲   Continue to the southwest.
           GPS: N34°53.30′ W112°11.87′

▼ 0.0   Continue to the northwest.

3.6 ▲ TR Turn right onto graded road, sign-post-
           ed to Chino Valley. Ahead is Northeast
           #15: Jerome–Perkinsville Road, CR
           72, to Jerome. Zero trip meter.
▼ 0.6 SO Corral on right; then cross over Verde
           River on steel bridge.
3.0 ▲ SO Cross over Verde River on steel bridge;
           then corral on left.
           GPS: N34°53.70′ W112°12.27′

▼ 0.7 TL Track on left is FR 9004M; cross over
           aqueduct; then turn left over cattle
           guard. Track on right goes to
           Perkinsville Railroad Station (located
           on private property).
2.9 ▲ TR Cattle guard; then turn right and cross

A view from the trail toward the Woodshute Wilderness

over aqueduct. Track straight on goes to Perkinsville Railroad Station (located on private property);then track on right is FR 9004M.

▼ 1.0   SO   Cross over railroad; then track on left.
2.6 ▲   SO   Track on right; then cross over railroad.
        GPS: N34°53.70' W112°12.57'

▼ 1.3   SO   Cross through wash.
2.3 ▲   SO   Cross through wash.
▼ 2.5   SO   Track on left.
1.1 ▲   SO   Track on right.
▼ 2.7   SO   Track on left.
0.9 ▲   SO   Track on right.
▼ 3.0   SO   Cattle guard.
0.6 ▲   SO   Cattle guard.
▼ 3.6   SO   Track on right is Northeast #14: Henderson Flat Trail, FR 181. Zero trip meter.
0.0 ▲   Continue to the south.
        GPS: N34°55.59' W112°12.33'

▼ 0.0   Continue to the north.
2.2 ▲   SO   Track on left is Northeast #14: Henderson Flat Trail, FR 181. Zero trip meter.
▼ 0.7   SO   Track on right is FR 9004T.

1.5 ▲   SO   Track on left is FR 9004T.
        GPS: N34°56.16' W112°12.60'

▼ 1.4   SO   Cross over Government Canyon Creek on bridge.
0.8 ▲   SO   Cross over Government Canyon Creek on bridge.
        GPS: N34°56.63' W112°12.75'

▼ 2.1   SO   Track on left; then cattle guard.
0.1 ▲   SO   Cattle guard; then track on right.
▼ 2.2   BL   Graded road on right is FR 354 to Sand Flat. This road is also part of the Great Western Trail. Zero trip meter.
0.0 ▲   Continue to the south on CR 70.
        GPS: N34°57.31' W112°12.75'

▼ 0.0   Continue to the west on CR 71.
3.0 ▲   BR   Graded road on left is FR 354 to Sand Flat. This road is also part of the Great Western Trail. Zero trip meter.
▼ 0.2   SO   Cross through wash.
2.8 ▲   SO   Cross through wash.
▼ 0.5   SO   Two tracks on left.
2.5 ▲   SO   Two tracks on right.
▼ 0.6   SO   Cross through wash.
2.4 ▲   SO   Cross through wash.

▼ 0.7	SO	Track on right is FR 9119A; then cross through wash.
2.3 ▲	SO	Cross through wash; then track on left is FR 9119A.

GPS: N34°57.35′ W112°13.37′

▼ 1.0	SO	Track on left is FR 492A to Bear Siding and Verde River. Track on right is FR 9116X.
2.0 ▲	SO	Track on right is FR 492A to Bear Siding and Verde River. Track on left is FR 9116X.

GPS: N34°57.50′ W112°13.64′

▼ 1.3	SO	Track on right; then cross over Bear Canyon Creek on bridge.
1.7 ▲	SO	Cross over Bear Canyon Creek on bridge; then track on left.
▼ 1.7	SO	Cross over creek on bridge; then track on left.
1.3 ▲	SO	Track on right; then cross over creek on bridge.
▼ 1.5	SO	Track on right; then cattle guard.
1.5 ▲	SO	Cattle guard; then track on left.
▼ 2.3	SO	Track on right.
0.7 ▲	SO	Track on left.
▼ 2.6	SO	Cross over wash; then track on left is FR 9711Y.
0.4 ▲	SO	Track on right is FR 9711Y; then cross over wash.

GPS: N34°57.74′ W112°15.39′

▼ 2.8	SO	Road turns to paved.
0.2 ▲	SO	Road turns to graded dirt.
▼ 3.0	SO	Trail ends immediately after the paved road where the graded road on the left from Drake and Arizona 89 enters. This intersection is signed to Drake. Turn left for Arizona 89; continue straight ahead on the paved road to Williams.
0.0 ▲		Trail commences on FR 173 (Perkinsville Road), 25 miles south of Williams at the intersection of CR 71 and Perkinsville Road. Zero trip meter at the intersection and continue southeast on paved Perkinsville Road, following the sign to Perkinsville and Jerome. Graded road on the right is the road to Drake and is signposted.

GPS: N34°57.96′ W112°15.76′

Henderson Flat Trail

STARTING POINT: Northeast #13: Perkinsville Road, 3 miles north of the Verde River crossing at Perkinsville

FINISHING POINT: Sycamore Basin Hiking Trailhead #63

TOTAL MILEAGE: 12.5 miles

UNPAVED MILEAGE: 12.5 miles

DRIVING TIME: 1.25 hours (one-way)

ELEVATION RANGE: 4,200–5,000 feet

USUALLY OPEN: Year-round

BEST TIME TO TRAVEL: Dry weather

DIFFICULTY RATING: 3

SCENIC RATING: 9

REMOTENESS RATING: +1

Special Attractions

■ Access to Sycamore Canyon hiking trails.

■ Spectacular red rock scenery.

Description

One of the most scenic and popular wilderness areas within Arizona is the Sycamore Canyon Wilderness, with its striking red rock canyons and mountains. Although there are more than 70 places with the name Sycamore in Arizona alone, Sycamore Canyon near Sedona is probably the best known. The canyon is 25 miles long and 7 miles across at its widest point. Scattered throughout are many cliff dwellings left behind by early Indians. Many people travel to Sedona to view the area, but a quieter yet equally pretty access comes in from the west side, through Prescott National Forest.

This trail leaves Northeast #13: Perkinsville Road to travel a roughly graded, single-track trail toward the wilderness boundary. The trail winds through the predominant pinyon and juniper vegetation, crossing through a number of small canyons as it travels toward Henderson Flat. The red bluffs of Sycamore Canyon come into view. The trail continues past the cabin at Henderson Flat to finish at the trailhead for the Sycamore Basin Hiking Trail #63, which is

Rock formations reach skyward as the trail nears Sycamore Canyon

Northeast Trail #14: Henderson Flat Trail

the main trail leading into the Sycamore Canyon Wilderness.

The road surface, especially at the far end, gradually turns into red clay. The addition of water turns the clay into a thick, greasy mess that quickly fills tire treads and makes traction impossible. Traveling along this trail in wet weather is not recommended. There are a couple of nice camping spots, particularly near the trailhead at the end.

Current Road Information

Prescott National Forest
Chino Valley Ranger District
735 North Hwy 89
Chino Valley, AZ 86323
(928) 777-2200

Map References

BLM   Prescott
USFS   Prescott National Forest: Chino
       Valley Ranger District
USGS   1:24,000   Perkinsville, Sycamore
       Basin
       1:100,000 Prescott
Maptech CD-ROM: Flagstaff/Sedona/Prescott
Arizona Atlas & Gazetteer, p. 41
Arizona Road & Recreation Atlas, pp. 34, 68

Route Directions

▼ 0.0   From Northeast #13: Perkinsville Road, 3 miles north of the Verde River crossing at Perkinsville, zero trip meter and turn northeast on FR 181 signed to Henderson Flat. Trail is roughly graded dirt road.
         GPS: N34°55.59' W112°12.33'

▼ 0.6   SO Cattle guard; entering canyon.
▼ 0.7   SO Cross through wash.
▼ 0.9   SO Track on left.
▼ 1.2   BL Track on right is FR 9000P.
         GPS: N34°56.01' W112°11.53'

▼ 2.6   SO Track on right.
▼ 2.8   SO Track on right; then cross through wash.
▼ 3.1   SO Track on left through fence.
         GPS: N34°56.48' W112°09.92'

▼ 3.6   SO Cattle guard.
▼ 3.8   SO Track on right is FR 639. Zero trip meter.
         GPS: N34°56.39' W112°09.57'

▼ 0.0   Continue to the east.
▼ 0.7   SO Track on right is FR 9710R.
         GPS: N34°56.71' W112°09.01'

▼ 0.8   SO Track on right.
▼ 0.9   SO Track on right.

A summer thunderstorm darkens the sky above Sycamore Canyon

▼ 1.6   SO   Cattle guard.

▼ 2.3   BL   Small track on right and viewpoint over the Sycamore Canyon Wilderness.
       GPS: N34°57.75′ W112°07.94′

▼ 2.6   SO   Track on left; entering the line of Railroad Draw.

▼ 2.8   SO   Cross through Railroad Draw.
       GPS: N34°57.78′ W112°07.87′

▼ 3.3   SO   Track on right is FR 639. Zero trip meter.
       GPS: N34°57.81′ W112°07.51′

▼ 0.0   Continue to the east.

▼ 0.2   SO   Lonesome Pocket Hiking Trail #61 on left to Sand Flat; then entrance to old cabin on left and track on right; water catchment on left. This is Henderson Flat.
       GPS: N34°57.78′ W112°07.34′

▼ 0.3   SO   Cattle guard.
▼ 0.6   SO   Cross through wash.
▼ 0.9   SO   Track on left.
▼ 1.0   SO   Cross through wash.
▼ 1.3   SO   Cross through wash.
▼ 1.6   SO   Cross through wash.
▼ 2.9   SO   Cross through wash.

       GPS: N34°56.19′ W112°06.11′

▼ 3.0   SO   Cross through wash.
▼ 3.8   SO   Cross through wash; then track on right; then track on left.
▼ 4.4   SO   Track on right; then cattle guard; then cross through wash.
       GPS: N34°55.24′ W112°05.25′

▼ 4.7   SO   Track on right.
▼ 5.4   BR   The trail finishes at Sycamore Basin Hiking Trailhead #63 into Sycamore Canyon Wilderness. The main trail continues as a smaller formed trail for a short distance before finishing at the wilderness boundary.
       GPS: N34°55.51′ W112°04.27′

NORTHEAST REGION TRAIL #15

Jerome–Perkinsville Road

STARTING POINT: Northeast #13: Perkinsville Road, immediately south of Perkinsville

FINISHING POINT: Jerome

Negotiating an old railroad cut

TOTAL MILEAGE: 14.8 miles
UNPAVED MILEAGE: 14.8 miles
DRIVING TIME: 1.25 hours
ELEVATION RANGE: 4,000–6,000 feet
USUALLY OPEN: Year-round
BEST TIME TO TRAVEL: Dry weather
DIFFICULTY RATING: 2
SCENIC RATING: 8
REMOTENESS RATING: +0

Special Attractions

- Many varied views, including the Woodchute Wilderness, Jerome, and the Verde Valley.
- Route follows a section of the historic United Verde & Pacific Railroad.
- Rockhounding for Perkinsville agate.

Description

This graded dirt road travels through fascinating scenery between Perkinsville and the former ghost town of Jerome. The trail travels on ridge tops and on a section of the old United Verde & Pacific Railroad grade as it makes its final descent into Jerome.

The trail, which also forms part of the Great Western Trail, is roughly graded along its length, although a few rough spots make it more suitable for high-clearance vehicles.

Six miles south of Perkinsville, rock hounds may be able to find some samples of agate by scouring in the washes and areas surrounding them.

From the intersection with Northeast #16: United Verde & Pacific Railroad Grade Trail, the route follows along the old railroad bed into Jerome. The shelf road is wide enough for two vehicles to pass with care, and the gentle grade winds around Woodchute Mountain before passing through a cut and the highest point of the railroad (5,935 feet). On the south side of the cut is First View. Travelers in this direction get their first view of Jerome and the Verde Valley. From here, the trail winds its way down to Jerome, passing through property still owned by Phelps Dodge. It passes by the entrance of the Gold King Mine, Museum, and Ghost Town before finishing in the center of Jerome.

The road can be negotiated by any high-clearance vehicle in dry weather, but 4WD or chains are recommended for winter travel when there might be a sprinkling of snow on the higher elevations.

Current Road Information

Prescott National Forest
Chino Valley Ranger District
735 North Hwy 89
Chino Valley, AZ 86323
(928) 777-2200

Prescott National Forest
Verde Ranger District
300 East Hwy 260
PO Box 670
Campe Verde, AZ 86322
(928) 567-4121

Map References

BLM   Prescott
USFS   Prescott National Forest: Chino
       Valley and Verde Ranger Districts
USGS   1:24,000 Perkinsville, Munds
       Draw, Clarkdale
       1:100,000 Prescott
Maptech CD-ROM: Flagstaff/Sedona/Prescott
Arizona Atlas & Gazetteer, p. 41
Arizona Road & Recreation Atlas, pp. 34, 68
Recreational Map of Arizona

Route Directions

▼ 0.0   From the intersection of Northeast
         #13: Perkinsville Road, CR 70, and CR
         72 immediately south of Perkinsville,
         zero trip meter and turn southeast on
         graded dirt road CR 72, following the
         sign to Jerome. The route is designated
         as part of the Great Western Trail.

1.5 ▲   Trail ends at the intersection of
         CR 70 and CR 72, Northeast #13:
         Perkinsville Road, immediately south
         of Perkinsville. Continue north to exit
         to Williams or Drake; turn left to exit
         to Chino Valley.

         GPS: N34°53.30′ W112°11.87′

The bustling Jerome Mine Museum below the trail with mine tailings in the background

Northeast Trail #15: Jerome–Perkinsville Road

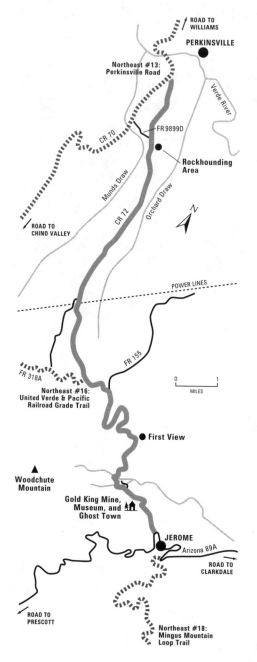

▼ 1.5   SO   Track on right is FR 9899D to Chino Valley. Zero trip meter.

0.0 ▲   Continue to the northwest, following the sign to Drake and Williams.

GPS: N34°52.02' W112°11.53'

▼ 0.0   Continue to the southeast and cross cattle guard. Around this cattle guard is the agate rockhounding area.

6.0 ▲   BR   Cattle guard; then track on left is FR 9899D to Chino Valley. Zero trip meter at intersection. Around this cattle guard is an agate rockhounding area.

▼ 0.7   SO   Cattle guard; then track on right.

5.3 ▲   SO   Track on left; then cattle guard.

▼ 2.7   SO   Track on right.

3.3 ▲   SO   Track on left.

▼ 4.1   SO   Cattle guard; then track on right. Pass under power lines; then track on left under power lines.

1.9 ▲   SO   Track on right under power lines; then pass under power lines. Track on left; then cattle guard.

GPS: N34°48.44' W112°11.40'

▼ 4.4   SO   Track on right.

1.6 ▲   SO   Track on left.

▼ 4.7   SO   Track on left.

1.3 ▲   SO   Track on right.

▼ 5.4   SO   Track on left.

0.6 ▲   SO   Track on right.

▼ 6.0   BL   Track on right is Northeast #16: United Verde & Pacific Railroad Grade Trail, FR 318A. Zero trip meter.

0.0 ▲   Continue to the northwest, following sign to Williams and Chino Valley.

GPS: N34°47.11' W112°10.34'

▼ 0.0   Continue to the east.

3.8 ▲   BR   Track on left is Northeast #16: United Verde & Pacific Railroad Grade Trail, FR 318A. Zero trip meter.

▼ 0.8   BR   Track on left is FR 155.

3.0 ▲   SO   Track on right is FR 155.

GPS: N34°47.14' W112°09.69'

▼ 2.5   SO   Pass through cutting.

1.3 ▲   SO   Pass through cutting.

▼ 3.8 SO Cattle guard; then track on left. First View of the Verde Valley, Cottonwood and Clarkdale, and then Jerome. Zero trip meter at sign.

0.0 ▲ Continue to the west on FR 318.

GPS: N34°46.59′ W112°08.50′

▼ 0.0 Continue to the south.

3.5 ▲ SO First View of Jerome and the Verde Valley; then track on right; then cattle guard. Signpost in other direction for First View. Zero trip meter.

▼ 0.2 SO Cutting; then view of Jerome.

3.3 ▲ SO Cutting.

▼ 1.2 SO Track on right; then cutting.

2.3 ▲ SO Cutting; then track on left.

▼ 1.3 SO Cross over creek.

2.2 ▲ SO Cross over creek.

GPS: N34°45.69′ W112°08.59′

▼ 1.6 SO Cross over creek on bridge.

1.9 ▲ SO Cross over creek on bridge.

▼ 1.9 SO Track on left.

1.6 ▲ BL Track on right.

▼ 2.0 SO Track on left.

1.5 ▲ SO Track on right.

▼ 2.7 TL Entrance to the Gold King Mine, Museum, and Ghost Town on right.

0.8 ▲ TR Entrance to the Gold King Mine, Museum, and Ghost Town ahead. Turn right in front of the entrance.

GPS: N34°45.45′ W112°07.74′

▼ 3.3 SO Cross old railroad; mine entrance on right and road on left.

0.2 ▲ SO Mine entrance on left and road on right; cross old railroad.

▼ 3.5 Trail ends in Jerome on Arizona 89A at the fire station. Continue ahead for Clarkdale; turn right for Prescott.

0.0 ▲ In Jerome on Arizona 89A, at the fire station, on a sharp switchback in the main street, zero trip meter and turn west on Perkinsville Road. The road goes to the Gold King Mine, Museum, and Ghost Town.

GPS: N34°45.11′ W112°07.01′

United Verde & Pacific Railroad Grade Trail

STARTING POINT: Northeast #13: Perkinsville Road, 6.2 miles east of Chino Valley
FINISHING POINT: Northeast #15: Jerome–Perkinsville Road, 7.3 miles north of Jerome
TOTAL MILEAGE: 13.1 miles
UNPAVED MILEAGE: 13.1 miles
DRIVING TIME: 1 hour
ELEVATION RANGE: 5,000–5,600 feet
USUALLY OPEN: Year-round
BEST TIME TO TRAVEL: Dry weather
DIFFICULTY RATING: 2
SCENIC RATING: 8
REMOTENESS RATING: +0

Special Attractions

■ Trail that follows the route of the United Verde & Pacific Railroad.
■ Views of Jerome and the Verde Valley.
■ Long, extremely scenic shelf road.

History

The trail bears evidence of the sidings and turnaround points for the old United Verde & Pacific Railroad. Near the easern end of the trail, an open area beside the road is Horseshoe Siding, which is believed to be the site of a sawmill that milled timber from Woodchute Mountain. Timber was used to fire the smelters before coke was brought in.

Description

For the most part, this trail follows along the grade of the United Verde & Pacific Railroad as it travels between Chino Valley and Jerome. The trail leaves from Northeast #13: Perkinsville Road, turning south on the small graded dirt road, FR 318A. There is a forest road number post at the intersection, and a large corral can be seen a short distance down the road. Initially, the trail crosses the broad, flat plain, joining the railroad grade to head in a straight line toward Woodchute Mountain.

Northeast Trail #16: United Verde & Pacific Railroad Grade Trail

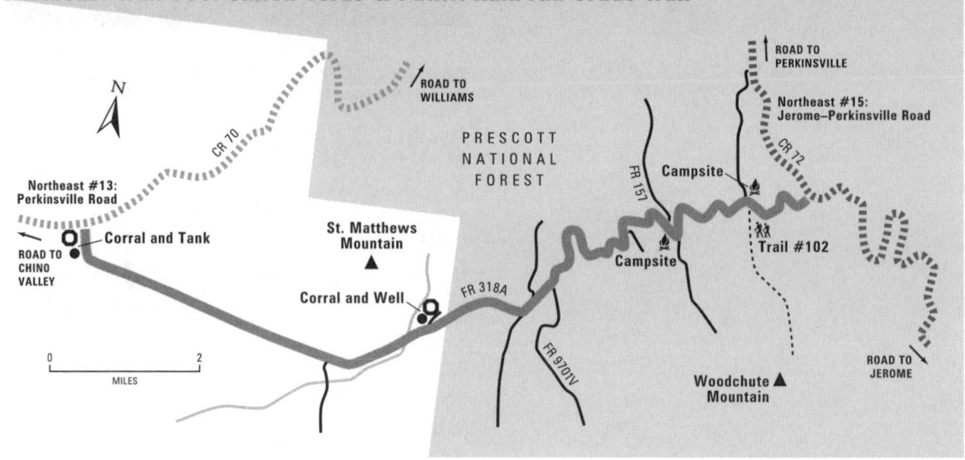

Past the intersection of FR 9701V (which appears on the Prescott National Forest Map as FR 642), the trail becomes narrower and starts to wind along a shelf road around the north face of Woodchute Mountain. It closely follows the original railroad grade, and you will pass through many of the cuttings made for the train. The grade is easy and the shelf road is wide enough for a single vehicle; there are good passing places.

Surprisingly, given that the trail is mainly a shelf road, there are a couple of good campsites where you can pull off the trail and enjoy the panoramic view north toward the Sycamore Canyon Wilderness and the San Francisco Peaks north of Williams.

The trail ends at the intersection with Northeast #15: Jerome–Perkinsville Road, which then continues to follow the path of the railroad grade into Jerome.

Current Road Information

Prescott National Forest
Chino Valley Ranger District
735 North Hwy 89
Chino Valley, AZ 86323
(928) 777-2200

Map References

BLM Prescott
USFS Prescott National Forest: Chino Valley Ranger District
USGS 1:24,000 King Canyon, Prescott Valley North, Munds Draw
1:100,000 Prescott
Maptech CD-ROM: Flagstaff/Sedona/Prescott
Arizona Atlas & Gazetteer, p. 41
Arizona Road & Recreation Atlas, pp. 34, 68

Route Directions

▼ 0.0 From Northeast #13: Perkinsville Road, 6.2 miles east of Chino Valley, zero trip meter and turn south on graded dirt road marked FR 318A.
5.3 ▲ Trail ends at the intersection with Northeast #13: Perkinsville Road. Turn right for Williams; turn left for Chino Valley and Prescott.

GPS: N34°45.83' W112°20.45'

▼ 0.1 SO Corral and tank on right.
5.2 ▲ SO Corral and tank on left.
▼ 0.4 SO Join railroad grade.
4.9 ▲ SO Leave railroad grade.
▼ 1.7 SO Cattle guard.
3.6 ▲ SO Cattle guard.
▼ 2.2 SO Cattle guard.
3.1 ▲ SO Cattle guard.
▼ 2.4 SO Track on right to dam.
2.9 ▲ SO Track on left to dam.
▼ 2.8 SO Cattle guard.
2.5 ▲ SO Cattle guard.
▼ 3.7 SO Track on right.
1.6 ▲ SO Track on left.

The trail commences along the dead straight course of the old railroad grade

THE UNITED VERDE & PACIFIC RAILWAY COMPANY

The Sinagua Indians roamed the hills around what is now known as Jerome, long before the United Verde Copper Company gained prominence in the area on and around Mingus Mountain. The natives collected and utilized blue azure residue for their body paints and pottery decorations. In the late 1500s and early 1600s, Spanish explorers took a minor interest in the area and collected some ore specimens to take back to Mexico. However they were unimpressed and bypassed the ore because it was not gold.

Americans began to mine the area in 1876. One of the first owners of the mines was the territorial governor of Arizona Frederick Tritle. The governor gained much-needed financial backing from New Yorker Eugene Murray Jerome, who insisted the town be named after him. Under the direction of their new United Verde Copper Company, the town of Jerome began to form. By 1883, Jerome bustled with 50 homes, 3 stores, several saloons, and about 400 residents, but that was only the beginning.

The United Verde & Pacific depot in Jerome, circa 1900

In 1884, Montana Senator William A. Clark purchased the mine and Jerome experienced great changes. The multimillionaire spent more than $1 million over a 12-year period to renovate the mine and town. The United Verde & Pacific Railway Company was chartered in March 1894. It cost $600,000 to lay the 26 miles of track that connected the Senator's copper mine in Jerome to the Santa Fe, Prescott & Phoenix Railway in the Chino Valley. The narrow-gauge railway began operating in January 1895 and was called the "crookedest railroad in the world" by the miners who rode along its 3-foot-wide tracks. With 126 curves along its route, the name described the railroad perfectly. Clark also built a large hotel called Montana House and erected a new smelter down-valley in Clarkdale. By 1900, Jerome boasted the fourth largest population in Arizona.

The hauling of coke for firing smelter furnaces was the primary function of the United Verde. Passengers (mainly miners) and necessities were carried to Jerome. At the junction of the two railroads, the town of Jerome Junction shot up to service the freight and passengers transferring to the United Verde for the short journey east. Rain was often a problem on the tracks, and the route was washed out several times. Fire also caused stoppages—engine sparks frequently ignited the wooden trestles that crossed gullies. Twenty-three trestles were replaced between 1898 and 1901 by the built-up grade that you see today. The project cost a quarter of a million dollars. Then in 1920, when the standard-gauge railroad was extended to Jerome from the east, the United Verde & Pacific Railway was abandoned and Jerome Junction was left for the ghosts. In 1923, its name was changed to Chino Valley.

Thanks to the forethought of the Jerome Historical Society, that town did not meet the same fate and end up a ghost town. Museums, shops, and a state historical park remain to weave the tale of this once-booming mining town. Travelers can follow the route of the abandoned railway on Northeast #16: United Verde & Pacific Railroad Trail.

▼ 4.9   SO   Cross over wash; corral and well on left.

0.4 ▲   SO   Cross over wash; corral and well on right.

▼ 5.1   SO   Cattle guard; then track on left.

0.2 ▲   SO   Track on right; then cattle guard.

▼ 5.3   SO   Entering Prescott National Forest at sign. Zero trip meter.

0.0 ▲   Continue to the west.

GPS: N34º45.28' W112º15.24'

▼ 0.0   Continue to the east on FR 318A.

1.5 ▲   SO   Leaving Prescott National Forest. Zero trip meter.

▼ 0.4   SO   Track on left under power lines.

1.1 ▲   SO   Track on right under power lines.

▼ 0.6   SO   Track on left.

0.9 ▲   SO   Track on right.

▼ 1.1   SO   Track on right through wire gate.

0.4 ▲   SO   Track on left through wire gate.

▼ 1.2   SO   Track on left.

0.3 ▲   SO   Track on right.

▼ 1.5   SO   Track on right is FR 9701V, part of the Great Western Trail. Zero trip meter.

0.0 ▲   Continue to the southwest, remaining on FR 318A. End of shelf road.

GPS: N34º45.80' W112º13.84'

▼ 0.0   Continue to the northeast, remaining on FR 318A. Start of shelf road.

3.2 ▲   SO   Track on left is FR 9701V, part of the Great Western Trail. Zero trip meter.

▼ 0.9   SO   Cattle guard.

2.3 ▲   SO   Cattle guard.

▼ 1.2   SO   Cross over creek.

2.0 ▲   SO   Cross over creek.

▼ 1.4   SO   Track on left.

1.8 ▲   SO   Track on right.

▼ 1.8   SO   Cross over wash; then track on right.

1.4 ▲   SO   Track on left; then cross over wash.

▼ 2.1   SO   Track on right.

1.1 ▲   SO   Track on left.

▼ 2.7   SO   Cross over creek; dam on right.

0.5 ▲   SO   Cross over creek; dam on left.

GPS: N34º46.59' W112º12.50'

▼ 3.2   SO   Track on left is FR 157. Zero trip meter. Campsite at intersection.

0.0 ▲   Continue to the northwest.

GPS: N34º46.56' W112º12.29'

▼ 0.0   Continue to the southeast.

3.1 ▲   SO   Track on right is FR 157. Zero trip meter. Campsite at intersection.

▼ 0.1   SO   Track on right; then cross over creek.

3.0 ▲   SO   Cross over creek; then track on left.

▼ 0.4   SO   Cattle guard.

2.7 ▲   SO   Cattle guard.

▼ 1.4   SO   Cross over creek.

1.7 ▲   SO   Cross over creek.

▼ 1.7   SO   Track on left; campsite at intersection.

1.4 ▲   SO   Track on right; campsite at intersection.

GPS: N34º46.97' W112º11.22'

▼ 1.8   SO   Trail on right (#102) for hiking and horses only. The open area on the left is Horseshoe Siding.

1.3 ▲   SO   Trail on left (#102) for hiking and horses only. The open area on the right is Horseshoe Siding.

GPS: N34º46.97' W112º11.18'

▼ 3.1   Trail ends at the intersection with Northeast #15: Jerome–Perkinsville Road. Turn left to continue to Perkinsville; turn right to continue to Jerome.

0.0 ▲   Trail commences at the intersection with Northeast #15: Jerome–Perkinsville Road, 7.3 miles from Jerome. Zero trip meter and proceed southwest on FR 318A. Trail is a shelf road.

GPS: N34º47.11' W112º10.34'

NORTHEAST REGION TRAIL #17

Goat Peak Trail

STARTING POINT: Arizona 89A, west of Jerome, opposite Potato Patch Campground
FINISHING POINT: FR 372, 1 mile west of Cherry
TOTAL MILEAGE: 14.6 miles
UNPAVED MILEAGE: 14.5 miles
DRIVING TIME: 1.5 hours

Northeast Trail #17: Goat Peak Trail

ELEVATION RANGE: 5,200–7,500 feet
USUALLY OPEN: March to November
BEST TIME TO TRAVEL: Dry weather
DIFFICULTY RATING: 2
SCENIC RATING: 8
REMOTENESS RATING: +0

Special Attractions
- Mingus Lake.
- Long, scenic ridge-top trail.
- Backcountry campsites and developed camping on Mingus Mountain.

Description
This trail connects the small settlement of Cherry with Mingus Mountain to the north. It leaves from Arizona 89A west of Jerome and travels up Mingus Mountain to within a mile of Mingus Lake, which is a small but pretty lake that is a popular spot for fishing or relaxing on a hot summer day. Initially, the trail travels on a wide, graded dirt road past many well-used backcountry campsites. In addition, there is a campground on Mingus Mountain. The trail then travels along FR 132, which is definitely for dry weather travel only. The road becomes totally impassable in wet weather, and a sign at the start warns that wet weather travel is prohibited and violators are subject to prosecution.

The northern end of the trail passes through cool ponderosa pine country on Mingus Mountain, but as it descends it enters the lower vegetation zone—manzanita and small oak trees predominate. Much of the trail travels along a ridge top, and there

are great views to the west over the Prescott National Forest as well as Goat Peak. After passing below the summit of Goat Peak, the trail drops down farther to follow along a creek before joining FR 372 near Cherry.

Current Road Information
Prescott National Forest
Verde Ranger District
300 East Hwy 260
PO Box 670
Campe Verde, AZ 86322
(928) 567-4121

Map References
BLM   Prescott
USFS   Prescott National Forest: Verde Ranger District
USGS 1:24,000 Hickey Mtn., Cottonwood, Cherry
       1:100,000 Prescott
Maptech CD-ROM: Flagstaff/Sedona/Prescott
Arizona Atlas & Gazetteer, p. 41
Arizona Road & Recreation Atlas, pp. 40, 74

Route Directions

▼ 0.0   From Arizona 89A west of Jerome, zero trip meter on the saddle at the entrance to Summit Picnic Area and Potato Patch Campground and turn east on paved FR 104 signposted to Mingus Springs Camp. Summit Picnic Area is immediately on the left. The road is also marked for the Great Western Trail.

Mingus Lake, a popular spot for fishing or just relaxing

Tree tunnel near the southern end of the trail

| 1.4 ▲ | | Trail finishes at the intersection with Arizona 89A. Turn right for Jerome; turn left for Prescott. |
| | | **GPS: N34°42.44′ W112°08.94′** |

▼ 0.1	SO	Road turns to graded gravel.
1.3 ▲	SO	Road is now paved.
▼ 1.4	TR	Turn right onto FR 413, following the sign for Cherry. Road straight on goes 0.6 miles to Mingus Lake. Zero trip meter.
0.0 ▲		Continue to the west.
		GPS: N34°41.88′ W112°08.29′

▼ 0.0		Continue to the south.
2.1 ▲	TL	T-intersection; turn left onto FR 104, following the sign to Arizona 89A. Road on right goes 0.6 miles to Mingus Lake. Zero trip meter.
▼ 1.9	SO	Track on left.
0.2 ▲	SO	Track on right.
▼ 2.1	TR	Cattle guard; then turn right onto FR 105/FR 132, following the sign to Cherry. Northeast #18: Mingus Mountain Loop Trail is straight ahead. Zero trip meter.
0.0 ▲		Continue to the northwest.
		GPS: N34°40.39′ W112°09.02′

▼ 0.0		Continue to the south.
9.0 ▲	TL	Turn left onto FR 413. Track on right is FR 413, Northeast #18: Mingus Mountain Loop Trail. Zero trip meter.
▼ 0.4	SO	Track on right is FR 105 to Mingus Springs Camp. Tank on left. Continue on FR 132.
8.6 ▲	SO	Track on left is FR 105 to Mingus Springs Camp. Tank on right. Continue on FR 132.
		GPS: N34°40.08′ W112°09.18′

▼ 0.7	SO	Cross through wash.
8.3 ▲	SO	Cross through wash.
		GPS: N34°39.86′ W112°08.92′

▼ 1.0	SO	Track on left.
8.0 ▲	SO	Track on right.
▼ 1.1	SO	Track on right.
7.9 ▲	SO	Track on left.
▼ 1.6	SO	Trail #9029 on right for hikers, horses, and mountain bikes.

| 7.4 ▲ | SO | Trail #9029 on left for hikers, horses, and mountain bikes. |
| | | **GPS: N34°39.52′ W112°08.35′** |

▼ 1.7	SO	Track on left.
7.3 ▲	SO	Track on right.
▼ 3.4	SO	Entering private land. Track on left; then Brindle Pup Mine on left.
5.6 ▲	SO	Brindle Pup Mine on right; then track on right. Leaving private land.
		GPS: N34°38.74′ W112°07.01′

▼ 3.8	SO	Leaving private land; then track on left.
5.2 ▲	SO	Track on right; then entering private land.
▼ 4.2	SO	Cross through wash.
4.8 ▲	SO	Cross through wash.
▼ 5.9	SO	Cattle guard; then track on left through fence line.
3.1 ▲	SO	Track on right through fence line; then cattle guard.
		GPS: N34°38.16′ W112°05.26′

▼ 6.6	SO	Track on right.
2.4 ▲	BR	Track on left.
▼ 6.7	SO	Turnout on left under Goat Peak.
2.3 ▲	SO	Turnout on right under Goat Peak.
		GPS: N34°37.80′ W112°04.78′

▼ 6.9	SO	Track on left.
2.1 ▲	SO	Track on right.
▼ 7.7	SO	Closure gate; then cattle guard.
1.3 ▲	SO	Cattle guard; then closure gate.
		GPS: N34°37.01′ W112°04.77′

▼ 8.0	BR	Track on left at wash.
1.0 ▲	BL	Track on right at wash.
▼ 8.1	SO	Cross through wash.
0.9 ▲	SO	Cross through wash.
▼ 8.6	SO	Track on left.
0.4 ▲	SO	Track on right.
▼ 8.8	SO	Track on right.
0.2 ▲	SO	Track on left.
▼ 9.0	SO	Cross through Cherry Creek; then track on right is FR 9004A. Zero trip meter.
0.0 ▲		Continue to the north and cross through Cherry Creek.
		GPS: N34°36.09′ W112°04.36′

▼ 0.0		Continue to the south; then track on left.
2.1 ▲	SO	Track on right; then track on left is FR 9004A. Zero trip meter.
▼ 0.2	SO	Track on left.
1.9 ▲	SO	Track on right.
▼ 1.1	SO	Graded road on left.
1.0 ▲	BL	Graded road on right.
		GPS: N34°36.02′ W112°03.51′

▼ 1.3	SO	Track on left.
0.8 ▲	SO	Track on right.
▼ 2.1		Trail ends at the intersection with FR 372. Turn left for Cherry; turn right for Dewey.
0.0 ▲		Trail starts on FR 372, 1 mile west of Cherry. Zero trip meter and turn north on FR 132 at the sign for the Great Western Trail, following the sign for Mingus Mountain.
		GPS: N34°35.14′ W112°03.43′

NORTHEAST REGION TRAIL #18

Mingus Mountain Loop Trail

STARTING POINT: Arizona 89A, on the east side of Jerome

FINISHING POINT: Northeast #17: Goat Peak Trail, 2.1 miles south of intersection with FR 104

TOTAL MILEAGE: 16.6 miles

UNPAVED MILEAGE: 16.6 miles

DRIVING TIME: 2.5 hours

ELEVATION RANGE: 4,800–6,900 feet

USUALLY OPEN: April to November

BEST TIME TO TRAVEL: Dry weather

DIFFICULTY RATING: 5

SCENIC RATING: 9

REMOTENESS RATING: +0

Special Attractions

- Historic mining town of Jerome.
- Very long section of narrow shelf road.
- Panoramic views over Verde Valley and the Red Rock Secret Mountain Wilderness.
- Old mining adits and tailings.

History

Mingus Mountain and the Jerome region have been visited by humans looking for minerals in the ground for more than a thousand years. The Sinagua Indians sought copper ore, argillite, azurite, and malachite for ornaments, tools, and as trading items.

The Spanish explorers who passed through the region in the 1500s were looking for gold, so they ignored the rich copper deposits. These deposits first attracted interest in 1876, but it was a few more years before investors could be persuaded to commit funds to the remote, seemingly inaccessible location. In 1882, the Atlantic & Pacific Railroad came within 60 miles of the region, making the deposits a more attractive proposition and a group of investors formed the United Verde Copper Company. The town of Jerome, named after Eugene Murray Jerome, one of the investors, was formed and continued to expand, despite its precarious location on the steep slopes of Mingus Mountain. The steep site caused many problems. For a start, construction was on the flattest section of ground on Cleopatra Hill, which happened to be near the smelter. Thus, the town was covered with smoke and the immediate area denuded of vegetation. Because of the steep slopes, landslip was, and still is, a continual problem. The original underground mine was unable to be worked after a fire in 1894, which burned for an incredible 33 years. To reach the rich ore body, ways were found around these problems. The smelter was relocated and the mine converted to an open-pit operation, which necessitated rerouting the twisting United Verde & Pacific Railroad, which connected the town to Jerome Junction (now Chino Valley) near Prescott.

Jerome continued to thrive, and in 1900 it was the fourth largest town in Arizona. In 1917, it was affected by labor disputes. The Industrial Workers of the World (known as the Wobblies) were in dispute with another union and a strike resulted. The Wobblies were unpopular in much of Jerome, and some of the townspeople took action, rounding up the Wobblies and shipping

A narrow section of shelf road above the Verde Valley

them out of town.

In 1935, mining giant Phelps Dodge purchased the United Verde Copper Company and continued churning out copper, recouping its initial investment in only five years. The mines finally closed in 1953.

For a time Jerome was quiet enough to be described as a ghost town, but over the years it has redefined itself as a center for the arts, a tourist town, and a historical center. It is now a thriving little place, packed on weekends with sightseers eager to explore the history and attractions of Jerome.

Description

This trail is not for the faint-hearted, as for most of its length it runs along an extremely narrow shelf road with precipitous drops. It leaves the ghost town of Jerome on narrow unpaved streets along the mountainside. There is no sign on the highway, and it is easy to miss the turn as well as the subsequent ones to the start of the shelf road; at first glance they look like private driveways. Once you reach the cattle guard with the yellow national forest marker, it is obvious that you are on the correct trail.

The trail leaves the outskirts of Jerome and immediately starts climbing along a narrow, rough shelf road. At the first saddle, you get a good view of the trail ahead and the last easy turning point for many miles. Passing places are extremely limited. If you see an oncoming vehicle and you are close to a passing point, pull in and wait. Uphill vehicles have the right of way, but common sense should always prevail. The trail continues as a shelf road for the next 13 miles as it winds around the steep eastern slope of Mingus Mountain. The first section of the shelf road is by far the narrowest and roughest; after the intersection with FR 493 the trail gradually widens until two vehicles can pass with care. Don't be surprised if you see hang gliders soaring above you on the east side of Mingus Mountain. A launch pad is located on the top of the mountain.

Originally, the trail was cut by miners, the evidence of whom can be seen in the tailings heaps and adits along the way. The trail surface is rough in places, but not exceptionally so, and there are several miles of smooth travel along red clay soils that become very greasy in wet weather.

The views are stunning all along this trail; initially, they look back to the houses straggling down the mountainside in Jerome and then later over the Verde Valley with the communities of Cottonwood and Clarkdale more than 2,000 feet below. Higher up still, you can see over the path of Northeast #19: Bill Gray–Buckboard Road to the red rock country near Sedona.

Initially, the shelf road is open and has low vegetation, but farther up the trail passes through patches of pine forest. Several hiking trails intersect the vehicle route, most of which climb up Mingus Mountain. Campers should note that there are no campsites near Jerome along this trail, but that there are many excellent ones in the ponderosa pines near the intersection with Northeast #17: Goat Peak Trail. This trail should not be attempted when it is wet or if there is snow or ice on the trail. Muddy sections, or lack of traction caused by snow or ice, make this trail extremely dangerous because of the low margin for error. Even in dry weather, care needs to be taken and the sightseeing should be left to the passengers.

Current Road Information

Prescott National Forest
Verde Ranger District
300 East Hwy 260
PO Box 670
Campe Verde, AZ 86322
(928) 567-4121

Map References

BLM   Prescott
USFS   Prescott National Forest: Verde
          Ranger District
USGS   1:24,000   Cottonwood, Hickey Mtn.
          1:100,000   Prescott
Maptech CD-ROM:
          Flagstaff/Sedona/Prescott
Arizona Atlas & Gazetteer, p. 41
Arizona Road & Recreation Atlas, pp. 40, 74

Northeast Trail #18: Mingus Mountain Loop Trail

Route Directions

▼ 0.0 From Arizona 89A on the east side of Jerome, turn east onto small Gulch Road; this turn is hard to spot—it is on a switchback on the east side of town and initially passes houses. The turn is opposite East Avenue and is immediately a graded narrow dirt road as it descends down into the gulch. Zero trip meter.

0.5 ▲ The trail ends on Arizona 89A on the east side of Jerome. Turn left to visit Jerome; turn right for Clarkdale.
  GPS: N34°44.83′ W112°06.64′

▼ 0.3 TR Turn onto unmarked dirt street that looks like a private drive and bear left.

0.2 ▲ TL Turn onto larger street.

▼ 0.5 SO Cattle guard; leaving Jerome. Zero trip meter.

0.0 ▲ End of shelf road; continue into the edge of Jerome.
  GPS: N34°44.53′ W112°06.60′

▼ 0.0 Continue south up rough shelf road.

7.7 ▲ SO Cattle guard; entering Jerome. Zero trip meter.

▼ 0.3 BR Track on left at saddle. Continue on FR 413 past primitive road sign.

7.4 ▲ BL Track on right at saddle. Trail is descending toward Jerome.
  GPS: N34°44.59′ W112°06.24′

▼ 0.6 SO Track on right and mine tailings on right up the hill.

7.1 ▲ SO Track on left and mine tailings on left up the hill.
  GPS: N34°44.46′ W112°06.47′

▼ 1.8 SO Track on right.

5.9 ▲ BR Track on left.
  GPS: N34°43.80′ W112°06.99′

▼ 2.1 SO Cross over Mescal Gulch on bridge.

5.6 ▲ SO Cross over Mescal Gulch on bridge.
  GPS: N34°43.63′ W112°07.16′

▼ 2.3 SO Adit on right.

5.4 ▲ SO Adit on left.
  GPS: N34°43.52′ W112°06.98′

▼ 2.4 SO Cross through creek fed by spring. Mine tailings on left.

5.3 ▲ SO Mine tailings on right. Cross through creek fed by spring.

▼ 3.1 SO Cross over wash.

4.6 ▲ SO Cross over wash.

Jerome Town Hall

▼ 3.6   SO   Trail levels off and runs around Mingus Mountain. Cottonwood and Clarkdale are visible far below.

4.1 ▲   SO   Trail starts to descend toward Jerome.

▼ 4.1   SO   Mine on left below trail.

3.6 ▲   SO   Mine on right below trail.

    GPS: N34°43.42' W112°06.15'

▼ 4.8   SO   Cross over wash; small tailings pile on the right.

2.9 ▲   SO   Cross over wash; small tailings pile on the left.

    GPS: N34°43.11' W112°06.10'

▼ 5.5   SO   Adit on left and mine below the trail.

2.2 ▲   SO   Adit on right and mine below the trail.

    GPS: N34°42.88' W112°05.67'

▼ 5.7   SO   Adit on right.

2.0 ▲   SO   Adit on left.

▼ 5.9   SO   Cross over creek.

1.8 ▲   SO   Cross over creek.

▼ 6.3   SO   Cross over creek on bridge.

1.4 ▲   SO   Cross over creek on bridge.

    GPS: N34°42.57' W112°05.93'

▼ 7.0   SO   Track on left; first track on right is Trail #106 to viewpoint. Also second small track on right. Trail #106 is hiking only and is blocked to vehicles after a short distance.

0.7 ▲   SO   Track on left; then second track on left is Trail #106 to viewpoint. Trail #106 is hiking only and is blocked to vehicles after a short distance. Track on right.

    GPS: N34°42.34' W112°05.61'

▼ 7.3   SO   Cross over creek.

0.4 ▲   SO   Cross over creek.

▼ 7.7   SO   Track on left is FR 493. Zero trip meter.

0.0 ▲   Continue to the northwest on FR 413.

    GPS: N34°42.02' W112°05.77'

▼ 0.0   Continue to the southeast on FR 413.

5.0 ▲   BL   Bear left, remaining on upper trail. Track on right is FR 493. Zero trip meter.

▼ 0.3   SO   Cross over creek.

4.7 ▲   SO   Cross over creek.

▼ 0.6   SO   Cross over creek.

4.4 ▲   SO   Cross over creek.

▼ 1.4   SO   Copper Chief Spring on right.

3.6 ▲   SO   Copper Chief Spring on left.

    GPS: N34°41.48' W112°06.17'

▼ 2.5   BR   Track on left.

2.5 ▲   SO   Track on right.

    GPS: N34°40.95' W112°05.89'

▼ 2.6   SO   Track on right.

2.4 ▲   SO   Track on left.

▼ 3.0   SO   Seasonal closure gate.

2.0 ▲   SO   Seasonal closure gate.

▼ 3.7   SO   Track on left through gate.

1.3 ▲   SO   Track on right through gate.

    GPS: N34°40.50' W112°05.69'

▼ 4.4   SO   Cattle guard; then Coleman Trail #108 on right to Mingus Mountain Lookout for hikers, horses, and mountain bikes only.

0.6 ▲   SO   Coleman Trail #108 on left to Mingus Mountain Lookout for hikers, horses, and mountain bikes only; then cattle guard.

    GPS: N34°40.12' W112°06.14'

▼ 4.9   SO   Cross over Gaddes Canyon creek.

0.1 ▲   SO   Cross over Gaddes Canyon creek.

▼ 5.0   SO   Track on right is Trail #110; then Black Canyon Trail #114 on left. Zero trip meter.

0.0 ▲   Continue to the north.

    GPS: N34°39.98' W112°06.55'

▼ 0.0   Continue to the south.

3.4 ▲   SO   Black Canyon Trail #114 on right; then track on left is Trail #110. Zero trip meter.

▼ 1.0   SO   Shelf road ends.

2.4 ▲   SO   Start of shelf road.

▼ 2.2   SO   Track on left.

1.2 ▲   SO   Track on right.

▼ 2.7   SO   Track on left is FR 9003V, Gaddes Canyon Trail #110 on right for hikers and horses.

0.7 ▲   SO   Track on right is FR 9003V, Gaddes Canyon Trail #110 on left for hikers and horses.

▼ 2.8	SO	Cross through creek.
0.6 ▲	SO	Cross through creek.
▼ 3.1	SO	Track on right; then second track on right is FR 9003T.
0.3 ▲	SO	Track on left is FR 9003T; then second track on left.

GPS: N34°40.31' W112°08.71'

| ▼ 3.4 | SO | Track on left; then trail ends at the intersection with Northeast #17: Goat Peak Trail, FR 413. Also track on right. Turn left to continue along Goat Peak Trail to Cherry; turn right to exit to Arizona 89A. |
| 0.0 ▲ | | Trail commences on Northeast #17: Goat Peak Trail, FR 413, 2.1 miles south of the intersection with FR 104. Zero trip meter and turn southeast on FR 413. The trail is a smooth graded road at this point. Track on right and track on left. |

GPS: N34°40.39' W112°09.02'

NORTHEAST REGION TRAIL #19

Bill Gray–Buckboard Road

STARTING POINT: Northeast #20: Boynton Pass Trail, 2.5 miles north of Arizona 89A
FINISHING POINT: Arizona 89A, south of Clarkdale
TOTAL MILEAGE: 18.5 miles
UNPAVED MILEAGE: 16.7 miles
DRIVING TIME: 1.25 hours
ELEVATION RANGE: 3,400–4,400 feet
USUALLY OPEN: Year-round
BEST TIME TO TRAVEL: Dry weather
DIFFICULTY RATING: 2
SCENIC RATING: 8
REMOTENESS RATING: +0

Special Attractions

- Views of Verde Valley and Mingus Mountain.
- Tuzigoot National Monument.

History

Tuzigoot, a small national monument set slightly above the Verde River, contains the stone remains of twelfth-century Sinagua Indian dwellings. Tuzigoot, which is an Apache word for "crooked water," was home to approximately 200 people and originally had 110 rooms in several 3-story complexes.

The Sinagua (Spanish for "without water") lived in the Verde Valley and on nearby plateaus. Originally pithouse dwellers and farmers dependent on rain to grow their crops, they integrated with the Hohokam Indians; the blending of cultures changed their farming techniques and their dwellings. The Sinagua adopted the Hohokam irrigation system and began to build aboveground stone houses.

The building of the hilltop houses began around 1150, and Tuzigoot probably reached its present size in the 1300s. The Sinagua were not as skillful at building as the Anasazi—the walls at Tuzigoot are large but often poorly constructed. However, the structures have stood for more than 600 years. The Sinagua abandoned the valley around 1400.

Description

This graded road connects Northeast #20: Boynton Pass Trail to Cottonwood without ever touching the highway. The trail surface is roughly graded dirt that becomes extremely greasy when wet and is often impassable, even to 4WD vehicles. The trail starts in red rock country and gradually wraps its way down to the Verde River Valley. The differing views from the ends of the trail provide great contrasts. As the road descends gradually toward Clarkdale along a wide shelf road, Jerome can be seen clinging to the side of Mingus Mountain on the other side of the Verde Valley. Below, the Verde River cuts a deep swath through the valley.

The final section of the trail follows the Verde River. The remains of the Tapco Power Station, which used to power the mines in Jerome, Prescott, and Crown King, can be seen on the far side of the river.

Just off the main trail is Tuzigoot National Monument, which has a small visitor center, a display of regional plants, and a wheelchair-accessible path around the ruins.

The Verde River flows near Tuzigoot National Monument

Current Road Information
Coconino National Forest
Red Rock Ranger District
PO Box 20429
Sedona, AZ 86341
(928) 282-4119

Map References
BLM   Sedona
USFS   Coconino National Forest: Sedona
  Ranger District
USGS   1:24,000   Page Springs, Loy Butte,
  Clarkdale
  1:100,000   Sedona
Maptech CD-ROM: Flagstaff/Sedona/Prescott
Arizona Atlas & Gazetteer, p. 41
Arizona Road & Recreation Atlas, pp. 34, 68
Recreational Map of Arizona
Other: Beartooth Maps—Sedona

Route Directions

▼ 0.0		From Northeast #20: Boynton Pass Trail, 2.5 miles north of Arizona 89A, zero trip meter and turn northwest on the graded dirt road, signposted to Bill Gray Road and Sycamore Pass, FR 525C.
3.0 ▲		Trail ends on Northeast #20: Boynton Pass Trail. Turn right to exit to Arizona 89A; turn left to continue along the Boynton Pass Trail to Sedona.
		GPS: N34°51.02' W111°54.94'

▼ 0.5	BR	Track on left is FR 525A; then cross through wash and immediately bear right. Unmarked graded road on left.
2.5 ▲	SO	Unmarked graded road on right. Cross through wash; then track on right is FR 525A.
		GPS: N34°50.92' W111°55.54'

Tuzigoot National Monument

Northeast Trail #19: Bill Gray–Buckboard Road

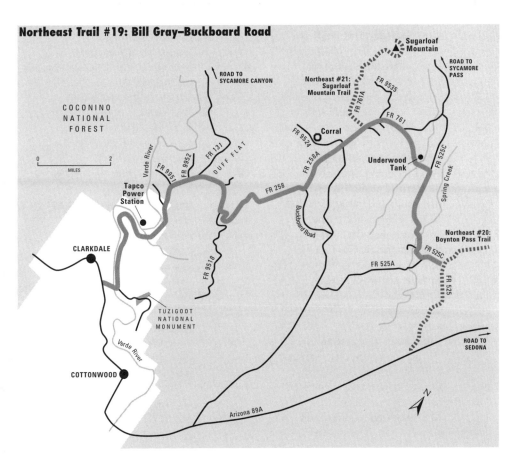

▼ 0.8   SO   Track on left to private property.

2.2 ▲   SO   Track on right to private property.

▼ 1.1   SO   Track on right; then cross through Spring Creek.

1.9 ▲   SO   Cross through Spring Creek; then track on left.

GPS: N34°51.19′ W111°56.01′

▼ 1.4   SO   Track on right.

1.6 ▲   SO   Track on left.

▼ 2.0   SO   Track on left is FR 9554.

1.0 ▲   SO   Track on right is FR 9554.

GPS: N34°51.69′ W111°56.62′

▼ 2.2   SO   Track on right.

0.8 ▲   SO   Track on left.

▼ 3.0   BL   Bear left onto Bill Gray Road at the sign. Graded road on right goes to Sycamore Pass. Zero trip meter.

0.0 ▲   Continue to the south on FR 525C.

GPS: N34°52.62′ W111°56.86′

▼ 0.0   Continue to the west on FR 761 and cross cattle guard.

2.5 ▲   BR   Cattle guard; then graded road on left goes to Sycamore Pass. Zero trip meter.

▼ 0.4   SO   Cross through wash.

2.1 ▲   SO   Cross through wash.

▼ 0.5   SO   Track on right to Underwood Tank and track on left.

2.0 ▲   SO   Track on left to Underwood Tank and track on right.

▼ 0.6   SO   Track on right is FR 9553.

1.9 ▲   SO   Track on left is FR 9553.

▼ 0.9   SO   Track on right; then cattle guard; then private road on left.

1.6 ▲   SO   Private road on right; then cattle guard; then track on left.

▼ 1.2   SO   Graded road on left.

1.3 ▲   SO   Graded road on right.

▼ 1.4   SO   Cattle guard; then track on right.
1.1 ▲   SO   Track on left; then cattle guard.
▼ 2.1   SO   Track on right over cattle guard is FR 9535 and track on left is FR 9534.
0.4 ▲   SO   Track on left over cattle guard is FR 9535 and track on right is FR 9534.
GPS: N34°52.85' W111°58.93'

▼ 2.5   SO   Track on left; track on right is Northeast #21: Sugarloaf Mountain Trail, FR 761A. Zero trip meter.
0.0 ▲   Continue to the north.
GPS: N34°52.50' W111°59.11'

▼ 0.0   Continue to the south.
0.6 ▲   SO   Track on right; track on left is Northeast #21: Sugarloaf Mountain Trail, FR 761A. Zero trip meter.
▼ 0.6   BR   Small track on right to corral is FR 9524; then bear right on FR 258A signposted to Buckboard Road. Zero trip meter. Graded road on left goes to Arizona 89A.
0.0 ▲   Continue to the north.
GPS: N34°51.96' W111°59.36'

▼ 0.0   Continue to the south.
1.7 ▲   SO   Graded road on right goes to Arizona 89A; then track on left is FR 9524 to corral. Zero trip meter and continue straight on.
▼ 1.0   SO   Two tracks on right; then cattle guard.
0.7 ▲   SO   Cattle guard; then two tracks on left.
▼ 1.1   SO   Track on right.
0.6 ▲   SO   Track on left.
▼ 1.5   SO   Track on right; then track on left.
0.2 ▲   SO   Track on right; then track on left.
▼ 1.7   TR   T-intersection with Buckboard Road. Turn right, following the sign to Duff Flat Road. Zero trip meter.
0.0 ▲   Continue to the north on FR 258A.
GPS: N34°50.53' W111°59.52'

▼ 0.0   Continue to the southwest on FR 258.
4.7 ▲   BL   Bear left, leaving Buckboard Road for FR 258A, following the sign to Bill Gray Road. Zero trip meter.
▼ 0.1   SO   Track on right.
4.6 ▲   SO   Track on left.

▼ 0.8   SO   Gas pipeline crosses.
3.9 ▲   SO   Gas pipeline crosses.
▼ 1.2   SO   Track on left; trail starts to descend toward Clarkdale.
3.5 ▲   SO   Track on right; end of climb.
▼ 2.3   SO   Track on left to tank.
2.4 ▲   SO   Track on right to tank.
▼ 3.3   SO   Track on left is FR 9518; then second track on left.
1.4 ▲   SO   Track on right; then second track on right is FR 9518.
GPS: N34°48.96' W112°01.09'

▼ 3.6   SO   Pipeline and power line cross.
1.1 ▲   SO   Pipeline and power line cross.
▼ 4.0   SO   Well-used track on right. End of descent; now crossing Duff Flat.
0.7 ▲   SO   Well-used track on left. Trail starts to climb.
GPS: N34°49.50' W112°01.50'

▼ 4.2   SO   Track on left.
0.5 ▲   SO   Track on right.
▼ 4.7   TL   T-intersection. Turn left onto graded dirt road, FR 131, signposted to Arizona 89A. Zero trip meter. Road on right goes to Sycamore Canyon.
0.0 ▲   Continue to the northeast on FR 258.
GPS: N34°49.31' W112°02.24'

▼ 0.0   Continue to the south.
5.6 ▲   TR   Turn right onto FR 258, signposted Buckboard Road to Bill Gray Road. Zero trip meter. Road ahead is FR 131 to Sycamore Canyon.
▼ 0.3   SO   Track on right is FR 9952.
5.3 ▲   SO   Track on left is FR 9952.
▼ 0.4   SO   Track on left follows pipeline.
5.2 ▲   SO   Track on right follows pipeline.
▼ 0.8   SO   Graded dirt road on right is FR 9951.
4.8 ▲   SO   Graded dirt road on left is FR 9951.
GPS: N34°48.78' W112°02.73'

▼ 1.2   SO   Track on left; then cattle guard. Exiting Coconino National Forest; no sign.
4.4 ▲   SO   Cattle guard; then track on right. Entering Coconino National Forest; no sign.
GPS: N34°48.43' W112°02.58'

The road gradually descends toward Clarkdale in the Verde Valley

▼ 1.3	BL	Track on right; then cross through wash.
4.3 ▲	BR	Cross through wash; then track on left.
▼ 1.4	SO	Track on right.
4.2 ▲	BR	Track on left.
▼ 1.7	SO	Cross through wash.
3.9 ▲	SO	Cross through wash.
▼ 2.4	SO	Cross through wash.
3.2 ▲	SO	Cross through wash.
▼ 3.4	BL	Two tracks on right.
2.2 ▲	BR	Two tracks on left.
▼ 3.5	SO	Track on right.
2.1 ▲	SO	Track on left.
▼ 3.6	SO	Track on right and track on left.
2.0 ▲	SO	Track on right and track on left.
▼ 3.7	SO	Track on right.
1.9 ▲	SO	Track on left.
▼ 4.0	SO	Track on left.
1.6 ▲	SO	Track on right.
▼ 4.2	SO	Road becomes paved. Remain on paved road.
1.4 ▲	SO	Road turns to graded dirt.
▼ 5.6	TR	T-intersection. Turn right onto paved road. Zero trip meter. Road on the left goes 0.7 miles to Tuzigoot NM.
0.0 ▲		Continue to the north.

GPS: N34°46.10′ W112°02.29′

▼ 0.0		Continue to the west and cross over the Verde River on bridge.
0.4 ▲	TL	Bridge over Verde River; then turn left on paved Sycamore Canyon Road. Road ahead goes 0.7 miles to Tuzigoot NM. Zero trip meter.
▼ 0.4		Trail ends at the T-intersection with Arizona 89A immediately south of Clarkdale. Turn left for Sedona; turn right for Jerome and Clarkdale.
0.0 ▲		Trail starts on Arizona 89A immediately to the south of Clarkdale. Zero trip meter and turn northeast on paved road sign-posted to Tuzigoot National Monument.

GPS: N34°45.99′ W112°02.71′

Boynton Pass Trail

STARTING POINT: Long Canyon Road, FR 152D

FINISHING POINT: Arizona 89A, 0.5 miles southwest of mile marker 365

TOTAL MILEAGE: 10.5 miles

UNPAVED MILEAGE: 9 miles

DRIVING TIME: 45 minutes

ELEVATION RANGE: 4,000–4,800 feet

USUALLY OPEN: Year-round

BEST TIME TO TRAVEL: Dry weather

DIFFICULTY RATING: 2

SCENIC RATING: 9

REMOTENESS RATING: +0

Special Attractions

- Palatki and Honanki Ruins and rock art.
- Very scenic road over Boynton Pass through red rock country.
- Boynton Canyon Vortex and Blue Door Vortex.

History

Palatki Ruins are a southern Sinagua cliff dwelling that was occupied from A.D. 1100 to 1300. Along with the Honanki Ruins, Palatki Ruins were first reported by Dr. Jesse Walter Fewkes of the Smithsonian Institution. He named the sites in the Hopi language: Palatki means "red house" and Honanki means "bear house." The sites are the two largest cliff dwellings in the Sedona area.

Palatki consists of two separate dwellings with many pictographs. The structures are pressed against natural alcoves in the cliff face, which acts as one wall for the buildings and provides a degree of protection from the elements. The walls are made from stones, held together by a mortar and clay plaster. The site, which has been stabilized by the forest service, also contains an agave roasting pit and many pictographs, including clan symbols and Barrier Canyon figures.

In addition to the remains of Indian occupation, the Palatki site also has the remains of a much later settler of the site, Charles

The Palatki cliff dwellings

Willard, who became the founder of Clark-dale. The remains of his stone dwelling and a number of catchments can be seen.

Description

This road leaves Sedona and travels through red rock country over Boynton Pass. Initially, the road is paved as it passes close to a resort and residential areas. It passes several hiking trailheads that lead into the wilderness areas to the north. The Boynton Canyon Trailhead also gives access to one of Sedona's more famous vortices—the Boynton Canyon Vortex. Some believe that a vortex is an outflowing of the earth's energy at a specific point and that each vortex has a unique energy. Vortices are often used as meditation sites and are thought to have spiritual qualities. The Boynton Canyon Vortex, a masculine-feminine vortex, is reputed to enhance the senses—in particular, psychic senses and past-life memories. To reach the vortex from the parking area at the trailhead, take Boynton Canyon Trail #47 and then fork right onto Vista Trail, which goes to a 30-foot-high knoll. The energy is believed to be strongest around the knoll.

The road turns to rough graded dirt as it travels over Boynton Pass. A high-clearance vehicle is preferred, and like all roads in this region it is not suitable for wet-weather travel. As the road crests the gentle pass, there are views back toward Sedona.

There are two Sinagua Indian ruins located just off the main trail. They are well signposted up FR 525. A small fee is charged to visit the closer Palatki Ruins, which are run by the forest service. The hiking trail to the pictographs and an intact agave roasting pit is approximately 0.2 miles long. Immediately past the pit, at the end of the trail, there is a tall vertical crack in the rock, which some people believe to be the Blue Door Vortex. People come from all over the world to visit the vortex.

A second hiking trail leads to the ruins of a five-room cliff dwelling. Honanki Ruins are larger and more spread out than the Palatki Ruins but they are not as well preserved. There is no fee at this site, but as at the Palatki Ruins, visitors are restricted to opening hours. Call ahead for

days and hours, which are subject to change; at the time of writing the ruins were only open from Friday to Sunday. The main trail continues down Red Canyon to finish on Arizona 89A.

Current Road Information

Coconino National Forest
Red Rock Ranger District
PO Box 20429
Sedona, AZ 86341
(928) 282-4119

Map References

BLM   Sedona
USFS   Coconino National Forest: Sedona
          Ranger District
USGS   1:24,000   Wilson Mtn., Loy Butte,
          Page Springs
          1:100,000 Sedona
Maptech CD-ROM: Flagstaff/Sedona/Prescott
Arizona Atlas & Gazetteer, p. 42
Arizona Road & Recreation Atlas, pp. 34,
          35, 68, 69
Recreational Map of Arizona
Other: Beartooth Maps—Sedona

Route Directions

▼ 0.0   From Arizona 89A in Sedona, turn
          north up Dry Creek Road through West
          Sedona. Remain on paved Dry Creek
          Road for 2.7 miles, passing the start of
          Northeast #22: Dry Creek Road after
          1.9 miles. At the T-intersection of
          Boynton Pass Road (FR 152C) and
          Long Canyon Road (FR 152D), zero trip
          meter and turn southwest on paved
          Boynton Pass Road, following the sign
          to Palatki and Honanki Ruins.

1.5 ▲   Trail ends at the intersection of
          Boynton Pass Road and Long Canyon
          Road (FR 152D). Turn south on Long
          Canyon Road, which leads to Dry
          Creek Road and West Sedona.
          GPS: N34°53.92' W111°49.69'

▼ 1.5   TL   At T-intersection, turn left. Zero trip
          meter. Paved road on right goes 0.3
          miles to the trailhead of Boynton
          Canyon Trail #47. This area is the site

Palatki cliff dwellings

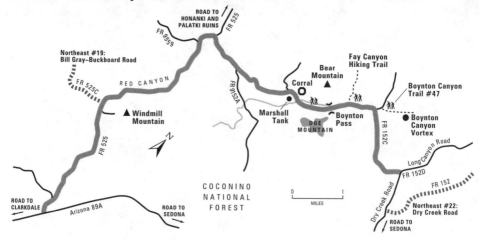

of the Boynton Canyon Vortex.

0.0 ▲   Continue to the southeast on paved road.

GPS: N34°54.38' W111°50.98'

▼ 0.0   Continue to the southwest on graded dirt road.

3.7 ▲   TR   Turn right onto paved Boynton Pass Road. Zero trip meter. Paved road ahead goes 0.3 miles to the trailhead of Boynton Canyon Trail #47. This area is the site of the Boynton Canyon Vortex.

▼ 0.3   SO   Track on left is FR 9587.

3.4 ▲   SO   Track on right is FR 9587.

GPS: N34°54.19' W111°51.29'

▼ 0.5   SO   Fay Canyon Hiking Trailhead parking on right; then track on left is FR 9586.

3.2 ▲   SO   Track on right is FR 9586; then Fay Canyon Hiking Trailhead parking on left.

GPS: N34°54.10' W111°51.43'

▼ 0.7   SO   Track on left.

3.0 ▲   SO   Track on right.

▼ 0.8   SO   Boynton Pass is at the saddle.

2.9 ▲   SO   Boynton Pass is at the saddle.

GPS: N34°53.85' W111°51.64'

▼ 1.2   SO   Doe Mountain Hiking Trail #60 on left and Bear Mountain Trail #54 on right. Trailhead parking on right; then cross

cattle guard.

2.5 ▲   SO   Cross cattle guard; then Doe Mountain Hiking Trail #60 on right and Bear Mountain Trail #54 on left. Trailhead parking on left.

GPS: N34°53.61' W111°51.88'

▼ 1.4   SO   Track on left is FR 9584 and track on right.

2.3 ▲   SO   Track on right is FR 9584 and track on left.

GPS: N34°53.52' W111°52.08'

▼ 1.5   SO   Cross through wash.

2.2 ▲   SO   Cross through wash.

▼ 1.6   SO   Track on right past corral on right.

2.1 ▲   SO   Track on left past corral on left.

▼ 1.7   SO   Track on left past Marshall Tank; then cattle guard; then track on right.

2.0 ▲   SO   Track on left; then cattle guard; then track on right past Marshall Tank.

▼ 1.9   SO   Well-used graded road on left is FR 9583, which goes 0.2 miles to a viewpoint overlooking Boynton Pass. The road continues a short distance to private property.

1.8 ▲   SO   Well-used graded road on right is FR 9583, which goes 0.2 miles to a viewpoint overlooking Boynton Pass. The road continues a short distance to private property.

GPS: N34°53.41' W111°52.53'

▼ 2.1 SO Track on left.

1.6 ▲ SO Track on right.

▼ 2.3 SO Track on right.

1.4 ▲ SO Track on left.

▼ 2.7 SO Private road on right; then cross through wash.

1.0 ▲ SO Cross through wash; then private road on left.

▼ 2.9 SO Well-used track on left is FR 9152A (shown on forest map as 152A).

0.8 ▲ SO Well-used track on right is FR 9152A (shown on forest map as 152A).

GPS: N34°53.16' W111°53.55'

▼ 3.2 SO Track on right.

0.5 ▲ SO Track on left.

▼ 3.3 SO Private paved road on right.

0.4 ▲ SO Private paved road on left.

▼ 3.7 TL T-intersection. Turn left onto graded road FR 525. Zero trip meter. Turn right here to go to Palatki Ruins (1.8 miles) and to Honanki Ruins (4 miles).

0.0 ▲ Continue to the east on FR 152C.

GPS: N34°53.29' W111°54.33'

▼ 0.0 Continue to the south on FR 525.

2.8 ▲ TR Turn right onto FR 152C, Boynton Pass Road. Zero trip meter. Continue straight to go to Palatki Ruins (1.8 miles) and to Honanki Ruins (4 miles).

▼ 0.2 SO Track on right.

2.6 ▲ SO Track on left.

▼ 0.3 SO Track on right is FR 9559.

2.5 ▲ SO Track on left is FR 9559.

GPS: N34°52.98' W111°54.49'

▼ 0.9 SO Track on right.

1.9 ▲ SO Track on left.

▼ 1.1 SO Track on right is FR 9558.

1.7 ▲ SO Track on left is FR 9558.

GPS: N34°52.33' W111°54.29'

▼ 1.4 SO Track on left is FR 9576.

1.4 ▲ SO Track on right is FR 9576.

GPS: N34°52.08' W111°54.21'

▼ 1.6 SO Track on right.

1.2 ▲ SO Track on left.

▼ 1.9 SO Track on left is FR 9575.

0.9 ▲ SO Track on right is FR 9575.

▼ 2.4 SO Track on left follows pipeline.

0.4 ▲ SO Track on right follows pipeline.

▼ 2.6 SO Pipeline trail on right.

0.2 ▲ SO Pipeline trail on left.

▼ 2.8 SO Graded road on right is Northeast #19: Bill Gray–Buckboard Road. Zero trip meter.

0.0 ▲ Continue to the northwest.

GPS: N34°51.02' W111°54.94'

▼ 0.0 Continue to the southeast and cross cattle guard.

2.5 ▲ BR Cattle guard; then graded road on left is Northeast #19: Bill Gray–Buckboard Road. Zero trip meter.

▼ 0.1 SO Track on left is FR 9574.

2.4 ▲ SO Track on right is FR 9574.

▼ 1.5 SO Track on left is FR 9573.

1.0 ▲ SO Track on right is FR 9573.

GPS: N34°49.85' W111°54.41'

▼ 2.2 SO Graded road on right is FR 761B.

0.3 ▲ BR Graded road on left is FR 761B.

GPS: N34°49.25' W111°54.23'

▼ 2.3 SO Track on right.

0.2 ▲ SO Track on left.

▼ 2.5 Cattle guard; then trail ends on Arizona 89A. Turn right for Clarkdale; turn left for Sedona.

0.0 ▲ Trail commences on Arizona 89A, 0.5 miles southwest of mile marker 365 between Sedona and Clarkdale. Zero trip meter and turn west on graded dirt road signposted FR 525. After the turn, there is a sign for Boynton Pass and other directional signs.

GPS: N34°48.97' W111°54.18'

Sugarloaf Mountain Trail

STARTING POINT: Northeast #19: Bill Gray–Buckboard Road, 5.5 miles from the eastern end
FINISHING POINT: Sugarloaf Mountain
TOTAL MILEAGE: 3.7 miles
UNPAVED MILEAGE: 3.7 miles
DRIVING TIME: 45 minutes (one-way)
ELEVATION RANGE: 4,400–5,200 feet
USUALLY OPEN: Year-round
BEST TIME TO TRAVEL: Year-round
DIFFICULTY RATING: 3
SCENIC RATING: 8
REMOTENESS RATING: +0

Special Attractions

■ Rarely used trail offering excellent views over the red rocks west of Sedona.

Description

This short, rough-surfaced trail provides a distant view of the red rock country west of Sedona. The trail, which leaves Northeast #19: Bill Gray–Buckboard Road, is initially narrow and quite eroded. As it gradually climbs around the side of Black Mountain, it becomes a shelf road that is wide enough for a single vehicle and has adequate places to pass other vehicles.

The panoramic views are excellent: back to the east over the Boynton Pass area and north toward Sycamore Pass and the Red Rock Secret Mountain Wilderness. Although this trail is shown as a loop on many maps, private property has blocked it at the point indicated. There are a couple of good camping spots a short distance from the trail on some of the side trails. Like most of the trails in the area, this one should not be attempted in wet weather. The red soil becomes extremely greasy and the road is likely to be impassable.

Current Road Information

Coconino National Forest
Red Rock Ranger District

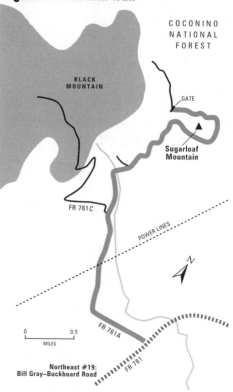

PO Box 20429
Sedona, AZ 86341
(928) 282-4119

Map References

BLM   Prescott, Sedona
USFS Coconino National Forest: Sedona Ranger District
USGS 1:24,000   Loy Butte, Sycamore Basin
       1:100,000 Prescott, Sedona
Maptech CD-ROM: Flagstaff/Sedona/Prescott
Arizona Atlas & Gazetteer, p. 41
Arizona Road & Recreation Atlas, pp. 34, 68
Other: Beartooth Maps—Sedona

Route Directions

▼ 0.0   From Northeast #19: Bill Gray–Buckboard Road, 2.5 miles northwest of the intersection of FR 525C and FR 761, zero trip meter and turn west on small formed trail

Red Rock Secret Wilderness in the distance

A view toward Sugarloaf Mountain, typical of the expansive scenic views along the trail

marked FR 761A.
GPS: N34°52.50′ W111°59.11′

▼ 0.9   BR   Track on right; then two tracks on left, one of which is FR 95241. Bear right. Do not follow track on right along power lines.
GPS: N34°52.94′ W111°59.89′

▼ 1.3   SO   Track on left is FR 761C, which climbs up Black Mountain. Zero trip meter.
GPS: N34°53.32′ W112°00.08′

▼ 0.0   Continue to the north.
▼ 0.4   SO   Cross through wash.
▼ 0.6   SO   Track on left.
GPS: N34°53.79′ W112°00.15′

▼ 1.7   SO   Track on right.
GPS: N34°54.30′ W111°59.50′

▼ 1.8   SO   Track on right.
▼ 2.4   Road is closed at this point. There is a turning point immediately before the gate.
GPS: N34°54.39′ W112°00.04′

Dry Creek Road

STARTING POINT: Dry Creek Road
FINISHING POINT: Vultee Arch and Dry Creek Hiking Trailheads
TOTAL MILEAGE: 4.2 miles
UNPAVED MILEAGE: 4.2 miles
DRIVING TIME: 45 minutes
ELEVATION RANGE: 4,600–4,800 feet
USUALLY OPEN: Year-round
BEST TIME TO TRAVEL: Dry weather
DIFFICULTY RATING: 2
SCENIC RATING: 9
REMOTENESS RATING: +0

Special Attractions

- Stunning views of red rock country.
- Access to a number of popular hiking trails.
- Historic cowboy cabin located a short distance from the main trail.

Description

This high-clearance road is immensely popular with photographers who like the diversity of the red rock scenery along its length. At sunset especially, the rocks take on a luminescent quality as the red color deepens. The scene often produces some wonderful atmospheric photographs.

The trail is roughly graded dirt along its entire length. There are many pull-ins at viewpoints along the trail, but because of the popularity of the area, camping is not allowed. The trail meanders alongside Dry Creek for much of the way, and the pull-ins can be used for picnicking or just relaxing amid some of the most beautiful scenery in Arizona.

A short 4-rated spur trail leads to an old cabin perched above Dry Creek. Only the final section of this spur is 4-rated; those who do not wish to tackle the rougher section can park before crossing Dry Creek and walk the final short distance. The old timber cabin consists of two connected rooms. Behind the cabin there is an underground dugout visible to the southwest. There is private property nearby. Please respect the signs. The coordinates of the cabin are: N34º54.99' W111º48.74'.

The trail passes the trailheads of many hiking trails into the Red Rock Secret Mountain Wilderness before finishing at the trailhead to Vultee Arch. This popular, easy hike (1.7 miles) with a gentle gradient climbs to the natural arch, which is named after Gerard and Sylvia Vultee, pioneer aviators who died in a plane crash in 1938. The crash site is farther north on East Picket Mesa.

The bed of Dry Creek runs parallel to the road—beware of flash floods

Northeast Trail #22: Dry Creek Road

Current Road Information

Coconino National Forest
Red Rock Ranger District
PO Box 20429
Sedona, AZ 86341
(928) 282-4119

Map References

BLM   Sedona
USFS   Coconino National Forest: Sedona
       Ranger District
USGS   1:24,000   Wilson Mtn.
       1:100,000   Sedona
Maptech CD-ROM:
       Flagstaff/Sedona/Prescott
Arizona Atlas & Gazetteer, p. 42
Arizona Road & Recreation Atlas, pp. 35, 69
Other: Beartooth Maps—Sedona

Route Directions

▼ 0.0   From the intersection of Arizona 89A in
         West Sedona, turn north on the paved
         Dry Creek Road and zero trip meter.
         Proceed for 1.9 miles; then turn north-
         east on FR 152 signposted Dry Creek
         Road to Vultee Arch Trail. Road is grad-
         ed dirt road. Zero trip meter.
         GPS: N34°53.26' W111°49.31'

▼ 0.2   SO Track on left goes 0.1 miles to excel-
         lent viewpoint.
▼ 0.5   SO Track on left to excellent viewpoint.
         GPS: N34°53.64' W111°49.11'

▼ 1.3   SO Devils Bridge Trailhead #120 and park-
         ing on right; then cross through wash.
         GPS: N34°54.18' W111°48.80'

▼ 1.9   SO Track on left.
         GPS: N34°54.68' W111°48.59'

▼ 2.2   SO Cross through wash.
         GPS: N34°54.88' W111°48.50'

▼ 2.2   SO Track on left goes 0.3 miles to old tim-
         ber cabin. To reach it, take this side
         trail; at 0.2 miles there is a rough
         rocky crossing of Dry Creek; then bear
         left up onto slickrock platform above
         Dry Creek.
         GPS: N34°54.92' W111°48.53'

▼ 2.4   SO Brins Mesa Hiking Trailhead #119 and
         parking on right. Zero trip meter.
         GPS: N34°55.01' W111°48.49'

▼ 0.0   Continue to the north.
▼ 0.1   SO Track on left to viewpoint.
         GPS: N34°55.10' W111°48.49'

▼ 0.9   SO Secret Canyon Hiking Trailhead #121
         on left; then track on left to Dry Creek.
         GPS: N34°55.78' W111°48.34'

▼ 1.8   Trail ends at the hiking trailheads for Dry
         Creek Trail and Vultee Arch Trail #22.
         GPS: N34°56.24' W111°47.62'

Red sand from Brins Mesa settles on the road below it

Soldier Pass Road

STARTING POINT: Arizona 89A, 1.2 miles west of the intersection with Arizona 179
FINISHING POINT: Hiking trail to Soldier Pass
TOTAL MILEAGE: 2.5 miles
UNPAVED MILEAGE: 1 mile
DRIVING TIME: 45 minutes (one-way)
ELEVATION RANGE: 4,400–4,600 feet
USUALLY OPEN: Year-round
BEST TIME TO TRAVEL: Year-round
DIFFICULTY RATING: 4 (main trail); 5 (Devils Kitchen)
SCENIC RATING: 8
REMOTENESS RATING: +0

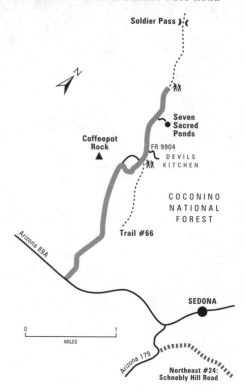

Special Attractions

- Devils Kitchen—a natural sinkhole.
- Popular, short rugged trail used by 4WD tour companies.
- Natural rock tanks of Seven Sacred Ponds.

Description

This very short trail is maintained by Red Rock Jeep Tours in conjunction with the Coconino National Forest, and you can expect to meet some of the tour jeeps along the trail as well as private vehicles. The trail does not go all the way to Soldier Pass but stops a short distance before it. It is suitable for high-clearance 4WD vehicles, because it is rough and sandy for most of the way. The main trail is rated a 4 for difficulty, but the short spur to the Devils Kitchen sinkhole rates a 5 because of the rough slickrock and short, steep sections.

The trail passes the side trail to Devils Kitchen, a very large and spectacular natural sinkhole, which is so regular it looks man-made. Farther along are the Seven Sacred Ponds—small natural rock holes that contain water year-round. These pools were important to local Indian tribes in the past and to local wildlife today.

The trail ends at a turnaround and the start of the hiking trail to Soldier Pass, which was used by General George Crook during the Apache Campaign in 1871–72. There is limited parking at the end of the trail. If you plan on hiking to the pass, you would be better off parking at the trailhead rather than obstructing the turnaround point.

Current Road Information

Coconino National Forest
Red Rock Ranger District
PO Box 20429
Sedona, AZ 86341
(928) 282-4119

Map References

BLM   Sedona
USFS   Coconino National Forest: Sedona Ranger District
USGS   1:24,000   Sedona, Wilson Mtn.
       1:100,000 Sedona
Maptech CD-ROM: Flagstaff/Sedona/Prescott
Arizona Atlas & Gazetteer, p. 42
Other: Beartooth Maps—Sedona

At the Seven Sacred Ponds

Route Directions

▼ 0.0   From Arizona 89A, 1.2 miles west of the intersection with Arizona 179, zero trip meter and turn north on Soldier Pass Road, which is a paved street. Remain on Soldier Pass Road, ignoring turns to the right and left.
GPS: N34°51.77′ W111°46.95′

▼ 1.3   TR   Turn right onto Rim Shadows Drive, following the sign for Soldier Pass Trail.
GPS: N34°52.93′ W111°47.15′

▼ 1.5   BR   Bear right, following the sign for Soldier Pass Trail. Canyon Shadows Drive is the first right; take the second right; then immediately turn left through gateway for Soldier Pass Trailhead. Parking area is closed 6 p.m. to 8 a.m.
GPS: N34°52.99′ W111°47.02′

▼ 1.6   SO   Parking area for Soldier Pass Road. Hiking Trail #66 on right. Soldier Pass Road, FR 9904, continues ahead out the back of the parking area. Zero trip meter.
GPS: N34°53.06′ W111°46.99′

▼ 0.0   Continue to the north.
▼ 0.2   SO   Track on right is FR 9904, which goes 0.3 miles to Devils Kitchen, a natural sinkhole. This spur is rated 5. Zero trip meter.
GPS: N34°53.19′ W111°47.02′

▼ 0.0   Continue to the north and pass the Teacup Hiking Trail on the left.
▼ 0.2   BR   Trail forks and rejoins almost immediately.
GPS: N34°53.32′ W111°47.13′

▼ 0.3   SO   Track on right goes 0.1 miles to the Seven Sacred Ponds. The pools are immediately below the slickrock platform. Zero trip meter.
GPS: N34°53.45′ W111°47.14′

▼ 0.0   Continue to the northwest.
▼ 0.3   SO   Cross through wash.
GPS: N34°53.69′ W111°47.22′

▼ 0.4   Vehicle trail ends at turnaround.
GPS: N34°53.77′ W111°47.21′

NORTHEAST REGION TRAIL #24

Schnebly Hill Road

STARTING POINT: I-17 at exit 320
FINISHING POINT: Arizona 179, south of Sedona
TOTAL MILEAGE: 11.4 miles
UNPAVED MILEAGE: 10.5 miles
DRIVING TIME: 1 hour
ELEVATION RANGE: 4,300–6,600 feet
USUALLY OPEN: Year-round
BEST TIME TO TRAVEL: Year-round
DIFFICULTY RATING: 2
SCENIC RATING: 9
REMOTENESS RATING: +0

Special Attractions
- Unequaled view of red rock country above Sedona.
- Deep Bear Wallow Canyon.

History
The red rock country around Sedona has seen a long history of human settlement, stretching back thousands of years. The earliest inhabitants appear to date back to 8000 B.C. when people hunted in the valley. Indians used the hot springs in Oak Creek Canyon and the Sedona area as a trading place for goods from the south. In the 1500s, Spanish explorers passed through the valley.

The earliest permanent settlement in the area was in Oak Creek Canyon. In 1876 John James Thompson took up squatters' rights in an area known as Indian Gardens. The Indians, who had planted the thriving gardens of corn and vegetables that Thompson found there, had been relocated to the San Carlos Reservation. Thompson's small farming settlement soon attracted other families.

The Schnebly family name is inextricably linked with Sedona. The town was named in 1902 after Sedona Schnebly, the wife of the

A view of the trail in Bear Wallow Canyon

first postmaster, Carl Schnebly, who had come from Missouri. The original name suggested for the town was Schnebly Station, but the post office would not accept the name because it was too long. When Carl's brother, Ellsworth, suggested the name Sedona after his sister-in-law, the post office accepted it.

Schnebly Hill is named after Theodore Carlton Schnebly, one of the first settlers in the Oak Creek Canyon area. In 1902 Schnebly constructed a rough road up Bear Wallow Canyon over the Mogollon Rim.

Description

This popular route linking I-17 and Sedona is best suited for a high-clearance vehicle because of the rockiness of the road around Bear Wallow Canyon. The best direction for travel is east to west because the descent into Bear Wallow Canyon gives the better views.

Initially, the trail passes through the ponderosa pine forest of Coconino National Forest on Schnebly Hill. There are many tracks off to the right and left on this section, most of which enter the Woods Wildlife Area. Motorized vehicles are not allowed within the wildlife area between December 15 and April 1 to protect the winter habitat for elk and other animals. Travel on Schnebly Hill Road is permitted year-round.

The Schnebly Hill Vista is reached at 5.4 miles, where there is a large pull-in. It is a good place to stop and appreciate the view. From the viewpoint, you can look down Casner Canyon to the highway far below. Wilson Mountain is ahead. Sedona can be glimpsed in the valley, 1,800 feet below.

Past the vista point, the trail is not recommended for passenger vehicles as it is rough and rocky, but a high-clearance vehicle will have no problems. The trail winds down a wide shelf road, providing unparalleled views of the red rock country that has made Sedona world famous. This road is extremely popular with jeep tours that operate out of Sedona as well as with individuals, and it can be busy. It descends gradually along an even grade, leaving behind the ponderosa pine forest and entering a band of vegetation dominated by prickly pears, century plants, and junipers.

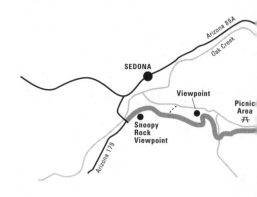

Several hiking trails lead from the lower end of the road. There is also a viewpoint for Snoopy Rock—the small rock to the southeast that looks unmistakably like the famous cartoon character lying on his back on the roof of his dog house.

Current Road Information

Coconino National Forest
Red Rock Ranger District
PO Box 20429
Sedona, AZ 86341
(928) 282-4119

Coconino National Forest
Mormon Lake Ranger District
4373 South Lake Mary Rd.
Flagstaff, AZ 86001
(928) 774-1147

Map References

BLM   Sedona
USFS   Coconino National Forest: Sedona and Mormon Lake Ranger Districts
USGS   1:24,000   Munds Park, Munds Mtn., Sedona
        1:100,000 Sedona
Maptech CD-ROM: Flagstaff/Sedona/Prescott
Arizona Atlas & Gazetteer, p. 42
Arizona Road & Recreation Atlas, pp. 35, 69
Recreational Map of Arizona
Other: Beartooth Maps—Sedona

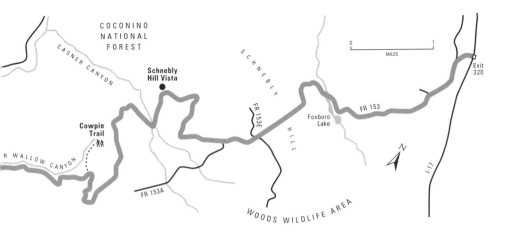

Route Directions

▼ 0.0　From I-17 at exit 320, proceed to the west side of the freeway; zero trip meter and proceed west on Schnebly Hill Road, FR 153. The road turns to dirt immediately after a cattle guard. Bear immediately left after the cattle guard, following the sign for Sedona.

5.4 ▲　Bear right over the cattle guard to finish at exit 320 on I-17.

　　　　GPS: N34°54.73' W111°38.48'

▼ 0.2　SO Track on right.
5.2 ▲　SO Track on left.

▼ 0.5　SO Track on left into Woods Wildlife Area.
4.9 ▲　SO Track on right into Woods Wildlife Area.

Foxboro Lake, high above Sedona in the Coconino National Forest

▼ 0.7　　SO　Graded road on right.
4.7 ▲　　SO　Graded road on left.
▼ 0.8　　SO　Track on right.
4.6 ▲　　SO　Track on left.
▼ 1.1　　SO　Track on left.
4.3 ▲　　SO　Track on right.
▼ 1.5　　SO　Graded road on left.
3.9 ▲　　SO　Graded road on right.
　　　　　　GPS: N34°53.84′ W111°39.45′

▼ 2.2　　SO　Graded road on left; then Foxboro Lake on left; then track on right and track on left into Woods Wildlife Area.
3.2 ▲　　BL　Track on right into Woods Wildlife Area and track on left; then Foxboro Lake on right; then graded road on right.
　　　　　　GPS: N34°53.88′ W111°40.06′

▼ 2.6　　SO　Two tracks on left.
2.8 ▲　　SO　Two tracks on right.
▼ 2.8　　SO　Track on left into Woods Wildlife Area.

2.6 ▲　　SO　Track on right into Woods Wildlife Area.
　　　　　　GPS: N34°53.69′ W111°40.36′

▼ 3.1　　SO　Track on left; no motorized access.
2.3 ▲　　SO　Track on right; no motorized access.
　　　　　　GPS: N34°53.48′ W111°40.58′

▼ 3.2　　SO　Track on right is FR 153E. Closed to vehicles from December 15 to April 1 to minimize disturbance to big-game winter habitat.
2.2 ▲　　SO　Track on left is FR 153E. Closed to vehicles from December 15 to April 1 to minimize disturbance to big-game winter habitat.
　　　　　　GPS: N34°53.44′ W111°40.62′

▼ 3.4　　SO　Track on left is FR 801 into Woods Wildlife Area; then track on right.
2.0 ▲　　SO　Track on left; then track on right is FR 801 into Woods Wildlife Area.

Looking across Casner Canyon towards Wilson Mountain

▼ 3.5   SO Track on left is closed to vehicles from December 15 to April 1.

1.9 ▲   SO Track on right is closed to vehicles from December 15 to April 1.

▼ 3.9   SO Track on left is FR 153A into Woods Wildlife Area; closed to vehicles from December 15 to April 1.

1.5 ▲   SO Track on right is FR 153A into Woods Wildlife Area; closed to vehicles from December 15 to April 1.

▼ 5.0   SO Cattle guard.

0.4 ▲   SO Cattle guard.

▼ 5.4   SO Schnebly Hill Vista on the right. Camping and fires prohibited past this point. Zero trip meter.

0.0 ▲   Continue to the east.

GPS: N34°53.39' W111°42.15'

▼ 0.0   Continue to the west. Not recommended for passenger vehicles past this point.

5.1 ▲   SO Schnebly Hill Vista on the left. Zero trip meter.

▼ 0.4   SO Cross through wash.

4.7 ▲   SO Cross through wash.

GPS: N34°53.05' W111°42.13'

▼ 0.7   SO Turnout on right.

4.4 ▲   SO Turnout on left.

▼ 1.1   SO Saddle between Casner Canyon and Bear Wallow Canyon.

4.0 ▲   SO Saddle between Casner Canyon and Bear Wallow Canyon.

▼ 1.6   SO Closure gate.

3.5 ▲   SO Closure gate.

GPS: N34°52.52' W111°42.41'

▼ 2.6   SO Pull-in on left is parking for Cowpie Trail on the right.

2.5 ▲   SO Pull-in on right is parking for Cowpie Trail on the left.

GPS: N34°52.32' W111°42.74'

▼ 3.4   SO Cross over wash.

1.7 ▲   SO Cross over wash.

▼ 4.1   SO Picnic tables on right below road alongside creek. Hiking trail on far side.

1.0 ▲   SO Picnic tables on left below road alongside creek. Hiking trail on far side.

GPS: N34°52.08' W111°44.05'

▼ 4.5   SO Cross through wash.

0.6 ▲   SO Cross through wash.

GPS: N34°51.90' W111°44.44'

▼ 4.8   SO Viewpoint on right over Sedona.

0.3 ▲   SO Viewpoint on left over Sedona.

GPS: N34°52.05' W111°44.73'

▼ 5.1   SO Road becomes paved. Trailhead parking for Huckaby and Margs Draw Trails on right (hiking, horses, mountain bikes). Zero trip meter.

0.0 ▲   Continue to the east.

GPS: N34°51.96' W111°44.87'

▼ 0.0   Continue to the west.

0.9 ▲   SO Road turns to graded dirt. Trailhead parking for Huckaby and Margs Draw Trails on left (hiking, horses, mountain bikes). Zero trip meter.

▼ 0.2   SO Munds Mountain Wilderness on left and hiking trail on right.

0.7 ▲   SO Munds Mountain Wilderness on right and hiking trail on left.

GPS: N34°51.97' W111°45.03'

▼ 0.3   SO Pull-in on left is viewpoint for Snoopy Rock.

0.6 ▲   SO Pull-in on right is viewpoint for Snoopy Rock.

GPS: N34°51.92' W111°45.18'

▼ 0.4   SO Track on right and track on left; then cattle guard.

0.5 ▲   SO Cattle guard; then track on left and track on right.

▼ 0.9   Trail ends at the intersection with Arizona 179 in Sedona, immediately south of the bridge over Oak Creek.

0.0 ▲   From Arizona 179, zero trip meter and turn northeast on the paved Schnebly Hill Road at the well-marked intersection, immediately south of the bridge over Oak Creek in Sedona.

GPS: N34°51.74' W111°45.64'

Broken Arrow Trail

STARTING POINT: Arizona 179, south of Sedona, 1.3 miles from intersection with Arizona 89A
FINISHING POINT: Chicken Point
TOTAL MILEAGE: 3.1 miles (round-trip)
UNPAVED MILEAGE: 2.6 miles
DRIVING TIME: 2 hours
ELEVATION RANGE: 4,200–4,600 feet
USUALLY OPEN: Year-round
BEST TIME TO TRAVEL: Year-round
DIFFICULTY RATING: 7
SCENIC RATING: 9
REMOTENESS RATING: +0

Special Attractions

- Challenging and scenic sand and slickrock trail.
- Submarine Rock and other prominent rock formations.
- Exceptional views from Chicken Point and all along the trail.
- Devils Dining Room—a natural sinkhole.

Description

This extremely popular short trail encompasses the best of Sedona—panoramic views, red rock formations, and a challenging 4WD trail. You won't find solitude along this trail. It is heavily used by individuals and by Pink Jeep Tours, one of Sedona's popular Jeep tour companies. Pink Jeep Tours helps to maintain the trail in conjunction with the Coconino National Forest.

Although this trail is very short, it is extremely rugged; the main challenge comes from the extensive slickrock. The trail is best suited to small or mid-sized SUVs with high clearance. Vehicles with long overhangs will probably connect with the slickrock ledges—and vehicle underbodies bend before slickrock does.

The trail lets you know what you are in for at the first slickrock step, which is actually easier than it looks; most vehicles will slowly advance with no problem. If you don't like the look of this step, or you think that your front or rear overhangs will catch, go no farther as there are more difficult sections to come. There is a turning point before the step if you decide to go back.

The trail, a mix of sand and slickrock steps, winds its way toward Chicken Point. Side trails lead to the large natural sinkhole of Devils Dining Room and the aptly named Submarine Rock. The viewpoint at Chicken Point is a large slickrock platform that looks out to the southwest over the red rock cliffs.

A portion of the return trip takes a detour to allow one-way travel on this part of the ascent. A highlight of the return trip, a slickrock knob that makes a tight natural "roundabout," is a great place from which to photograph Submarine Rock.

The most challenging part of the trail is the end of the one-way section, which descends a very steep, ledgy slickrock hill. This section is not easy in wet weather, when slickrock lives up to its name. This hill is rated a 7 for difficulty; the rest of the trail is rated a 6. You can view this hill from the bottom at the start of the one-way section by walking the hundred yards to the base of the hill. If you don't feel comfortable piloting your vehicle down the hill, turn back at this point. Please respect the one-way system, which is designed to reduce congestion on the trail. Do not continue to Chicken Point if you do not wish to tackle the steep downhill.

Once down the hill, the trail retraces its path back to Arizona 179.

Current Road Information

Coconino National Forest
Red Rock Ranger District
PO Box 20429
Sedona, AZ 86341
(928) 282-4119

Map References

BLM   Sedona
USFS   Coconino National Forest: Sedona Ranger District
USGS   1:24,000   Sedona, Munds Mtn.
         1:100,000 Sedona
Maptech CD-ROM: Flagstaff/Sedona/Prescott
Arizona Atlas & Gazetteer, p. 42
Other: Beartooth Maps—Sedona

These steps are the most diffficult part of the trail

Route Directions

▼ 0.0   From the intersection of Arizona 179 and Arizona 89A, proceed south on Arizona 179 for 1.3 miles; then turn southeast on Morgan Road at the sign for Broken Arrow Estates. Zero trip meter. Remain on paved Morgan Road, ignoring roads on right and left.
GPS: N34°50.92' W111°45.90'

▼ 0.5   SO   Road turns to graded dirt; then cattle guard.

▼ 0.6   SO   Parking area on left for Margs Draw Trailhead. Hiking trail on the right. Road is now designated FR 179F and is a 4WD road.
GPS: N34°50.73' W111°45.40'

▼ 0.8   SO   Climb up large rock step; then cross through wash. This is the start of the 4WD section.
GPS: N34°50.56' W111°45.28'

▼ 0.9   SO   Track on right goes 0.1 miles to the large natural sinkhole of Devils Dining Room. Zero trip meter.
GPS: N34°50.50' W111°45.26'

▼ 0.0   Continue to the southeast on the main trail.

▼ 0.1   BR   Start of one-way section.
GPS: N34°50.45' W111°45.15'

▼ 0.2   SO   End of one-way section.

▼ 0.4   SO   Hiking trail crosses vehicle trail. Submarine Rock is on the left, among the junipers.
GPS: N34°50.29' W111°44.96'

▼ 0.5   BL   Start of one-way section. Track on right is end of loop. Walk a short distance to the right to view the final steep descent, which is the most difficult section of the trail. You can turn around here if you do not want to descend the rock steps. Past this point, the trail is one-way.

▼ 0.6   BR   Track on left goes 0.2 miles to a viewpoint on the top of Submarine Rock.

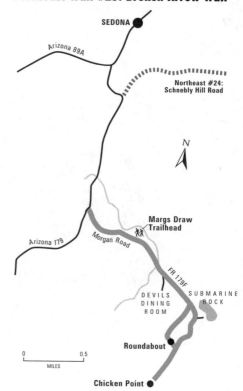

Zero trip meter.
GPS: N34°50.21' W111°44.89'

▼ 0.0   Continue to the southeast.

▼ 0.4   BL   Track on right is start of return loop. Zero trip meter.
GPS: N34°49.97' W111°45.05'

▼ 0.0   Continue to the south.

▼ 0.3   UT   Chicken Point. Make a U-turn and return along the trail the way you came.
GPS: N34°49.76' W111°45.23'

▼ 0.6   BL   Track on right. Zero trip meter.
GPS: N34°49.97' W111°45.05'

▼ 0.0   Continue to the north.

▼ 0.1   SO   Steep climb up slickrock to a "roundabout" around a large rock.
GPS: N34°50.03' W111°45.09'

A high-clearance vehicle is necessary to climb the rock steps

Vehicles approaching Chicken Point, at the southern end of the trail

The end of the trail

▼ 0.2	TR	Trail does a sharp right turn at a high point, then twists on slickrock with some tight turns. **GPS: N34°50.05′ W111°45.14′**
▼ 0.3	SO	Hiking trail on left.
▼ 0.5	SO	Very steep, short downhill section. Most difficult section of trail. **GPS: N34°50.23′ W111°44.99′**
▼ 0.6	TL	Two-way section of trail resumes. Turn left and retrace your steps to Arizona 179. **GPS: N34°50.24′ W111°44.94′**

NORTHEAST REGION TRAIL #26

Rattlesnake Canyon Trail

STARTING POINT: FR 239, 2.1 miles south of junction with I-17
FINISHING POINT: Stoneman Lake Road, FR 213
TOTAL MILEAGE: 4.4 miles
UNPAVED MILEAGE: 4.4 miles
DRIVING TIME: 1.25 hours

ELEVATION RANGE: 6,200–6,700 feet
USUALLY OPEN: January 1–August 15
BEST TIME TO TRAVEL: January 1–August 15
DIFFICULTY RATING: 5
SCENIC RATING: 8
REMOTENESS RATING: +0

Special Attractions

- Moderately rated, lightly used trail.
- Views over Rattlesnake Canyon and red rock country near Sedona.

Description

This trail is short, but because the surface is rough, it takes more than an hour to drive less than 5 miles. The trail is contained within the Rattlesnake Quiet Area, which is closed to vehicles between August 15 and December 31 to allow for non-motorized hunting, hiking, and horseback riding.

The main difficulty of the trail comes from the large rocks embedded in the surface. At some sections, particularly as the trail descends to cross through Rattlesnake Canyon, you will need to place your wheels carefully. If you have low-hanging brush bars or side steps, you should be particularly careful.

The descent into Rattlesnake Canyon is rough and rocky

South of the Rattlesnake Canyon crossing, there is an excellent viewpoint to the southwest down the canyon. Other great views are to be found earlier on the trail as it crosses through an open area where you can look west toward the red rock country around Sedona, and across Horse Mesa to Lee Mountain.

This trail sees little use, and in places it can be faint and hard to follow, particularly around an open area 1.1 miles from the start of the trail.

Current Road Information
Coconino National Forest
Red Rock Ranger District
PO Box 20429
Sedona, AZ 86341
(928) 203-7500

Map References
BLM   Sedona
USFS Coconino National Forest: Beaver
        Creek Ranger District
USGS 1:24,000 Stoneman Lake
        1:100,000 Sedona
Maptech CD-ROM: Flagstaff/Sedona/Prescott
Arizona Atlas & Gazetteer, p. 42

Arizona Road & Recreation Atlas, pp. 35, 69

Route Directions

▼ 0.0   From I-17, exit 315, proceed to the east
           side of the interstate and head south
           along FR 80 for 2.1 miles. Zero trip
           meter at the intersection of FR 80 and
           FR 239 and proceed to the south. Enter
           Rattlesnake Quiet Area through gate.
4.4 ▲   Trail finishes at the intersection of FR
           239 and FR 80. Bear left to exit to I-17.
           GPS: N34°49.47' W111°35.65'

▼ 0.1   SO   Stock tank on left.
4.3 ▲   SO   Stock tank on right.
▼ 1.1   BL   Faint track on right; continue on small
             faint trail.
3.3 ▲   BR   Faint track on left; continue on main
             trail, which is faint at this point.
             GPS: N34°48.53' W111°35.78'

▼ 1.8   SO   Gate on right; trail is beside the freeway.
2.6 ▲   SO   Gate on left; trail is beside the freeway.
▼ 1.9   SO   Gate.
2.5 ▲   SO   Gate.

The trail is indistinct because of its light use

Northeast Trail #26: Rattlesnake Canyon Trail

GPS: N34°47.93' W111°35.37'

▼ 2.3   SO   Trail follows alongside the edge of a tributary of Rattlesnake Canyon.

2.1 ▲   SO   Trail follows alongside the edge of a tributary of Rattlesnake Canyon.

GPS: N34°47.56' W111°35.34'

▼ 2.7   SO   Cross through Rattlesnake Canyon wash.

1.7 ▲   SO   Cross through Rattlesnake Canyon wash.

GPS: N34°47.29' W111°35.33'

▼ 2.9   SO   Wire gate. Red Hill is on the right.

1.5 ▲   SO   Wire gate. Red Hill is on the left.

GPS: N34°47.19' W111°35.32'

▼ 3.0   SO   Cross through wash.

1.4 ▲   SO   Cross through wash.

▼ 3.4   SO   Faint track on left.

1.0 ▲   SO   Faint track on right.

▼ 4.0   SO   Cross through wash.

0.4 ▲   SO   Cross through wash.

GPS: N34°46.45' W111°34.50'

▼ 4.1   SO   Track on left goes sharply back to the left.

0.3 ▲   BL   Trail forks; take left-hand fork down to cross wash.

GPS: N34°46.41' W111°34.42'

▼ 4.3   SO   Faint track on left.

0.1 ▲   SO   Faint track on right.

▼ 4.4   Cross cattle guard; information board for the Palatkwapi Indian Trail immediately on right and seasonal closure gate. Trail ends at the intersection with paved Stoneman Lake Road. Turn left for Stoneman Lake; turn right for I-17.

0.0 ▲   Trail commences on paved Stoneman Lake Road, FR 213, 5.1 miles east of I-17, exit 306. Zero trip meter and turn northwest through seasonal closure gate and across a cattle guard. There is an information board for the old Palatkwapi Indian Trail immediately after the gate. Proceed northeast on formed lumpy trail, FR 80. The route marker is a few hundred yards along the trail.

GPS: N34°46.27' W111°34.56'

NORTHEAST REGION TRAIL #27

Cedar Flat Road

STARTING POINT: Intersection of FR 618 and FR 214, 4 miles north of the General Crook Trail (Arizona 260)

FINISHING POINT: Intersection with Northeast #28: Home Tank Draw Trail (FR 214)

TOTAL MILEAGE: 10.8 miles

UNPAVED MILEAGE: 10.8 miles

DRIVING TIME: 1 hour

ELEVATION RANGE: 3,900–6,000 feet

USUALLY OPEN: May to October

BEST TIME TO TRAVEL: Dry weather

DIFFICULTY RATING: 1

SCENIC RATING: 9

REMOTENESS RATING: +0

Special Attractions
- Views into West Clear Creek Canyon and south to the Verde Valley.
- Connects to Northeast #28: Home Tank Draw Trail.

Description
This trail, basically a continuation of Northeast #28: Home Tank Draw Trail, connects with it to form a loop that returns to more-used roads. However, this portion of the loop is a highly scenic trail in its own right for those without the high-clearance 4WD necessary to tackle the rocky Home Tank Draw Trail. Cedar Flat Road, a wide, graded dirt road, can be driven by passenger vehicles in dry weather.

The highlight of the trail is the section of wide shelf road near the western end, which has panoramic views into West Clear Creek Canyon and south to the Verde Valley. These views are best appreciated when driving the trail in the reverse direction.

The remainder of the trail crosses the wide plateau of Cedar Ridge to connect with the start of Northeast #28: Home Tank Draw Trail.

Current Road Information
Coconino National Forest
Red Rock Ranger District
PO Box 20429
Sedona, AZ 86341
(928) 203-7500

Map References
BLM   Sedona
USFS   Coconino National Forest: Beaver Creek Ranger District
USGS   1:24,000   Buckhorn Mtn., Walker Mtn.
           1:100,000   Sedona
Maptech CD-ROM: Flagstaff/Sedona/Prescott
Arizona Atlas & Gazetteer, p. 42
Arizona Road & Recreation Atlas, pp. 41, 75
Recreational Map of Arizona

Route Directions

▼ 0.0   Trail commences at the intersection of FR 618 and FR 214. Zero trip meter and turn east on roughly graded road. Turn is marked Cedar Flat Road and is 4 miles north of the General Crook Trail

The easy trail runs high above West Clear Creek Canyon

(Arizona 260).

5.0 ▲   Trail ends at the intersection with FR 618. Turn left for Camp Verde; turn right for I-17.
GPS: N34°34.28′ W111°44.10′

▼ 0.1   SO   Cattle guard and closure gate; then track on right.

4.9 ▲   SO   Track on left; then cattle guard and closure gate.

▼ 0.2   SO   Cross through wash.

4.8 ▲   SO   Cross through wash.

▼ 0.8   SO   Track on right.

4.2 ▲   SO   Track on left.

▼ 1.5   SO   Track on left is FR 9201S and track on right.

3.5 ▲   SO   Track on right is FR 9201S and track on left.
GPS: N34°34.33′ W111°42.66′

▼ 2.6   SO   Track on left.

2.4 ▲   SO   Track on right.

▼ 2.7   SO   Track on left.

2.3 ▲   SO   Track on right.

▼ 3.2   SO   Track on right.

1.8 ▲   SO   Track on left.

▼ 3.9   SO   Track on right goes to Blodgett Basin Trail #31 (initially suitable for vehicles); then cattle guard.

1.1 ▲   SO   Cattle guard; then track on left goes to Blodgett Basin Trail #31 (initially suitable for vehicles).
GPS: N34°33.78′ W111°40.33′

▼ 4.9   SO   Viewpoint on right on left-hand bend into West Clear Creek Canyon.

0.1 ▲   SO   Viewpoint on left on right-hand bend into West Clear Creek Canyon.

▼ 5.0   SO   Track on right is FR 214A; then track on left through gate. Zero trip meter.

0.0 ▲   Continue to the northwest.
GPS: N34°33.58′ W111°39.25′

▼ 0.0   Continue to the northeast.

5.8 ▲   SO   Track on left is FR 214A; then track on right through gate. Zero trip meter.

▼ 0.9   SO   Track on left is FR 9201V; then track on right.

4.9 ▲   SO   Track on left; then track on right is FR 9201V.
GPS: N34°34.35′ W111°38.88′

▼ 1.1   SO   Track on left is FR 9201W.

4.7 ▲   SO   Track on right is FR 9201W.
GPS: N34°34.53′ W111°38.89′

▼ 1.8   SO   Cattle guard; then track on left is FR 214B, also marked Walker Basin Trail #81 (hiking); then track on right is FR 9263N; then cattle guard.

4.0 ▲   SO   Cattle guard; then track on left is FR 9263N; then track on right is FR 214B, also marked Walker Basin Trail #81 (hiking); then cattle guard.
GPS: N34°35.10′ W111°38.51′

▼ 3.9   SO   Track on left through wire gate.

1.9 ▲   SO   Track on right through wire gate.

▼ 4.0   SO   Cattle guard.

1.8 ▲   SO   Cattle guard.

The trail climbs Bald Hill

▼ 4.1 SO Corral on right at Cedar Flat; then cattle guard; then track on right and track on left.

1.7 ▲ SO Track on right and track on left; then cattle guard; then corral on left at Cedar Flat.

GPS: N34°36.30' W111°36.51'

▼ 5.0 SO Track on right.
0.8 ▲ SO Track on left.
▼ 5.2 SO Track on left.
0.6 ▲ SO Track on right.
▼ 5.3 TR Two tracks on left; remain on main trail. Trail is now a roughly graded road.
0.5 ▲ TL Two tracks on right. Remain on main trail.

GPS: N34°36.46' W111°35.18'

▼ 5.8 Trail finishes at the intersection with Northeast #28: Home Tank Draw Trail, FR 214. Turn left over the cattle guard and continue northeast to continue along the Home Tank Draw Trail.

0.0 ▲ Trail commences at the western end of Northeast #28: Home Tank Draw Trail, FR 214. Zero trip meter and turn north on unmarked trail. To the south is FR 9236K.

GPS: N34°36.02' W111°35.39'

NORTHEAST REGION TRAIL #28

Home Tank Draw Trail

STARTING POINT: Intersection of FR 229 and Northeast #29: Apache Maid Fire Lookout Trail (FR 620)
FINISHING POINT: Eastern end of Northeast #27: Cedar Flat Road
TOTAL MILEAGE: 14.1 miles
UNPAVED MILEAGE: 14.1 miles
DRIVING TIME: 2 hours
ELEVATION RANGE: 5,900–6,600 feet
USUALLY OPEN: May to October
BEST TIME TO TRAVEL: Dry weather
DIFFICULTY RATING: 4
SCENIC RATING: 8
REMOTENESS RATING: +1

Special Attractions
- Little-used trail that passes through interesting scenery in the Coconino National Forest.
- Alternative entry and exit to the Apache Maid Fire Lookout.

Description
This trail sees surprisingly little traffic considering that it is a very scenic (although fairly slow) alternative route into the Coconino National Forest. For the most part, the lumpy, rock-embedded surface ensures a slow pace. The rocks are not difficult to negotiate; a little care with wheel placement is all that is needed. Between the rocky sections, the trail is smooth although there are deep ruts caused by wet weather travel. This is not a good place to be in wet weather.

The single-track trail runs alongside Jacks Canyon for a short way and crosses through the very pretty Brady Canyon before running through open countryside, which is dotted with alligator junipers and oaks. Elk can often be seen in the area. There are many small trails leading off from the main trail, but it is fairly easy to remain on track, despite the limited route markers.

The trail finishes at the eastern end of Northeast #27: Cedar Flat Road, which is the way to Camp Verde. This trail is 1-rated so it is dealt with separately, but the two trails combine to form a complete route.

Current Road Information
Coconino National Forest
Red Rock Ranger District
PO Box 20429
Sedona, AZ 86341
(928) 203-7500

Coconino National Forest
Mogollon Rim Ranger District
HC 31 Box 300
Happy Jack, AZ 86024
(928) 477-2255

Map References
BLM Sedona
USFS Coconino National Forest: Beaver Creek Ranger District

Northeast Trail #28: Home Tank Draw Trail

USGS 1:24,000 Apache Maid Mtn.,
Happy Jack, Buckhorn Mtn.
1:100,000 Sedona
Maptech CD-ROM: Flagstaff/Sedona/Prescott
Arizona Atlas & Gazetteer, p. 42
Arizona Road & Recreation Atlas, pp. 41, 75

Route Directions

▼ 0.0   From the intersection of FR 229 and FR 620, Northeast #29: Apache Maid Fire Lookout Trail, zero trip meter and turn southeast on formed trail marked FR 229.

3.3 ▲   Trail ends at the intersection of FR 229 and FR 620, Northeast #29: Apache Maid Fire Lookout Trail. Turn left to exit via Mullican Canyon; turn right to exit via the graded road.
GPS: N34°42.76′ W111°31.22′

▼ 0.1 SO Cattle guard.
3.2 ▲ SO Cattle guard.
▼ 0.5 SO Cross through Jacks Canyon wash.
2.8 ▲ SO Cross through Jacks Canyon wash.
GPS: N34°42.58′ W111°30.83′

▼ 1.1 BR Track on left and faint track on right.
2.2 ▲ SO Track on right and faint track on left.
GPS: N34°42.29′ W111°30.48′

▼ 1.6 SO Track on left is second entrance to FR 229. Continue ahead on FR 214.
1.7 ▲ SO Track on right is FR 229. Continue straight on to join FR 229.
GPS: N34°41.98′ W111°30.06′

▼ 2.0 BL Cattle guard; then faint track on right.
1.3 ▲ BR Faint track on left; then cattle guard.
GPS: N34°41.78′ W111°29.68′

▼ 2.1 SO Track on right to stock tank.
1.2 ▲ SO Track on left to stock tank.
▼ 2.2 SO Cross through wash.
1.1 ▲ SO Cross through wash.
GPS: N34°41.68′ W111°29.48′

▼ 3.2 SO Cross through wash.
0.1 ▲ SO Cross through wash.
▼ 3.3 TR Track ahead is FR 83. Turn right, remaining on FR 214, and zero trip meter. Route markers at intersection.
0.0 ▲   Continue to the northeast.
GPS: N34°40.84′ W111°29.02′

▼ 0.0   Continue to the west.
4.4 ▲ TL Track on right is FR 83. Turn left, remaining on FR 214, and zero trip meter. Route markers at intersection.
▼ 0.2 SO Cross through Brady Canyon.
4.2 ▲ SO Cross through Brady Canyon.

A typical view of the meadows dotted with pines

▼ 1.6   SO   Cattle guard; then track on right.
2.8 ▲   SO   Track on left; then cattle guard.
GPS: N34º40.17' W111º30.32'

▼ 2.5   SO   Pass through wire gate.
1.9 ▲   SO   Pass through wire gate.
GPS: N34º40.07' W111º31.26'

▼ 3.7   SO   Cross over creek.
0.7 ▲   SO   Cross over creek.
▼ 3.9   SO   Faint track on right.
0.5 ▲   BR   Faint track on left.
GPS: N34º39.20' W111º32.25'

▼ 4.4   BL   Track on right to Tinny stock tanks and cabin; bear left and cross cattle guard. Zero trip meter. The intersection is unmarked.
0.0 ▲   Continue to the northeast.
GPS: N34º39.04' W111º32.69'

▼ 0.0   Continue to the south; track on left.
6.4 ▲   BR   Track on right; then cross cattle guard; then track on left to Tinny stock tanks and cabin. Bear right, remaining on main trail. Zero trip meter. The intersection is unmarked.
▼ 0.1   SO   Cross through wash; then track on right. This section can be muddy.
6.3 ▲   SO   Track on left; then cross through wash. This section can be muddy.
▼ 0.2   SO   Track on right.
6.2 ▲   SO   Track on left.
▼ 0.6   SO   Track on right through gate.
5.8 ▲   SO   Track on left through gate.
GPS: N34º38.51' W111º33.01'

▼ 1.0   BL   Two tracks on right; road through gates goes to Fivemile Pass and stock tanks. Bear left, remaining on main trail.
5.4 ▲   BR   Two tracks on left; road through gates goes to Fivemile Pass and stock tanks. Bear right, remaining on main trail.
GPS: N34º38.22' W111º33.07'

▼ 1.6   TR   Track on left; turn right after cattle guard.
4.8 ▲   TL   Cattle guard; then turn left. Track continues ahead after cattle guard.

▼ 2.0   BR   Track on left.
4.4 ▲   SO   Track on right.
GPS: N34º37.61' W111º32.27'

▼ 2.1   SO   Track on right.
4.3 ▲   SO   Track on left.
▼ 2.3   SO   Stock tank on left.
4.1 ▲   SO   Stock tank on right.
▼ 2.6   BR   Well-used track on left; bear right and cross cattle guard.
3.8 ▲   BL   Cattle guard; then well-used track on right.
GPS: N34º37.09' W111º32.16'

▼ 3.3   SO   Pass through fence line.
3.1 ▲   SO   Pass through fence line.
▼ 3.6   SO   Track on right to stock tank.
2.8 ▲   SO   Track on left to stock tank.
▼ 3.8   SO   Track on left.
2.6 ▲   SO   Track on right.
GPS: N34º36.43' W111º33.12'

▼ 3.9   SO   Pass through wire gate.
2.5 ▲   SO   Pass through wire gate.
▼ 4.0   SO   Cross through wash.
2.4 ▲   SO   Cross through wash.
▼ 4.1   SO   Cross through wash.
2.3 ▲   SO   Cross through wash.
GPS: N34º36.25' W111º33.41'

▼ 4.4   SO   Track on left.
2.0 ▲   BL   Track on right.
GPS: N34º36.04' W111º33.52'

▼ 4.5   SO   Track on left; then cross through wash.
1.9 ▲   SO   Cross through wash; then track on right.
GPS: N34º36.02' W111º33.55'

▼ 5.2   SO   Cross through wash.
1.2 ▲   SO   Cross through wash.
▼ 5.8   SO   Well-used track on left.
0.6 ▲   BL   Well-used track on right.
GPS: N34º36.02' W111º34.84'

▼ 5.9   SO   Track on left.
0.5 ▲   SO   Track on right.
▼ 6.4   Trail ends at the T-intersection at the eastern end of the Northeast #27:

Cedar Flat Road. Turn right to continue down Cedar Flat Road to Camp Verde. Track on left is FR 9236K. Stock tank at the intersection.

0.0 ▲ Trail commences at the eastern end of the easier Northeast #27: Cedar Flat Road. Zero trip meter and turn east over the cattle guard onto FR 214, which is unmarked but has a yellow road sign: "Not maintained for low clearance vehicles." The trail that continues to the west at that point is FR 9236K. There is a stock tank at the intersection.

GPS: N34°36.02' W111°35.39'

Apache Maid Fire Lookout Trail

STARTING POINT: Intersection of Northeast #28: Home Tank Draw Trail (FR 229) and FR 620
FINISHING POINT: Apache Maid Fire Lookout
TOTAL MILEAGE: 4 miles
UNPAVED MILEAGE: 4 miles
DRIVING TIME: 30 minutes
ELEVATION RANGE: 6,500–7,200 feet
USUALLY OPEN: May to October
BEST TIME TO TRAVEL: May to October
DIFFICULTY RATING: 2
SCENIC RATING: 9
REMOTENESS RATING: +0

Special Attractions
- Panoramic 360-degree views from the Apache Maid Fire Lookout.
- Connects with other 4WD trails within the Coconino National Forest.

Description
This short trail climbs up the twisting road to the Apache Maid Fire Lookout in the Coconino National Forest. The trail, maintained by the forest service as access for the tower, is normally slightly rutted but is generally suitable for high-clearance vehicles.

Northeast Trail #29: Apache Maid Fire Lookout Trail

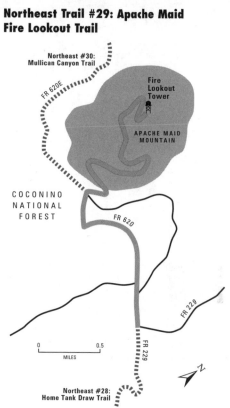

The lookout tower, which was built in 1961 to protect the Beaver Creek Watershed, is manned during the fire season. Usually, you are welcome to climb the tower with the lookout's permission. The gate to the tower is closed when the tower is not manned and at night. "No Camping" signs are on the far side of the gate, but there are some good campsites scattered among the oaks and pines along this trail.

Current Road Information
Coconino National Forest
Red Rock Ranger District
PO Box 20429
Sedona, AZ 86341
(928) 203-7500

Map References
BLM Sedona
USFS Coconino National Forest: Beaver Creek Ranger District

The view from the Apache Maid Fire Lookout

USGS 1:24,000 Apache Maid Mtn.
    1:100,000 Sedona
Maptech CD-ROM: Flagstaff/Sedona/Prescott
Arizona Atlas & Gazetteer, p. 42
Arizona Road & Recreation Atlas, pp. 41, 75

Route Directions

▼ 0.0   From the intersection of FR 229 and FR 620, zero trip meter and turn west on formed trail marked FR 620. Northeast #28: Home Tank Draw Trail leads off to the east.

1.5 ▲   Trail ends at the intersection of Northeast #28: Home Tank Draw Trail (FR 229) and FR 620.
    GPS: N34°42.76′ W111°31.22′

▼ 0.3 SO Track on right.
1.2 ▲ SO Track on left.
▼ 0.4 SO Track on left opposite dam; then track on right to dam.
1.1 ▲ SO Track on left to dam; then track on right opposite dam.
▼ 0.8 SO Track on right.
0.7 ▲ SO Track on left.
▼ 1.0 SO Track on right is FR 620D.
0.5 ▲ SO Track on left is FR 620D.
    GPS: N34°42.94′ W111°32.19′

▼ 1.3 BR Track on left; then cross over creek.
0.2 ▲ BL Cross over creek; then track on right.
▼ 1.5 SO Track on left is Northeast #30: Mullican Canyon Trail, FR 620E; track on right to camping area. Zero trip meter.
0.0 ▲   Proceed southeast on FR 620.
    GPS: N34°42.85′ W111°32.55′

▼ 0.0   Continue to the northwest on FR 620.
▼ 0.6 SO Closure gate; no camping beyond closure gate.
▼ 2.5   Trail ends at Apache Maid Fire Lookout. There is a picnic table at the top.
    GPS: N34°43.53′ W111°32.99′

Mullican Canyon Trail

STARTING POINT: Northeast #29: Apache Maid Fire Lookout Trail, 1.5 miles from the intersection with FR 229

FINISHING POINT: Intersection of FR 229 and FR 644, immediately north of the Watershed Camp Station

TOTAL MILEAGE: 6.5 miles

UNPAVED MILEAGE: 6.5 miles

DRIVING TIME: 1 hour

ELEVATION RANGE: 6,000–6,600 feet

USUALLY OPEN: May to October

BEST TIME TO TRAVEL: Dry weather

DIFFICULTY RATING: 3

SCENIC RATING: 8

REMOTENESS RATING: +0

Special Attractions

■ Rugged and scenic Mullican Canyon.
■ Views of Apache Maid Mountain.

Description

This short trail runs between Northeast #29: Apache Maid Fire Lookout Trail and FR 229. The trail, which is rough and rutted in places, describes a wide loop around Apache Maid Mountain. Initially, it runs over the open plateau, falling off gradually toward Wet Beaver Creek and Hog Hill. After the intersection with FR 9243H, the trail dips gradually into Mullican Canyon, a narrow, fairly shallow canyon that is rimmed with the black lava rocks that abound in this region.

The trail standard gradually improves until it joins the graded road that completes the loop to FR 229.

Current Road Information

Coconino National Forest
Red Rock Ranger District
PO Box 20429
Sedona, AZ 86341
(928) 203-7500

A small stock tank at the head of Mullican Canyon

Northeast Trail #30: Mullican Canyon Trail

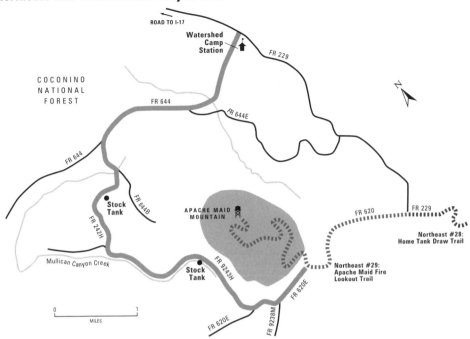

Map References

BLM   Sedona
USFS   Coconino National Forest: Beaver
         Creek Ranger District
USGS   1:24,000   Apache Maid Mtn.,
         Stoneman Lake
         1:100,000 Sedona
Maptech CD-ROM: Flagstaff/Sedona/Prescott
Arizona Atlas & Gazetteer, p. 42
Arizona Road & Recreation Atlas, pp. 41, 75

Route Directions

▼ 0.0   From Northeast #29: Apache Maid
            Fire Lookout Trail, (FR 620), zero trip
            meter and turn west on the small
            formed trail marked FR 620E.
0.8 ▲   Trail ends at Northeast #29: Apache
            Maid Fire Lookout Trail, 1.5 miles from
            the start. Turn left to visit the lookout;
            turn right to exit the forest.
            GPS: N34°42.85′ W111°32.55′

▼ 0.4   BR   Track on left is FR 9238M.
0.4 ▲   SO   Track on right is FR 9238M.
            GPS: N34°42.71′ W111°33.03′

▼ 0.5   SO   Cross through wash.
0.3 ▲   SO   Cross through wash.

▼ 0.8   TR   Turn right onto FR 9243H. FR 620E
                 continues ahead. Zero trip meter.
0.0 ▲   Continue to the east.
            GPS: N34°42.75′ W111°33.37′

▼ 0.0   Continue to the north.
2.0 ▲   TL   Turn left onto FR 620E. Zero trip meter.
                 Track on right is also 620E.

▼ 0.7   SO   Trail follows alongside Mullican
                 Canyon Creek.
1.3 ▲   SO   Trail follows alongside Mullican
                 Canyon Creek.

▼ 0.8   SO   Stock tank on left.
1.2 ▲   SO   Stock tank on right.
            GPS: N34°43.47′ W111°33.60′

▼ 1.0   SO   Cross through Mullican Canyon wash.
1.0 ▲   SO   Cross through Mullican Canyon wash.
            GPS: N34°43.54′ W111°33.83′

▼ 2.0   SO   Pass through gate; private property on
                 left. Zero trip meter. Trail is now
                 marked as FR 242H.

0.0 ▲		Continue to the south. Standard improves at this point—still a formed trail but a lot smoother. **GPS: N34°43.98' W111°34.53'**

▼ 0.0		Continue to the north and cross through small wash.
1.5 ▲	BL	Cross through small wash; then private property on right; pass through gate. Trail is now marked FR 9243H. Zero trip meter.
▼ 0.8	SO	Stock tank on right.
0.7 ▲	SO	Stock tank on left.
▼ 1.1	SO	Track on right is FR 644A; then cross through wash.
0.4 ▲	SO	Cross through wash; then track on left is FR 644A.
▼ 1.2	SO	Track on right is FR 644B; bear left, remaining on FR 242H.
0.3 ▲	BR	Track on left is FR 644B; bear right, remaining on FR 242H. **GPS: N34°44.69' W111°33.98'**

▼ 1.5	TR	T-intersection with FR 644. Turn right onto FR 644 and zero trip meter. Faint track ahead.
0.0 ▲		Continue to the south. **GPS: N34°44.96' W111°33.93'**

▼ 0.0		Continue to the northeast.
2.2 ▲	TL	Turn left from FR 644 onto FR 644A and zero trip meter. Faint track on right.
▼ 0.5	SO	Track on right to campsite.
1.7 ▲	SO	Track on left to campsite.
▼ 0.6	SO	Track on right.
1.6 ▲	SO	Track on left.
▼ 0.7	SO	Track on left.
1.5 ▲	SO	Track on right.
▼ 1.1	SO	Track on right is FR 644E and track on left.
1.1 ▲	SO	Track on left is FR 644E and track on right. **GPS: N34°44.82' W111°32.89'**

▼ 1.2	SO	Track on right.
1.0 ▲	SO	Track on left.
▼ 1.4	SO	Track on right; then cross over creek on bridge.

The trail heading toward Hog Hill

0.8 ▲	SO	Cross over creek on bridge; then track on left.
		GPS: N34°44.73' W111°32.58'

▼ 1.5	SO	Cross over creek.
0.7 ▲	SO	Cross over creek.
▼ 2.2		Trail ends at the T-intersection with FR 229, immediately north of the Watershed Camp Station. Turn left for I-17.
0.0 ▲		Trail commences on FR 229, immediately north of Watershed Camp Station, 9 miles east of I-17, exit 306. Zero trip meter and turn southwest on graded FR 644.
		GPS: N34°45.19' W111°31.87'

Coulter Hill Trail

STARTING POINT: Mormon Lake Road, immediately south of mile marker 8
FINISHING POINT: Lake Mary Road, near Lower Lake Mary
TOTAL MILEAGE: 18.1 miles
UNPAVED MILEAGE: 17.6 miles
DRIVING TIME: 1.25 hours
ELEVATION RANGE: 6,800–7,500 feet
USUALLY OPEN: April to October
BEST TIME TO TRAVEL: April to October
DIFFICULTY RATING: 2
SCENIC RATING: 7
REMOTENESS RATING: +0

Special Attractions
■ Elk can often be seen in the area.
■ Open area of Antelope Park.
■ The mainly dry area of Mormon Lake.

History
A lake in this region was first noted in 1864 when one called Carleton Lake appeared on a map made by General James Henry Carleton. Oral histories contradict the presence of a lake and say that Mormon Lake was not formed until Mormons came to the area and clogged the natural drainage channels to the basin with their farming and grazing activities.

However it formed, Mormon Lake is recognized as the largest natural lake in Arizona. The lake is shallow and for much of the time, especially in recent years, it has been marshland or dry. However, at one time it was deep enough for a boat tour company to operate.

In the late 1870s, Brigham Young was encouraging Mormons to settle in Arizona, partly for colonization and expansion and partly to provide a refuge for polygamous families that were being hounded in Utah. There was an active Mormon settlement in the area, then known as Pleasant Valley, including a dairy built by Hyrum Judd at Dairy Springs, near the present-day campground. The cows grazed near Mormon Lake, and butter and cheese were produced to supply the towns of Brigham City, Sunset, and Joseph. The dairy closed in 1886 and Judd and his family moved to Mexico to avoid prosecution for polygamy.

Description
This roughly graded, narrow dirt road travels between Mormon Lake and Lower Lake Mary. Much of the route passes through the Pinegrove Quiet Area, which is closed to vehicles from August to January to protect elk habitat and allow for non-motorized quiet recreation. The trails that lead into the quiet area are clearly marked.

The main Coulter Hill Trail is a roughly graded dirt road with patches of gravel. It travels through the pine forest, which is dotted with small stands of aspens. In early spring, wild irises carpet many of the meadows along the way, and in November and December the brilliant fall colors of aspens and oaks contrast with the dark green of ponderosa pines.

FR 236 goes past Coulter Cabin, a forest service guard station, at 10.3 miles from the start of the trail. To reach the cabin, turn down FR 236 and proceed for 0.3 miles before turning right down an unmarked small track that goes to the cabin. You can walk past the gate on the trail to see the old cabin plus the new guard station, which is often occupied in summer months.

The trail finishes on Lake Mary Road, just to the northwest of Lower Lake Mary.

A stand of aspens make Weimer Springs a particularly scenic spot

Current Road Information

Coconino National Forest
Mormon Lake Ranger District
4373 South Lake Mary Rd.
Flagstaff, AZ 86001
(928) 774-1147

Map References

BLM   Sedona, Flagstaff
USFS   Coconino National Forest:
       Mormon Lake Ranger District
USGS   1:24,000   Mormon Lake, Mormon
       Mtn., Lower Lake Mary
       1:100,000 Sedona, Flagstaff
Maptech CD-ROM: Flagstaff/Sedona/Prescott
Arizona Atlas & Gazetteer, p. 42
Arizona Road & Recreation Atlas, pp. 35, 69

Route Directions

▼ 0.0   From Mormon Lake Road, north of the
          settlement of Mormon Lake, and
          immediately south of mile marker 8,
          zero trip meter and turn west on grad-
          ed dirt road, FR 132, following the sign
          to Weimer Springs and Antelope Park.

4.2 ▲   Trail ends on Mormon Lake Road, north

of the settlement of Mormon Lake.
Turn right for Mormon Lake; turn left
for Flagstaff.

GPS: N34°58.88′ W111°28.56′

▼ 0.1   SO   Track on right is FR 9466Y into
             Pinegrove Quiet Area, which extends
             on the right side of the trail.

4.1 ▲   SO   Track on left is FR 9466Y into
             Pinegrove Quiet Area.

▼ 0.2   SO   Track on left is FR 9459C.

4.0 ▲   SO   Track on right is FR 9459C.

▼ 0.4   SO   Track on right is FR 9459 and track
             on left.

3.8 ▲   SO   Track on left is FR 9459 and track
             on right.

▼ 0.6   SO   Track on left.

3.6 ▲   SO   Track on right.

▼ 0.7   SO   Track on right.

3.5 ▲   SO   Track on left.

▼ 0.9   SO   Track on left is FR 9466X.

3.3 ▲   SO   Track on right is FR 9466X.

GPS: N34°59.63′ W111°29.10′

▼ 1.1   SO   Track on left; then track on right is
             FR 9459A.

3.1 ▲   SO   Track on left is FR 9459A; then track

Old Coulter Cabin

on right.

▼ 1.3	SO	Track on right is FR 1320.
2.9 ▲	SO	Track on left is FR 1320.
▼ 1.4	SO	Cattle guard.
2.8 ▲	SO	Cattle guard.
▼ 1.7	SO	Corral on right; then track on right is FR 6077.
2.5 ▲	SO	Track on left is FR 6077; then corral on left.

GPS: N34°59.87′ W111°29.79′

▼ 2.4	SO	Track on right.
1.8 ▲	SO	Track on left.
▼ 2.6	SO	Track on left.
1.6 ▲	SO	Track on right.
▼ 3.4	SO	Track on right is FR 132D.
0.8 ▲	SO	Track on left is FR 132D.

GPS: N34°58.99′ W111°31.32′

▼ 3.9	SO	Track on left is FR 9466X.
0.3 ▲	SO	Track on right is FR 9466X.
▼ 4.2	BR	Graded road on left is FR 132A to Munds Park and Mormon Mountain. Bear right, remaining on FR 132, and zero trip meter.
0.0 ▲		Continue to the east.

GPS: N34°58.48′ W111°31.65′

▼ 0.0		Continue to the north, following the sign to Antelope Park and Lake Mary. Weimer Springs on left.
3.3 ▲	BL	Weimer Springs on right; then graded

road on right is FR 132A to Munds Park and Mormon Mountain. Bear left, remaining on FR 132, and zero trip meter.

▼ 0.2	SO	Track on right.
3.1 ▲	SO	Track on left.
▼ 0.3	SO	Track on right.
3.0 ▲	SO	Track on left.
▼ 1.0	SO	Track on right.
2.3 ▲	SO	Track on left.
▼ 1.3	SO	Track on right.
2.0 ▲	SO	Track on left.
▼ 2.0	SO	Entering Antelope Park.
1.3 ▲	SO	Leaving Antelope Park.
▼ 2.3	SO	Track on left is FR 9410X.
1.0 ▲	SO	Track on right is FR 9410X.

GPS: N34°59.55′ W111°33.54′

▼ 2.4	SO	Cattle guard; then tank on left.
0.9 ▲	SO	Tank on right; then cattle guard.
▼ 2.5	SO	Track on right.
0.8 ▲	SO	Track on left.
▼ 2.6	SO	Track on right; then cross over creek.
0.7 ▲	SO	Cross over creek; then track on left.
▼ 2.7	SO	Leaving Antelope Park.
0.6 ▲	SO	Entering Antelope Park.
▼ 3.3	SO	Small graded road on left is FR 133. Zero trip meter.
0.0 ▲		Continue to the east.

GPS: N35°00.07′ W111°34.46′

▼ 0.0		Continue to the west.

ELK

Elk are large, hoofed cousins of deer with brown bodies, tawny-colored rumps, thick necks, and sturdy legs. Cows range in weight from 500 to 600 pounds. Bulls range from 600 to 1,000 pounds and average about 6 feet in height. Only males have antlers, which they shed each year. Once widely ranged, elk are primarily mountain dwellers in the summer and valley dwellers in the winter. They remain in herds throughout the year and feed on grasses, shrubs, and trees. In the late summer and early fall, bulls display mating behavior caused by their high levels of testosterone: They begin thrashing bushes and "bugling"—making a sound that begins as a bellow, changes to a shrill whistle or scream, and ends with a series of grunts. This vocalization broadcasts a bull's presence to other bulls and functions as a call of domination to the cows. Bulls become territorial and make great efforts to keep the cows together (a harem may consist of up to 60 cows), mating as they come into heat and keeping other bulls at a distance. Bulls often clash antlers in jousts but are seldom hurt. Calves are born in the late spring after a gestation period of about nine months. Elk calves are primarily brown with light spots until the early fall of their first year.

Bull elk bugling

2.4 ▲	SO	Small graded road on right is FR 133. Zero trip meter.
▼ 0.1	SO	Track on right.
2.3 ▲	SO	Track on left.
▼ 0.3	SO	Track on right.
2.1 ▲	SO	Track on left.
▼ 0.4	SO	Track on right.
2.0 ▲	SO	Track on left.
▼ 0.9	SO	Track on right.
1.5 ▲	SO	Track on left.
▼ 1.1	SO	Track on left is FR 9412G.
1.3 ▲	SO	Track on right is FR 9412G.
		GPS: N35°00.29′ W111°35.47′

▼ 1.3	SO	Track on right is FR 132B.
1.1 ▲	SO	Track on left is FR 132B.
		GPS: N35°00.36′ W111°35.63′

▼ 2.2	SO	Track on left to Lockett Ranch. Hard-to-spot, old metal sign at intersection.
0.2 ▲	SO	Track on right to Lockett Ranch. Hard-to-spot, old metal sign at intersection.
		GPS: N35°00.92′ W111°36.27′

▼ 2.3	BL	Track on right; then cattle guard.
0.1 ▲	BR	Cattle guard; then track on left.
▼ 2.4	BR	Graded dirt road on left is FR 236. Bear right, remaining on FR 132. Zero trip meter.
0.0 ▲		Continue to the southeast.
		GPS: N35°01.08′ W111°36.38′

▼ 0.0		Continue to the northwest.
4.9 ▲	BL	Graded dirt road on right is FR 236. Bear left, remaining on FR 132. Zero trip meter.
▼ 0.1	SO	Second entrance to FR 236 on left.
4.8 ▲	SO	Road on right is FR 236.
▼ 0.9	SO	Track on right is FR 132K.
4.0 ▲	SO	Track on left is FR 132K.
		GPS: N35°01.76′ W111°36.08′

▼ 1.2	SO	Track on left is FR 9487X.
3.7 ▲	SO	Track on right is FR 9487X.
▼ 1.8	SO	Track on left.
3.1 ▲	SO	Track on right.
▼ 2.3	SO	Track on right.

2.6 ▲	SO	Track on left.
▼ 2.7	BL	Well-used track on right.
2.2 ▲	BR	Well-used track on left.

GPS: N35°03.11′ W111°36.00′

▼ 3.1	SO	Cattle guard.
1.8 ▲	SO	Cattle guard.
▼ 3.2	SO	Track on left is FR 9483W.
1.7 ▲	SO	Track on right is FR 9483W.

GPS: N35°03.50′ W111°36.44′

▼ 3.8	SO	Track on left; then track on right.
1.1 ▲	SO	Track on left; then track on right.
▼ 4.1	SO	Track on left; then track on right.
0.8 ▲	SO	Track on left; then track on right.
▼ 4.9	TL	Graded road on right is FR 132D; also small track straight on. Zero trip meter.
0.0 ▲		Continue to the south, following the sign for Weimer Springs and Mormon Mountain.

GPS: N35°04.79′ W111°35.54′

▼ 0.0		Continue to the west, following the sign for Lake Mary Road and Flagstaff; graded road on right is FR 296A.
3.3 ▲	TR	Graded road on left is FR 296A; then 4-way intersection. Graded road ahead is FR 132D. Small track on left. Turn right, remaining on FR 132. Zero trip meter.
▼ 0.3	BR	Track on left is FR 235.
3.0 ▲	BL	Track on right is FR 235.

GPS: N35°05.01′ W111°35.71′

▼ 0.5	SO	Lake View Drive on right.
2.8 ▲	SO	Lake View Drive on left.
▼ 1.0	SO	Track on left.
2.3 ▲	SO	Track on right.
▼ 1.9	SO	Track on right.
1.4 ▲	SO	Track on left.
▼ 2.0	SO	Track on left.
1.3 ▲	SO	Track on right.
▼ 2.2	SO	Cattle guard.
1.1 ▲	SO	Cattle guard.
▼ 2.3	SO	Track on left.
1.0 ▲	SO	Track on right.
▼ 2.8	SO	Track on right; then road becomes paved.
0.5 ▲	SO	Road turns to graded dirt; then track on left.

GPS: N35°06.74′ W111°35.53′

▼ 3.2	SO	Graded road on right.
0.1 ▲	SO	Graded road on left.
▼ 3.3		Trail finishes at the intersection with Lake Mary Road. Turn left for Flagstaff; turn right for Mormon Lake.
0.0 ▲		Trail starts on the Lake Mary Road immediately north of mile marker 338. Zero trip meter and turn southwest on the graded primitive road, FR 132. Turn is not marked apart from a primitive road sign. There are mailboxes at the intersection.

GPS: N35°07.10′ W111°35.69′

NORTHEAST REGION TRAIL #32

Mormon to Kinnikinick Lakes Trail

STARTING POINT: Lake Mary Road at Mormon Lake
FINISHING POINT: Kinnikinick Lake
TOTAL MILEAGE: 8.7 miles
UNPAVED MILEAGE: 8.5 miles
DRIVING TIME: 45 minutes
ELEVATION RANGE: 7,100–7,300 feet
USUALLY OPEN: March to November
BEST TIME TO TRAVEL: March to November
DIFFICULTY RATING: 2
SCENIC RATING: 8
REMOTENESS RATING: +0

Special Attractions
- Kinnikinick Lake—trout fishing and camping.
- Mormon Lake—duck hunting in season.
- Mud Lake.
- Can be driven as a loop with Northeast #34: Long Lake Road and Northeast #33: Soldier and Kinnikinick Lakes Trail.

Description
This 2-rated trail is rough enough that a high-clearance vehicle is recommended to negotiate a few embedded rocks and vehicle ruts caused by wet-weather travel. It goes

from the paved Lake Mary Road at Mormon Lake to Kinnikinick Lake.

Mormon Lake, the largest natural lake in Arizona, encompasses more than 5,000 acres. Early in the 1900s, the lake was consistently deep enough for sailing, which became a popular activity. There was even a boat tour company. In 1924 the lake started to dry up, and now it is mostly dry. Some years it remains marshy enough to attract wildfowl, and it is a popular area for duck hunting. The small community of Mormon Lake sells gas and has a post office, country store, lodge, and restaurant.

At the end of the trail Kinnikinick Lake, which is stocked annually, is a popular spot for trout fishing. There is also a small national forest campground along the lake shore (fee area), which is open from May to October. From the lake, the trail winds through open forest, passing shallow Mud Lake, which is set just below the densely wooded and aptly named Pine Hill. Along the east side of Pine Hill, there are many shady campsites to be found.

Current Road Information

Coconino National Forest
Mormon Lake Ranger District
4373 South Lake Mary Rd.
Flagstaff, AZ 86001
(928) 774-1147

Map References

BLM   Sedona
USFS   Coconino National Forest:
       Mormon Lake Ranger District
USGS   1:24,000   Mormon Lake,
       Kinnikinick Lake
       1:100,000 Sedona
Maptech CD-ROM: Flagstaff/Sedona/Prescott
Arizona Atlas & Gazetteer, p. 42
Arizona Road & Recreation Atlas, pp. 35, 69
Recreational Map of Arizona

Route Directions

▼ 0.0   Trail commences at the intersection of FH 3 (Lake Mary Road) and FR 125 on the east side of Mormon Lake, 0.4 miles north of mile marker 316. Zero trip meter and turn southeast on paved

Mud Lake

Mormon Lake, now rarely more than marshland

FR 125, following the sign for
Kinnikinick Lake.

4.5 ▲ Trail ends at the T-intersection with FH
3 (Lake Mary Road) on the east side of
Mormon Lake. Turn left for Mormon
Lake; turn right for Flagstaff.
GPS: N34°55.50′ W111°25.82′

▼ 0.2 SO Cattle guard and seasonal closure
gate. Road turns to graded dirt.
4.3 ▲ SO Cattle guard and seasonal closure
gate. Road is now paved.
GPS: N34°55.39′ W111°25.77′

▼ 0.4 SO Track on left.
4.1 ▲ SO Track on right.
▼ 0.6 BL Small track on right goes to Wallace
Lake; then second track on right, FR
9483, over cattle guard.
3.9 ▲ BR Track on left over cattle guard is FR
9483; then second small track on left
goes to Wallace Lake.
GPS: N34°55.06′ W111°25.50′

▼ 0.8 SO Track on left.
3.7 ▲ SO Track on right.
▼ 1.4 SO Track on right is FR 104 and track on left.

3.1 ▲ SO Track on left is FR 104 and track
on right.
GPS: N34°55.29′ W111°24.82′

▼ 1.5 SO Cross over Ashurst Run.
3.0 ▲ SO Cross over Ashurst Run.
GPS: N34°55.36′ W111°24.72′

▼ 1.7 SO Cattle guard.
2.8 ▲ SO Cattle guard.
▼ 2.0 SO Track on left is FR 9117V.
2.5 ▲ SO Track on right is FR 9117V.
GPS: N34°55.61′ W111°24.19′

▼ 2.8 SO Track on right and track on left.
1.7 ▲ SO Track on right and track on left.
▼ 3.1 SO Track on left; then track on right.
1.4 ▲ SO Track on left; then track on right.
▼ 3.4 SO Track on right and left under power
lines. Track on left is closed to motorized vehicles from April 20 to June 15
to protect wildlife.
1.1 ▲ SO Track on right and left under power
lines. Track on right is closed to motorized vehicles from April 20 to June 15
to protect wildlife.
GPS: N34°56.10′ W111°22.75′

Northeast Trail #32: Mormon-to-Kinnikinick Lakes Trail

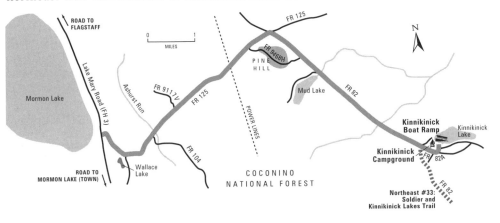

▼ 3.5   SO   Cattle guard.

1.0 ▲   SO   Cattle guard.

▼ 4.0   SO   Track on right is FR 9468H.

0.5 ▲   SO   Track on left is FR 9468H.
        GPS: N34°56.33' W111°22.32'

▼ 4.5   TR   Turn right onto FR 82, following the sign to Kinnikinick Lake. FR 125 continues ahead to Twin Arrows. Small track on left is closed to motorized vehicles from April 20 to June 15 to protect wildlife. Zero trip meter.

0.0 ▲   Continue to the southwest.
        GPS: N34°56.46' W111°21.72'

▼ 0.0   Continue to the southeast. Many small tracks on right and left for next 0.5 miles, mainly to campsites.

3.7 ▲   TL   Turn left onto FR 125, following the sign to Mormon Lake. FR 125 to the right goes to Twin Arrows. Small track ahead, which is closed to motorized vehicles from April 20 to June 15 to protect wildlife. Zero trip meter.

▼ 0.5   SO   Track on left.

3.2 ▲   SO   Track on right. Many small tracks on right and left for next 0.5 miles, mainly to campsites.

▼ 0.8   SO   Track on right. Pine Hill on the right.

2.9 ▲   SO   Track on left. Pine Hill on the left
        GPS: N34°55.95' W111°21.21'

▼ 1.0   SO   Cattle guard.

2.7 ▲   SO   Cattle guard.

▼ 1.2   SO   Track on right.

2.5 ▲   SO   Track on left.

▼ 1.3   SO   Cross over creek; then track on right. Pine Hill is the small, tree-covered hill to the northwest. Mud Lake on the right.

2.4 ▲   SO   Track on left; then cross over creek. Mud Lake on the left. Pine Hill is the small, tree-covered hill to the northwest.
        GPS: N34°55.51' W111°20.84'

▼ 2.1   SO   Track on left; then cattle guard.

1.6 ▲   SO   Cattle guard; then track on right.

▼ 2.9   SO   Track on left; then cross over creek.

0.8 ▲   SO   Cross over creek; then track on right.

▼ 3.3   SO   Track on left.

0.4 ▲   SO   Track on right.

▼ 3.7   SO   Cattle guard; then track on right is Northeast #33: Soldier and Kinnikinick Lakes Trail, FR 82. Zero trip meter.

0.0 ▲   Continue to the northwest and cross cattle guard.
        GPS: N34°53.84' W111°19.08'

▼ 0.0   Continue to the southeast toward Kinnikinick Lake; small track on left.

0.5 ▲   SO   Small track on right; then track on left is Northeast #33: Soldier and Kinnikinick Lakes Trail, FR 82. Zero trip meter.

▼ 0.3   BL   Small track on right; then second track on right.

0.2 ▲   BR   Track on left; then second smaller track on left.

▼ 0.4	SO	Track on right and Kinnikinick NFS Campground on the left.
0.1 ▲	SO	Kinnikinick NFS Campground on the right and track on left.
▼ 0.5		Trail ends at Kinnikinick Lake boat ramp. Return the way you came, or take Northeast #33: Soldier and Kinnikinick Lakes Trail to the south.
0.0 ▲		At Kinnikinick Lake boat ramp, zero trip meter and proceed south on the roughly graded road away from the lake. There is a picnic site at the end.

GPS: N34°53.82′ W111°18.66′

Soldier and Kinnikinick Lakes Trail

STARTING POINT: Long Lake, at the intersection with Northeast #34: Long Lake Road

FINISHING POINT: Kinnikinick Lake, at the intersection with Northeast #32: Mormon to Kinnikinick Lakes Trail

TOTAL MILEAGE: 9.4 miles

UNPAVED MILEAGE: 9.4 miles

DRIVING TIME: 1.5 hours

ELEVATION RANGE: 6,700–7,200 feet

USUALLY OPEN: March to December

BEST TIME TO TRAVEL: Dry weather

DIFFICULTY RATING: 3

SCENIC RATING: 7

REMOTENESS RATING: +0

Special Attractions

- Elk can often be seen grazing in the meadows.
- Trout fishing in the stocked waters of Kinnikinick and Soldier Lakes.
- Rough but scenic trail that crosses meadows.

Description

A rough but scenic trail that links two lakes best describes this route, which follows part of FR 82. It commences at the north end of Northeast #34: Long Lake Road, at Long Lake, and is a continuation of the graded, 1-rated road from Arizona 87. Although this trail shares the same forest route number as Long Lake Road, the similarity ends there. This trail crosses the rough plateau strewn with lava rocks to the north and is definitely not suitable for low-clearance or passenger vehicles. The trail leaves behind the expanse of Long Lake and passes around the top end of Soldier Lake. Although not directly visible from the main trail, Soldier Lake can be reached by driving 0.1 miles along a side trail. Fishermen can angle for bass and catfish there. Only boats powered by single electric motors are permitted on Soldier Lake.

Immediately past Soldier Lake, the route is extremely rocky and rough. Lava boulders and rocks make for a rough, slow ride as the trail winds its way along the side of Jaycox Mountain, which is more of a small rise than a mountain. However, it provides enough elevation for good views west over the Coconino National Forest to the Hutch Mountain area. This section of the trail is also the most vegetated as it meanders through junipers and pinyon pines. Jaycox Mountain is named after Henry H. Jaycox, a scout on two of King S. Woolsey's expeditions in 1864. He camped in a spot known as Jaycox Tank.

Once past Jaycox Mountain, the trail passes through more open country. Large grassy meadows, lightly scattered with pinyons and junipers, provide a very good chance of seeing elk herds that often come to the meadows to graze. The area north of Cow Lake is often fruitful. Elk also often come to drink at Kinnikinick Lake. This section of the trail, as it crosses the meadows, can be impassable and is best avoided in wet weather.

The trail finishes at Northeast #32: Mormon to Kinnikinick Lakes Trail, FR 82. Turn right onto the graded dirt road to go to Kinnikinick Lake (only 0.5 miles away), another good spot for catfish and trout fishing. There is a national forest campground at Kinnikinick Lake, which is open from May to October (fee required), and undeveloped campsites at Long Lake. These places are suggested for tent campers who might otherwise have a hard time finding a flat spot along the lava rock–studded trail.

Northeast Trail #33: Soldier and Kinnikinick Lakes Trail

Current Road Information
Coconino National Forest
Mogollon Rim Ranger District
HC 31 Box 300
Happy Jack, AZ 86024
(928) 477-2255

Map References
BLM   Sedona
USFS   Coconino National Forest: Blue
          Ridge Ranger District
USGS 1:24,000   Chavez Mtn. West,
          Jaycox Mtn., Kinnikinick Lake
          1:100,000 Sedona
Maptech CD-ROM: Flagstaff/Sedona/Prescott
Arizona Atlas & Gazetteer, p. 42
Arizona Road & Recreation Atlas, pp. 35, 69

Route Directions

▼ 0.0   From the northern end of Northeast
                 #34: Long Lake Road (at the northern
                 end of Long Lake), at the intersection
                 of FR 82 and the small FR 9719P, zero
                 trip meter and turn west on the more
                 frequently used FR 82. FR 82 is
                 unmarked at this point.

5.6 ▲   Trail ends at the north end of Long Lake
                 at the northern end of Northeast #34:
                 Long Lake Road. Continue on along FR
                 82 to connect with Arizona 87.
                 GPS: N34°48.04' W111°13.24'

▼ 0.1   SO   Cattle guard.
5.5 ▲   SO   Cattle guard.

▼ 0.9   SO   Track on left is FR 653, which goes 0.1
                 miles to Soldier Lake and on to Soldier
                 Annex Lake.
4.7 ▲   SO   Track on right is FR 653, which goes
                 0.1 miles to Soldier Lake and on to
                 Soldier Annex Lake.
                 GPS: N34°48.07' W111°14.17'

▼ 1.0   SO   Track on right is FR 126A to Crater
                 Lake. Continue on FR 82.
4.6 ▲   SO   Track on left is FR 126A to Crater Lake.
                 Continue on FR 82.
                 GPS: N34°48.08' W111°14.29'

▼ 1.2   SO   Stock tank on right.

The volcanic rock on the trail often makes a road rough

Kinnikinick Lake

4.4 ▲	SO	Stock tank on left.
▼ 1.4	SO	Well-used track on left.
4.2 ▲	SO	Well-used track on right.
▼ 1.8	SO	Cross through Sawmill Wash.
3.8 ▲	SO	Cross through Sawmill Wash.
		GPS: N34°48.42′ W111°15.05′

▼ 2.0	SO	Track on right.
3.6 ▲	SO	Track on left.
		GPS: N34°48.55′ W111°15.19′

▼ 2.3	SO	Stock tank on right.
3.3 ▲	SO	Stock tank on left.
▼ 3.3	SO	Well-used track on left.
2.3 ▲	SO	Well-used track on right.
		GPS: N34°49.31′ W111°16.24′

▼ 4.4	SO	Cattle guard. Views ahead to the San Francisco Peaks.
1.2 ▲	SO	Cattle guard.
		GPS: N34°50.01′ W111°16.92′

▼ 5.2	SO	Small track on right; then track on left.
0.4 ▲	SO	Track on right; then small track on left.
		GPS: N34°50.67′ W111°17.23′

▼ 5.6	BR	Bear right, remaining on FR 82. Track

on left is FR 82B. Zero trip meter. There is a seep at the intersection, which can be muddy.

0.0 ▲		Continue to the southeast.
		GPS: N34°50.88′ W111°17.45′

▼ 0.0		Continue to the north.
3.8 ▲	BL	Bear left, remaining on FR 82. Track on right is FR 82B. Zero trip meter. There is a seep at the intersection, which can be muddy.

▼ 0.3	SO	Track on right; then pass through wire gate.
3.5 ▲	SO	Pass through wire gate; then track on left.
		GPS: N34°51.15′ W111°17.48′

▼ 1.4	SO	Track on right.
2.4 ▲	SO	Track on left.
▼ 3.0	SO	The seasonal Cow Lake is on the right.
0.8 ▲	SO	The seasonal Cow Lake is on the left.
▼ 3.3	SO	Well-used track on left is FR 124.
0.5 ▲	SO	Well-used track on right is FR 124.
		GPS: N34°53.38′ W111°18.98′

▼ 3.4	SO	Cattle guard; then track on right.
0.4 ▲	SO	Track on left; then cattle guard.
▼ 3.8		Trail ends at the T-intersection of FR 82

and FR 82A, Northeast #32: Mormon to Kinnikinick Lakes Trail. Kinnikinick Lake is visible to the right, 0.5 miles down FR 82A.

0.0 ▲ Trail commences along Northeast #32: Mormon to Kinnikinick Lakes Trail at the intersection of FR 82 and FR 82A, 0.5 miles west of Kinnikinick NFS Campground. Immediately west of a cattle guard, zero trip meter and turn southeast on the formed trail, marked FR 82.

GPS: N34°53.84′ W111°19.08′

Long Lake Road

STARTING POINT: Arizona 87, 0.2 miles northeast of the Blue Ridge Ranger Station
FINISHING POINT: Northeast #33: Soldier and Kinnikinick Lakes Trail, at Long Lake
TOTAL MILEAGE: 16.2 miles
UNPAVED MILEAGE: 16.2 miles
DRIVING TIME: 1 hour
ELEVATION RANGE: 6,700–6,900 feet
USUALLY OPEN: April to October
BEST TIME TO TRAVEL: Dry weather
DIFFICULTY RATING: 1
SCENIC RATING: 7
REMOTENESS RATING: +0

Special Attractions
■ Varied fishing opportunities at Long and Soldier Annex Lakes.
■ Easy scenic trail passing through the open forest on the Mogollon Plateau.
■ Undeveloped camping at Long Lake.

Description
The trail to Long Lake travels along a graded dirt road through a pinyon-juniper forest and meadows in the Coconino National Forest. The trail is easygoing for the most part, with only a couple of slightly rough patches. In dry weather, it is suitable for a passenger vehicle. In wet weather, the dirt sections crossing meadows can become difficult even for 4WD vehicles.

The trail crosses through Jacks Canyon at a more gentle gradient and at a less dramatic place than Northeast #35: Chavez Draw Trail, but it is pretty nevertheless. There are many smaller trails to explore off the main trail. One of the nicest is the Chavez Draw Trail which follows a formed road down Chavez Draw to Arizona 87.

Long Lake at the end of the trail is a popular spot for trout fishing. Periodically, the lake is stocked with trout, and fishermen can also catch bass and catfish. There are some primitive campsites spread along the lakeshore as well as a boat ramp. The smaller Soldier Annex Lake on the west side of the trail is reached by a rocky high-clearance road. This lake is not stocked with trout, but there is fishing for catfish and bluegill. The third lake of the group is the smallest—Soldier Lake, which is a short distance farther on, just off Northeast #33: Soldier and Kinnikinick Lakes Trail. Only boats powered by single electric motors are allowed on Soldier and Soldier Annex Lakes.

Most years this area of the Coconino National Forest can receive up to 100 inches of snow, causing the closure of forest roads and trails. Exact closure dates depend on snowfall, and the trails can be open past the date given above.

Current Road Information
Coconino National Forest
Mogollon Rim Ranger District
HC 31 Box 300
Happy Jack, AZ 86024
(928) 477-2255

Map References
BLM   Sedona
USFS   Coconino National Forest: Blue
         Ridge Ranger District
USGS   1:24,000   Blue Ridge Reservoir,
         Hay Lake, Chavez Mtn. West
         1:100,000 Sedona
Maptech CD-ROM: Flagstaff/Sedona/Prescott
Arizona Atlas & Gazetteer, p. 42
Arizona Road & Recreation Atlas, pp. 41, 75
Recreational Map of Arizona

Jacks Canyon

Route Directions

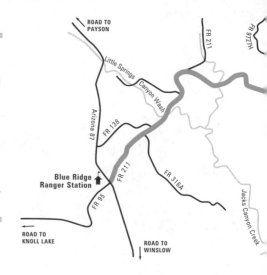

▼ 0.0   From Arizona 87, 0.2 miles northeast of the Blue Ridge Ranger Station, zero trip meter and turn west on the graded gravel road, FR 211, marked to Long Lake. The turn is opposite FR 95 to Knoll Lake.

3.0 ▲   Trail ends at the intersection with Arizona 87. Turn right for Payson; turn left for Winslow. The Blue Ridge Ranger Station is 0.2 miles to the right.

GPS: N34°36.80′ W111°11.18′

▼ 0.1   SO   Track on right to county work station.
2.9 ▲   SO   Track on left to county work station.
▼ 0.2   SO   Cattle guard and work station on right.
2.8 ▲   SO   Cattle guard and work station on left.
▼ 1.3   SO   Track on right is FR 316A.
1.7 ▲   SO   Track on left is FR 316A.
▼ 1.4   SO   Arizona Hiking Trail crosses the road.
1.6 ▲   SO   Arizona Hiking Trail crosses the road.

GPS: N34°37.43′ W111°12.45′

▼ 1.5   SO   Track on left is FR 138.
1.5 ▲   SO   Track on right is FR 138.

GPS: N34°37.49′ W111°12.52′

▼ 1.7   SO   Cross through Little Springs Canyon wash.
1.3 ▲   SO   Cross through Little Springs Canyon wash.
▼ 2.4   SO   Track on right is FR 9726J; then track on left.

Long Lake, popular with fisherman

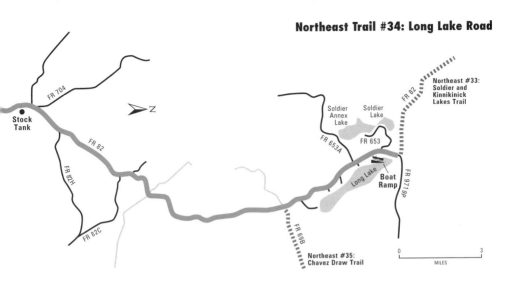

0.6 ▲	SO	Track on right; then track on left is FR 9726J.	
		GPS: N34°38.02' W111°13.27'	

▼ 2.6 SO Track on right.
0.4 ▲ SO Track on left.
▼ 2.9 SO Track on left.
0.1 ▲ SO Track on right.
▼ 3.0 BR Graded road ahead is FR 211 to FH 3. Bear right onto FR 82, following the sign for Long Lake. Zero trip meter.
0.0 ▲ Continue to the southeast.
GPS: N34°37.94' W111°13.84'

▼ 0.0 Continue to the north.
6.4 ▲ TL Graded road on right is FR 211 to FH 3. Turn left onto FR 211. Zero trip meter.
▼ 0.8 SO Track on left; then cross through Jacks Canyon Creek.
5.6 ▲ SO Cross through Jacks Canyon Creek; then track on right.
GPS: N34°38.66' W111°13.59'

▼ 1.2 SO Track on right to campsite.
5.2 ▲ SO Track on left to campsite.
▼ 1.5 SO Arizona Hiking Trail crosses road.
4.9 ▲ SO Arizona Hiking Trail crosses road.
GPS: N34°39.18' W111°13.98'

▼ 1.7 SO Cattle guard.
4.7 ▲ SO Cattle guard.

▼ 2.3 SO Track on left is FR 9727H.
4.1 ▲ SO Track on right is FR 9727H.
GPS: N34°39.63' W111°13.58'

▼ 3.4 SO Stock tank on right.
3.0 ▲ SO Stock tank on left.
▼ 3.6 SO Track on right and small track on left.
2.8 ▲ SO Track on left and small track on right.
▼ 3.7 SO Track on left is FR 704.
2.7 ▲ SO Track on right is second entrance to FR 704.
GPS: N34°40.82' W111°13.70'

▼ 3.8 SO Track on left is second entrance to FR 704.
2.6 ▲ SO Track on right is FR 704.
▼ 4.1 SO Track on right.
2.3 ▲ SO Track on left.
▼ 4.3 SO Track on right.
2.1 ▲ SO Track on left.
▼ 4.5 SO Track on right is FR 82H.
1.9 ▲ SO Track on left is FR 82H.
GPS: N34°41.37' W111°13.25'

▼ 4.8 SO Track on left.
1.6 ▲ SO Track on right.
▼ 4.9 SO Cattle guard; then track on left.
1.5 ▲ SO Track on right; then cattle guard.
▼ 5.0 SO Track on right.
1.4 ▲ SO Track on left.
▼ 5.7 SO Cattle guard.
0.7 ▲ SO Cattle guard.

▼ 6.2   SO Track on right is FR 82C.

0.2 ▲   SO Track on left is FR 82C.
         GPS: N34°42.66' W111°12.26'

▼ 6.4   TR Road ahead goes to Hay Lake Ranch.
             Zero trip meter.

0.0 ▲   Continue to the southeast on FR 82.
             GPS: N34°42.88' W111°12.37'

▼ 0.0   Continue to the northeast on FR 82.

3.9 ▲   TL Road on right goes to Hay Lake Ranch.
             Zero trip meter.

▼ 0.3   SO Cattle guard.

3.6 ▲   SO Cattle guard.

▼ 0.6   SO Track on right is FR 9718G; then cross
             over creek. Route number is hard to
             read and may be incorrect.

3.3 ▲   SO Cross over creek; then track on left is
             FR 9718G. Route number is hard to
             read and may be incorrect.
             GPS: N34°43.25' W111°11.93'

▼ 0.7   SO Cattle guard; then track on right.

3.2 ▲   SO Track on left; then cattle guard.

▼ 1.6   SO Track on right is FR 9718N.

2.3 ▲   SO Track on left is FR 9718N.

▼ 2.4   SO Track on right.

1.5 ▲   SO Track on left.

▼ 2.8   SO Track on left; then cattle guard.

1.1 ▲   SO Cattle guard; then track on right.

▼ 3.9   SO Track on right is Northeast #35:
             Chavez Draw Trail, FR 69B. Small track
             on left. Zero trip meter.

0.0 ▲   Continue to the southeast toward
             Arizona 87.
             GPS: N34°45.93' W111°11.90'

▼ 0.0   Continue to the northwest toward
             Long Lake.

2.9 ▲   SO Track on left is Northeast #35: Chavez
             Draw Trail, FR 69B. Small track on
             right. Zero trip meter.

▼ 0.4   SO Track on right is marked by a faded for-
             est route marker.

2.5 ▲   SO Track on left is marked by a faded for-
             est route marker.

▼ 0.7   SO Track on left.

2.2 ▲   SO Track on right.

▼ 1.0   SO Track on right goes to shore of Long
             Lake where there is parking and a cou-

ple of campsites.

1.9 ▲   SO Track on left goes to shore of Long
             Lake where there is parking and a cou-
             ple of campsites.
             GPS: N34°46.68' W111°12.38'

▼ 1.1   SO Track on right.

1.8 ▲   SO Track on left.

▼ 1.4   SO Track on right.

1.5 ▲   SO Track on left.

▼ 1.8   SO Track on left is FR 653A, which goes
             0.5 miles to Soldier Annex Lake.

1.1 ▲   SO Track on right is FR 653A, which goes
             0.5 miles to Soldier Annex Lake.
             GPS: N34°47.19' W111°13.01'

▼ 1.9   SO Track on right to camping area by Long
             Lake and boat ramp.

1.0 ▲   SO Track on left to camping area by Long
             Lake and boat ramp.

▼ 2.1   SO Track on right to lakeside. There are
             many small tracks on right to lakeside
             for next 0.8 miles.

0.8 ▲   SO Track on left to lakeside.

▼ 2.4   SO Cross through wash.

0.5 ▲   SO Cross through wash.

▼ 2.6   SO Track on left is FR 653 to Soldier Lake.

0.3 ▲   SO Track on right is FR 653 to Soldier Lake.
             GPS: N34°47.78' W111°13.37'

▼ 2.9   Trail ends at the intersection of FR
             9719P and FR 82, Northeast #33:
             Soldier and Kinnikinick Lakes Trail, at
             the north end of Long Lake. Turn left to
             follow the 3-rated Soldier and
             Kinnikinick Lakes Trail.

0.0 ▲   Trail commences on FR 82 at the north
             end of Long Lake, at the intersection of
             Northeast #33: Soldier and Kinnikinick
             Lakes Trail, FR 82, and the smaller FR
             9719P. Zero trip meter and proceed
             south down the roughly graded dirt
             road that runs along the west side of
             Long Lake. For the next 0.8 miles there
             are many small tracks on the left that
             lead to the lakeshore.
             GPS: N34°48.04' W111°13.24'

Chavez Draw Trail

STARTING POINT: Arizona 87, 4.7 miles south of the northern Coconino National Forest boundary, 0.2 miles south of mile marker 311

FINISHING POINT: Northeast #34: Long Lake Road, 2 miles south of Long Lake

TOTAL MILEAGE: 9 miles

UNPAVED MILEAGE: 9 miles

DRIVING TIME: 1 hour

ELEVATION RANGE: 6,200–6,700 feet

USUALLY OPEN: Year-round

BEST TIME TO TRAVEL: Dry weather in spring and fall

DIFFICULTY RATING: 3

SCENIC RATING: 8

REMOTENESS RATING: +0

Special Attractions

■ Scenic Jacks Canyon.

■ Moderate trail providing access to Long, Soldier, and Soldier Annex Lakes.

History

This trail follows a short section of what is known as the Palatkwapi Trail. The name is derived from a Hopi word meaning "red land to the south," a description of the area from which a number of their people came before they settled on the Hopi Mesas. The trail, which runs from Montezuma Castle and the Verde Valley to the Hopi Mesas, was used primarily as a trading route. Pottery, cotton, and parrots from the south were common trade items. Later, the trail was used by Antonio de Espejo, a Spanish explorer who was searching for gold. In 1863, Lt. Col. J. Francisco Chavez, who guided the Arizona territorial governor's party to Prescott, traveled along part of the Palatkwapi Trail on his return trip. Chavez Draw and Chavez Pass are named after him. In 1950, highway construction engineers searching for the best route for the new freeway, I-17, picked a similar route down the Mogollon Rim.

Description

Jacks Canyon is one of a number of canyons that cuts deep paths across the Mogollon Plateau. Chavez Draw drains into Jacks Canyon, and this trail follows the path of much of Chavez Draw. The trail leaves Arizona 87 a few miles south of the north boundary of the Coconino National Forest and travels as a rough formed trail that quickly descends into the scenic and rugged Jacks Canyon. It leaves the canyon, traveling alongside Chavez Draw and crossing it often in the next few miles.

The trail is impassable following heavy rain because of the long sections of deep, red mud at the higher end of Chavez Draw. It is best to avoid the trail when wet. Not only are you very likely to get stuck but you are also likely to damage the track and surrounding meadows and vegetation.

Once past the intersection with the Chavez Pass Road, the trail standard gradually improves until it is a roughly graded dirt road. It finishes at Northeast #34: Long Lake Road, immediately south of Long Lake.

Current Road Information

Coconino National Forest
Mogollon Rim Ranger District
HC 31 Box 300
Happy Jack, AZ 86024
(928) 477-2255

Map References

BLM   Sedona
USFS   Coconino National Forest: Blue Ridge Ranger District
USGS   1:24,000   Quayle Hill, Chavez Mtn. East, Chavez Mtn. West
       1:100,000 Sedona
Maptech CD-ROM: Flagstaff/Sedona/Prescott
Arizona Atlas & Gazetteer, pp. 43, 42
Arizona Road & Recreation Atlas, pp. 41, 75
Recreational Map of Arizona

Route Directions

▼ 0.0   From Arizona 87, 32 miles south of Winslow, 4.7 miles south of the national forest boundary, 0.2 miles

A bumpy descent into Jacks Canyon caused by the large, embedded rocks

Northeast Trail #35: Chavez Draw Trail

south of mile marker 311, zero trip meter and turn west on roughly formed dirt road marked FR 69 to Chavez Pass and Long Lake.

5.4 ▲ Trail ends on Arizona 87, 32 miles south of Winslow.
GPS: N34°43.08' W111°05.36'

▼ 0.1 BR Track on right; then immediately bear right, remaining on the main rocky trail.

5.3 ▲ BL Bear left, remaining on the main rocky trail; then track on left.

▼ 0.2 SO Track on left.

5.2 ▲ SO Track on right.
GPS: N34°43.28' W111°05.46'

▼ 1.0 SO Track on left.

4.4 ▲ SO Track on right.

▼ 1.2 SO Trail forks; take either one.

4.2 ▲ SO Trails rejoin.

▼ 1.4 SO Trails rejoin.

4.0 ▲ SO Trail forks; take either one.

▼ 1.5 SO Lumpy descent into Jacks Canyon.

3.9 ▲ SO Trail exits Jacks Canyon.

▼ 1.6 SO Track on left.

3.8 ▲ SO Track on right.

▼ 1.7 SO Cross through Jacks Canyon Wash.

3.7 ▲ SO Cross through Jacks Canyon Wash.
GPS: N34°44.46' W111°05.41'

▼ 1.8 SO Cattle guard; then cross through Chavez Draw; then track on right. Jacks Canyon leaves on right. Trail now follows Chavez Draw.

3.6 ▲ SO Track on left; then cross through Chavez Draw. Jacks Canyon leaves on left; then cattle guard.

▼ 2.2 SO Cross through Chavez Draw.

3.2 ▲ SO Cross through Chavez Draw.

▼ 2.3 SO Cross through wash.

3.1 ▲ SO Cross through wash.

▼ 2.4 SO Cross through wash.

3.0 ▲ SO Cross through wash.

▼ 2.5 SO Faint track on left.

2.9 ▲ SO Faint track on right.

▼ 2.6 SO Cross through wash.

2.8 ▲ SO Cross through wash.

▼ 2.8 SO Cross through wash.

2.6 ▲ SO Cross through wash.

▼ 3.4 SO Cross through wash.

2.0 ▲ SO Cross through wash.

▼ 3.5 SO Track on right is FR 9729.

1.9 ▲ SO Track on left is FR 9729.
GPS: N34°45.28' W111°07.00'

▼ 3.7 SO Chavez Draw Tank on left; then track on left is FR 9722M (sign is obliterated and hard to read).

1.7 ▲ SO Track on right is FR 9722M (sign is obliterated and hard to read). Chavez Draw Tank on right.
GPS: N34°45.42' W111°07.12'

▼ 4.1 SO Cross through Chavez Draw.

1.3 ▲ SO Cross through Chavez Draw.

▼ 4.3 BR Track on left is FR 9721H.

1.1 ▲ SO Track on right is FR 9721H.
GPS: N34°45.92' W111°07.38'

▼ 4.5	SO	Track on right is FR 9710A.
0.9 ▲	SO	Track on left is FR 9710A.

GPS: N34°46.01' W111°07.48'

▼ 4.7	SO	Track on left.
0.7 ▲	BL	Track on right.
▼ 5.3	SO	Entering motor travel restricted area at sign—travel only on designated roads.
0.1 ▲	SO	Leaving motor travel restricted area at sign.

GPS: N34°46.39' W111°08.26'

▼ 5.4	BL	Equally used track on right is FR 69. Bear left on FR 69B and zero trip meter.
0.0 ▲		Continue to the southeast.

GPS: N34°46.44' W111°08.34'

▼ 0.0		Continue to the northwest.
3.6 ▲	SO	Equally used track on left is second entrance to FR 69. Keep straight on and zero trip meter.
▼ 0.1	SO	Cross through Chavez Draw.
3.5 ▲	SO	Cross through Chavez Draw.
▼ 0.2	TL	T-intersection. Turn left and cross cattle guard, remaining on FR 69B. Track on right joins FR 69.
3.4 ▲	TR	Cattle guard; then turn right, remaining on FR 69B. Track ahead is first entrance to FR 69.

GPS: N34°46.46' W111°08.51'

▼ 0.3	SO	Cattle guard.
3.3 ▲	SO	Cattle guard.
▼ 0.4	SO	Leaving motor travel restricted area.
3.2 ▲	SO	Entering motor travel restricted area at sign—travel only on designated roads.
▼ 1.5	SO	Roadside Tank on left.
2.1 ▲	SO	Roadside Tank on right.

GPS: N34°46.42' W111°09.89'

▼ 1.8	SO	Track on right is FR 69G.
1.8 ▲	SO	Track on left is FR 69G.
▼ 2.1	SO	Track on left is FR 69F.
1.5 ▲	SO	Track on right is FR 69F.

GPS: N34°46.46' W111°10.48'

▼ 2.5	SO	Track on left.
1.1 ▲	SO	Track on right.
▼ 2.7	SO	Track on right; then cross over Chavez Pass Ditch.
0.9 ▲	SO	Cross over Chavez Pass Ditch; then track on left.

GPS: N34°46.24' W111°11.11'

▼ 2.9	SO	Small track on right.
0.7 ▲	SO	Small track on left.
▼ 3.0	SO	Track on right is FR 9724N and small track on left.
0.6 ▲	SO	Track on left is FR 9724N and small track on right.

GPS: N34°46.10' W111°11.38'

▼ 3.6		Trail ends at the intersection with Northeast #34: Long Lake Road, FR 82. Turn left to exit to Arizona 87 along graded gravel road; turn right to continue to Long Lake. Small track continues straight on.
0.0 ▲		Trail commences at the intersection of Northeast #34: Long Lake Road, FR 82, and FR 69B, 2 miles south of Long Lake and 15 miles north of Arizona 87. Zero trip meter and turn northeast on graded dirt road, following the sign to Chavez Pass.

GPS: N34°45.93' W111°11.90'

NORTHEAST REGION TRAIL #36

The Mogollon Rim Road

STARTING POINT: Arizona 87, 0.1 miles east of mile marker 281

FINISHING POINT: Arizona 260, opposite the Mogollon Rim Visitor Center

TOTAL MILEAGE: 41.3 miles

UNPAVED MILEAGE: 38.1 miles

DRIVING TIME: 3 hours

ELEVATION RANGE: 7,200–7,900 feet

USUALLY OPEN: April to October

BEST TIME TO TRAVEL: April to October

DIFFICULTY RATING: 1

SCENIC RATING: 9

REMOTENESS RATING: +0

Special Attractions

- Trail follows part of the historic route of the General George Crook Trail.
- Spectacular views of the rocky Mogollon Rim and the panoramic views to the south.
- Excellent, cool country camping opportunities.
- Access to many backcountry vehicle and hiking trails.

History

The present-day Mogollon Rim Road follows much of the original route put through by General George Crook as a military supply route to connect Fort Whipple at Prescott to Fort Apache and Camp Verde. The trail was constructed in 1872 as a wagon road and has been upgraded several times since. Fort Whipple and Fort Apache were established to protect settlers in the region against the frequent attacks by Apaches. The Apache were hunters and gatherers who resisted the takeover of their lands and efforts to confine them to the reservations. Far more skilled than the settlers at living in the trackless wilderness, they launched many successful surprise attacks.

General Crook arrived in Arizona Territory in 1871 as commander of the Army. His original journey from Fort Apache to Fort Whipple was the basis of the trail constructed in 1872. When completed, the trail was only the third major route constructed in northern Arizona. Today, a few old trees and rocks still bear the marks of the original blazes, which indicated the mileage along the trail. Many landmarks are named according to the mileage, such as Thirteen Mile Rock and Twentynine Mile Lake. Today the trail is popular for hiking and is well marked with cream and orange chevrons.

Approximately 15 miles from the western end and a short distance to the north of the main trail is the site of General Springs Cabin. The small wooden cabin, built between 1914 and 1915 by Louis Fisher, was used for many years as a guard station. It sits beside springs used by General Crook and reputedly was the spot at which he had a very narrow escape from the Apaches. The cabin, restored in 1989, is now listed as a historic site. Camping is prohibited in the immediate area around the cabin, but it makes for an exceedingly pretty picnic spot.

Opposite the turn to the cabin is the start of the Tunnel Hiking Trail. This trail leads down to the top of an ambitious project—a tunnel intended to burrow through the rock of the Mogollon Rim to connect the large town of Flagstaff to the rich mines of Globe. The Atlantic & Pacific Railroad already ran through Flagstaff in 1886 en route to the Pacific coast from Albuquerque. A proposal for the 160-mile Mineral Belt Railroad to Globe was floated and construction started through some incredibly rough terrain. The tunnel, situated at the mouth of General Springs Canyon, a low point in the rim, was to have been bored 3,100 feet through the rim. However, the promoters ran out of money after laying 40 miles of track and after tunneling only 70 feet into the rim.

Description

The Mogollon (pronounced "muggy-own") Rim is a 200-mile-long escarpment that cuts across the middle of Arizona, separating the lower desert country from the ponderosa pine and cedar forests of the higher elevations, and the scorching desert climate from the cooler, temperate zones. This "backbone of Arizona" forms the southern edge of the Colorado Plateau that extends to the north and east into Utah and New Mexico and is the result of a fault line that uplifted approximately 15 to 20 million years ago. It is named after Juan Ignacio Flores Mogollon, who was the governor of New Mexico from 1712 to 1715. Subsequent volcanic activity has deposited lava over the plateau and parts of the rim. Every summer, thousands of people from Phoenix and the south escape to the cooler climes above the rim.

The first part of the Rim Road—a national recreation route—follows a section of the General Crook Trail, which was blazed by Crook in the 1870s. The trail is a narrow graded gravel and dirt road for its entire length and although uneven in places, when it is dry it is suitable for a carefully driven

General Springs Cabin

passenger vehicle. Most of the trail runs through a cool ponderosa pine forest. There are many places along its length when it runs right at the edge of the rim, giving excellent views not only of the rugged rim itself but down to the lower elevations. Take care if you walk out on the edge of the rim, especially in wet conditions. Some of the trees at the edge carry memorial plaques to those who accidentally fell.

Backcountry campsites abound; some of the best are set under large pine trees right on the edge of the rim. One of the best is at Hi-View Point, an exceptionally beautiful scenic overlook set right on the rim. There are also developed national forest campgrounds at Kehl Spring, just off the trail at Knoll Lake, Bear Canyon Lake, several sites at Woods Canyon Lake, and along the final couple of miles of the trail.

Many smaller vehicle trails lead from the main rim road. Many to the south lead to additional, more secluded viewpoints and campsites on the rim. To the north, there are graded roads that will take a passenger vehicle back to Arizona 87 and smaller 4WD trails that lead to equally spectacular scenery.

Other sites worth seeing just off the main trail include the General Springs Cabin, a restored forest service cabin set on the edge of a flat grassy area next to General Springs. This area makes an excellent picnic spot. A passenger vehicle can negotiate the 0.4-mile spur to the cabin with care. Knoll Lake, Bear Canyon Lake, and Woods Canyon Lake are all just a few miles from the trail.

The eastern end of the trail within the Apache-Sitgreaves National Forest runs within the popular Rim Lakes Recreation Area. Inside this area, motorized travel is permitted on numbered roads only, ATVs are not permitted, and camping restrictions apply. In much of the area, camping is only permitted at designated backcountry campsites or developed campgrounds. The trail finishes on Arizona 260, opposite the Mogollon Rim Visitor Center.

The trail is closed each winter because of snow, but the dates are dependent on snowfall.

Most years it is closed for a shorter period of time than the approximate dates given above.

Current Road Information

Coconino National Forest
Mogollon Rim Ranger District
HC 31 Box 300
Happy Jack, AZ 86024
(928) 477-2255

Apache-Sitgreaves National Forest
Black Mesa Ranger District
PO Box 968
Overgaard, AZ 85933
(928) 535-4481

Map References

BLM   Payson, Show Low
USFS   Coconino National Forest: Long Valley and Blue Ridge Ranger Districts; Apache-Sitgreaves National Forest: Chevelon Ranger District (also shown on Tonto National Forest)
USGS 1:24,000 Pine, Kehl Ridge, Dane Canyon, Knoll Lake, Promontory Butte, Woods Canyon
     1:100,000 Payson, Show Low
Maptech CD-ROM: Flagstaff/Sedona/Prescott; East Central Arizona/White Mountains
Arizona Atlas & Gazetteer, pp. 50, 51
Arizona Road & Recreation Atlas, pp. 41, 75
Recreational Map of Arizona

Route Directions

▼ 0.0   From Arizona 87, 0.1 miles east of mile marker 281, 2.5 miles east of the intersection with Arizona 260, zero trip meter and turn southeast on FR 300 at the sign for Rim Road and Knoll Lake. Immediately cross cattle guard and continue on graded gravel road and pass Baker Lake on right.

3.4 ▲   Pass Baker Lake on left; then cattle guard; then trail finishes at the intersection with Arizona 87. Turn right for Winslow; turn left for Pine.

GPS: N34°27.31′ W111°23.75′

Northeast Trail #36: The Mogollon Rim Road

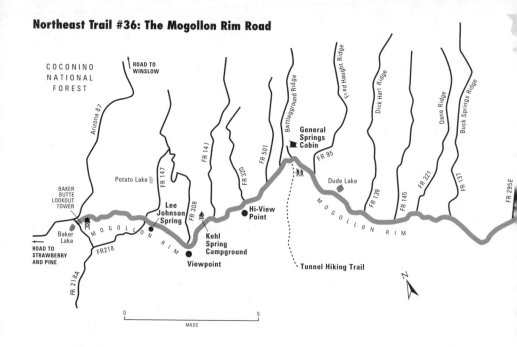

▼ 0.1   TL   Track ahead is FR 218A to Milk Ranch Point; small track on right. Turn left onto FR 300, following the sign for the Rim Road and Knoll Lake.

3.3 ▲   TR   Track on left is FR 218A to Milk Ranch Point; small track ahead. Turn right toward Arizona 87.

▼ 1.3   SO   Track on right to lookout tower; then track on left.

2.1 ▲   SO   Track on right; then track on left to lookout tower.
     GPS: N34°27.22′ W111°22.80′

▼ 1.7   SO   Track on left.
1.7 ▲   SO   Track on right.
▼ 1.8   SO   Track on right.
1.6 ▲   SO   Track on left.
▼ 2.1   SO   Cattle guard.
1.3 ▲   SO   Cattle guard.
▼ 2.2   SO   Track on right.
1.2 ▲   SO   Track on left.
▼ 2.3   SO   Track on left.
1.1 ▲   SO   Track on right.
▼ 2.4   SO   Track on left.
1.0 ▲   SO   Track on right.
▼ 2.6   SO   Track on left and track on right.
0.8 ▲   SO   Track on left and track on right.

▼ 2.9   SO   Track on left and track on right.
0.5 ▲   SO   Track on left and track on right.
▼ 3.2   SO   Track on right; then track on left.
0.2 ▲   SO   Track on right; then track on left.
▼ 3.4   SO   Cross roads. Graded road on right is FR 218; graded road on left is FR 147 to Potato Lake. Zero trip meter.

0.0 ▲   Continue to the west on FR 300, following the sign for Arizona 87.
     GPS: N34°26.75′ W111°21.04′

▼ 0.0   Continue to the east on FR 300, following the sign to Knoll Lake and Kehl Spring.

3.6 ▲   SO   Cross roads. Graded road on left is FR 218; graded road on right is FR 147 to Potato Lake. Zero trip meter.

▼ 0.3   SO   Cattle guard; then Lee Johnson Spring on right; track on right into spring.

3.3 ▲   SO   Lee Johnson Spring on left; track on left into spring; then cattle guard.
     GPS: N34°26.50′ W111°20.87′

▼ 0.9   SO   Track on left and track on right.
2.7 ▲   SO   Track on left and track on right.
▼ 1.7   SO   Track on right. Trail enters previously logged area.
1.9 ▲   SO   Track on left.

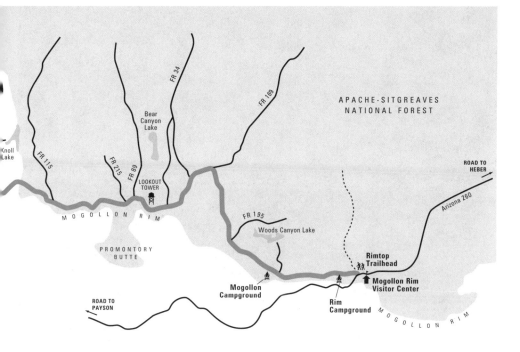

<table>
<tr><td>▼ 1.8</td><td>SO</td><td>Track on right.</td></tr>
<tr><td>1.8 ▲</td><td>SO</td><td>Track on left.</td></tr>
</table>

▼ 1.8   SO   Track on right.
1.8 ▲   SO   Track on left.
▼ 1.9   SO   Track on left is FR 308 to Potato Lake. Track on right goes out to a viewpoint along the rim. Continue on, following the sign to Kehl Spring.
1.7 ▲   SO   Track on right is FR 308 to Potato Lake. Track on left goes out to a viewpoint along the rim. Continue on, following the sign to Arizona 87. This viewpoint gives an excellent unobscured view of the rocky rim.

GPS: N34°25.56′ W111°19.81′

▼ 2.0   SO   View on right over rim.
1.6 ▲   SO   View on left over rim.
▼ 2.1   SO   Track on right.
1.5 ▲   SO   Track on left.
▼ 2.3   SO   Track on right.
1.3 ▲   SO   Track on left.
▼ 2.7   SO   Track on right.
0.9 ▲   SO   Track on left.
▼ 3.1   SO   Kehl Spring on left; then Kehl Spring Campground on left.
0.5 ▲   SO   Kehl Spring Campground on right; then Kehl Spring on right.

GPS: N34°26.09′ W111°18.97′

▼ 3.3   SO   Track on left.
0.3 ▲   SO   Track on right.
▼ 3.6   SO   Graded road on left is FR 141; small track on right. Zero trip meter.
0.0 ▲   Continue to the northwest on FR 300, following sign to Baker Butte Lookout.

GPS: N34°26.22′ W111°18.51′

▼ 0.0   Continue to the southeast on FR 300, following sign to Knoll Lake.
4.4 ▲   SO   Graded road on right is FR 141; small track on left. Zero trip meter.
▼ 0.1   SO   Track on left.
4.3 ▲   SO   Track on right.
▼ 0.2   SO   Track on right.
4.2 ▲   SO   Track on left.
▼ 0.4   SO   Track on left and track on right.
4.0 ▲   SO   Track on left and track on right.
▼ 1.2   SO   Excellent large campsite on right on edge of rim. This is Hi-View Point.
3.2 ▲   SO   Excellent large campsite on left on edge of rim. This is Hi-View Point.

GPS: N34°26.23′ W111°17.59′

▼ 1.7   SO   Track on left is FR 320.
2.7 ▲   SO   Track on right is FR 320.

A rock precipice along the Mogollon Rim

▼ 2.6   SO   Track on right.
1.8 ▲   SO   Track on left.
▼ 2.8   SO   Cattle guard; then track on left is FR 501.
1.6 ▲   SO   Track on right is FR 501; then cattle guard.

GPS: N34°26.73' W111°16.20'

▼ 2.9   SO   Track on right.
1.5 ▲   SO   Track on left.
▼ 3.0   SO   Track on right.
1.4 ▲   SO   Track on left.
▼ 3.1   SO   Track on left.
1.3 ▲   SO   Track on right.
▼ 3.6   SO   Graded road on left is FR 123 to Battleground Ridge and Battleground Monument.
0.8 ▲   SO   Graded road on right is FR 123 to Battleground Ridge and Battleground Monument.

GPS: N34°27.10' W111°15.53'

▼ 3.8   SO   Track on right.
0.6 ▲   SO   Track on left.

▼ 4.1   SO   Track on right.
0.3 ▲   SO   Track on left.
▼ 4.4   SO   Track on left goes 0.4 miles to General Springs Cabin and is also the Arizona Trail and Fred Haught Hiking Trail #22. Small track on right is start of Tunnel Hiking Trail and Colonel Devin Trail #290 also on right. Historical marker at the intersection for Battle of Big Dry Wash. Zero trip meter.
0.0 ▲   Continue to the south.

GPS: N34°27.23' W111°14.99'

▼ 0.0   Continue to the north.
4.1 ▲   SO   Track on right goes 0.4 miles to General Springs Cabin and is also the Arizona Trail and Fred Haught Hiking Trail #22. Track on left rejoins and is start of Tunnel Hiking Trail and Colonel Devin Trail #290 also on left. Historical marker at the intersection for Battle of Big Dry Wash. Zero trip meter.
▼ 0.2   SO   Track on right rejoins.
3.9 ▲   SO   Small track on left.
▼ 0.7   SO   Track on left is FR 393; then track on right.

Overlooking Dude Creek, site of the 1990 wildfire, one of Arizona's worst yet

3.4 ▲   SO   Track on left; then track on right is FR 393.
GPS: N34°26.85' W111°14.51'

▼ 1.0   SO   Graded road on left is FR 95 to Fred Haught Ridge and Arizona 87.
3.1 ▲   SO   Graded road on right is FR 95 to Fred Haught Ridge and Arizona 87.
GPS: N34°26.67' W111°14.30'

▼ 1.1   SO   Track on left is FR 398 and track on right.
3.0 ▲   SO   Track on right is FR 398 and track on left.
▼ 2.0   SO   Cattle guard.
2.1 ▲   SO   Cattle guard.
▼ 2.3   SO   Track on left.
1.8 ▲   SO   Track on right.
▼ 2.5   SO   Track on left to Dude Lake, just off the main trail.
1.6 ▲   SO   Track on right to Dude Lake, just off the main trail.
GPS: N34°25.80' W111°13.60'

▼ 3.9   SO   Houston Brothers Hiking Trail #171 on left.
0.2 ▲   SO   Houston Brothers Hiking Trail #171 on right.
GPS: N34°25.15' W111°12.92'

▼ 4.1   SO   Graded road on left is FR 139 to Dick Hart Ridge and Arizona 87. Zero trip meter.
0.0 ▲   Continue to the west following the sign to Arizona 87.
GPS: N34°25.05' W111°12.81'

▼ 0.0   Continue to the east on FR 300, following the sign for Knoll Lake.
6.4 ▲   SO   Graded road on right is FR 139 to Dick Hart Ridge and Arizona 87. Zero trip meter.
▼ 0.3   SO   Cattle guard.
6.1 ▲   SO   Cattle guard.
▼ 0.7   SO   Track on left.
5.7 ▲   SO   Track on right.
▼ 1.1   SO   Track on left.
5.3 ▲   SO   Track on right.
▼ 1.4   SO   Graded gravel road on left is FR 145, but there is no trail number.
5.0 ▲   SO   Graded gravel road on right is FR 145, but there is no trail number.
GPS: N34°24.49' W111°11.74'

▼ 2.2   SO   Graded road on left is FR 321 to Dane Ridge and Arizona 87.
4.2 ▲   SO   Graded road on right is FR 321 to Dane Ridge and Arizona 87.
GPS: N34°24.61' W111°10.89'

▼ 2.3   SO   Short section of rough ground; passenger vehicles will need to take it very carefully.
4.1 ▲   SO   Short section of rough ground; passenger vehicles will need to take it very carefully.
▼ 3.7   SO   Graded road on left is FR 137 to Buck Springs Ridge and Arizona 87.
2.7 ▲   SO   Graded road on right is FR 137 to Buck Springs Ridge and Arizona 87.
GPS: N34°24.23' W111°09.61'

▼ 3.8   SO   Cattle guard.
2.6 ▲   SO   Cattle guard.
▼ 5.2   SO   Two tracks on right.
1.2 ▲   SO   Two tracks on left.
▼ 5.3   SO   Track on left.
1.1 ▲   SO   Track on right.
▼ 5.7   SO   Track on left.
0.7 ▲   SO   Track on right.
▼ 6.4   SO   Graded road on left is FR 295E, which goes to Knoll Lake. Zero trip meter.
0.0 ▲   Continue to the west on FR 300, following sign to Arizona 87.
GPS: N34°23.50' W111°07.55'

▼ 0.0   Continue to the east on FR 300, following sign to Arizona 260.
7.4 ▲   SO   Graded road on right is FR 295E, which goes to Knoll Lake. Zero trip meter.
▼ 0.9   SO   Track on left.
6.5 ▲   SO   Track on right.
▼ 1.2   SO   Track on left.
6.2 ▲   SO   Track on right.
▼ 2.0   SO   Babe Haught Hiking Trail #143 on right; then track on left.
5.4 ▲   SO   Track on right; then Babe Haught Hiking Trail #143 on left.
GPS: N34°24.15' W111°05.76'

▼ 2.4   SO   Entering Apache-Sitgreaves National Forest; then closure gates. Entering motor-travel restricted area.

5.0 ▲	SO	Closure gates; then entering Coconino National Forest. Leaving motor-travel restricted area.

GPS: N34°24.07' W111°05.40'

▼ 3.8	SO	Graded road on left is FR 115, Chaco Loop (12 miles). Route is also a snow-mobile route in winter.
3.6 ▲	BL	Graded road on right is FR 115, Chaco Loop (12 miles). Route is also a snow-mobile route in winter.

GPS: N34°23.23' W111°04.51'

▼ 4.3	SO	Pass under power lines.
3.1 ▲	SO	Pass under power lines.
▼ 4.7	SO	Horton Spring Hiking Trail #292 on right.
2.7 ▲	SO	Horton Spring Hiking Trail #292 on left.

GPS: N34°22.88' W111°03.62'

▼ 4.9	SO	Cattle guard.
2.5 ▲	SO	Cattle guard.
▼ 7.1	SO	Track on left is FR 215.
0.3 ▲	SO	Track on right is FR 215.

GPS: N34°22.47' W111°01.62'

▼ 7.4	SO	Graded road on left is FR 89 to Bear Canyon Lake. Zero trip meter.
0.0 ▲		Continue to the northwest on FR 300, following sign to Knolls Lake.

GPS: N34°22.60' W111°01.37'

▼ 0.0		Continue to the southeast on FR 300, following sign to Woods Canyon Lake.
3.9 ▲	SO	Graded road on right is FR 89 to Bear Canyon Lake. Zero trip meter.
▼ 0.1	SO	Track on right is FR 76 to Promontory Butte.
3.8 ▲	SO	Track on left is FR 76 to Promontory Butte.

GPS: N34°22.53' W111°01.25'

▼ 0.5	SO	See Canyon Hiking Trail #184 on right.
3.4 ▲	SO	See Canyon Hiking Trail #184 on left.

GPS: N34°22.33' W111°01.00'

▼ 0.9	SO	Track on left is FR 208 and track on right.
3.0 ▲	SO	Track on right is FR 208 and track on left.

GPS: N34°22.02' W111°00.85'

▼ 1.0	SO	Promontory Lookout Tower on left.
2.9 ▲	SO	Promontory Lookout Tower on right.
▼ 1.6	SO	Graded road on left is FR 84, Bear Loop.
2.3 ▲	SO	Graded road on right is FR 84, Bear Loop.

GPS: N34°21.94' W111°00.15'

▼ 2.2	SO	Track on right is FR 9354 into USFS camping area.
1.7 ▲	SO	Track on left is FR 9354 into USFS camping area.
▼ 3.0	TR	Graded road ahead is FR 34.
0.9 ▲	TL	Graded road on right is FR 34.

GPS: N34°22.74' W110°59.07'

▼ 3.1	SO	Track on left.
0.8 ▲	SO	Track on right.
▼ 3.6	SO	Track on right is FR 9354 into USFS camping area.
0.3 ▲	SO	Track on left is FR 9354 into USFS camping area.
▼ 3.9	SO	Graded road on left is FR 169 to Chevelon Canyon Lake. Zero trip meter.
0.0 ▲		Continue to the northwest on FR 300, following the sign to Bear Canyon Lake.

GPS: N34°22.77' W110°58.15'

▼ 0.0		Continue to the southeast on FR 300, following the sign to Woods Canyon Lake.
4.9 ▲	SO	Graded road on right is FR 169 to Chevelon Canyon Lake. Zero trip meter.
▼ 0.1	SO	Closure gates.
4.8 ▲	SO	Closure gates.
▼ 2.7	SO	Graded road on left is FR 195 to USFS camping area; then tank on right.
2.2 ▲	SO	Tank on left; then graded road on right is FR 195 to USFS camping area.

GPS: N34°20.48' W110°58.30'

▼ 2.9	SO	Track on right is FR 9350 to USFS camping area.
2.0 ▲	SO	Track on left is FR 9350 to USFS camping area.
▼ 3.0	SO	General George Crook Hiking Trail crosses road.
1.9 ▲	SO	General George Crook Hiking Trail crosses road.

GPS: N34°20.18' W110°58.16'

▼ 4.3   SO   Mogollon Campground on right (fee area).

0.6 ▲   SO   Mogollon Campground on left (fee area).
              GPS: N34°19.33′ W110°57.27′

▼ 4.9   SO   Closure gates; then join paved road. Paved road on left goes to Woods Canyon Lake. Zero trip meter.

0.0 ▲   Continue to the northwest, following sign for Knolls Lake.
              GPS: N34°19.01′ W110°56.69′

▼ 0.0   Continue to the southeast toward Arizona 260.

3.2 ▲   BL   Bear left onto graded dirt road, FR 300. Paved road continues to Woods Canyon Lake. Zero trip meter.

▼ 0.1   SO   Parking area on right for Rim Lakes Vista Trail. Paved hiking trail, #622, suitable for wheelchairs next to the parking area.

3.1 ▲   SO   Parking area on left for Rim Lakes Vista Trail. Paved hiking trail, #622, suitable for wheelchairs next to the parking area.

▼ 0.5   SO   Parking area on right for Rim Lakes Vista Trail.

2.7 ▲   SO   Parking area on left for Rim Lakes Vista Trail.

▼ 1.3   SO   Parking area for Military Sinkhole Trail and Vista on right.

1.9 ▲   SO   Parking area for Military Sinkhole Trail and Vista on left.
              GPS: N34°18.56′ W110°55.52′

▼ 2.5   SO   Rim USFS Campground on right (fee area).

0.7 ▲   SO   Rim USFS Campground on left (fee area).
              GPS: N34°18.39′ W110°54.37′

▼ 2.9   SO   Hiking trail crosses left and right.

0.3 ▲   SO   Hiking trail crosses left and right.

▼ 3.1   SO   Closure gate; then Rimtop Trailhead on left.

0.1 ▲   SO   Rimtop Trailhead on right; then closure gate.

▼ 3.2   Trail ends at the intersection with Arizona 260, opposite the Mogollon Rim Visitor Center. Turn left for Heber; turn right for Payson.

0.0 ▲   Trail commences on Arizona 260, 0.6 miles west of mile marker 283, opposite the Mogollon Rim Visitor Center.

Zero trip meter and turn north on paved road, following the sign for Woods Canyon Lake. There is a sign at the turn for the Rim Lakes Recreation Area.
GPS: N34°18.17′ W110°53.73′

Hamilton Crossing Trail

STARTING POINT: Arizona 99 (FR 34), 6 miles south of the boundary of the Apache-Sitgreaves National Forest

FINISHING POINT: Viewpoint near Hamilton Crossing

TOTAL MILEAGE: 9.7 miles

UNPAVED MILEAGE: 9.7 miles

DRIVING TIME: 1 hour (one-way)

ELEVATION RANGE: 6,500–6,800 feet

USUALLY OPEN: March to November

BEST TIME TO TRAVEL: March to November

DIFFICULTY RATING: 4

SCENIC RATING: 8

REMOTENESS RATING: +0

Special Attractions

■ Panoramic views over Clear Creek.

■ Rough, moderately challenging trail.

Description

This trail within the Apache-Sitgreaves National Forest travels to the edge of steep Clear Creek Canyon and overlooks the site of historic Hamilton Crossing, which was originally a stock crossing of Clear Creek Canyon. The trail initially follows well-graded FR 63 before turning off onto FR 63B, a lumpy formed trail. This extremely twisty trail winds through oaks, cypress, pines, and junipers as it travels along the plateau. The embedded rocks make for a rough, slow ride for the first couple of miles. After that, there are some smoother sections, but these have deep wheel ruts. The trail can be impassable when wet; the red soil becomes very greasy. A couple of short, loose sections and rock ledges may cause some vehicles to lose traction, but this

Northeast Trail #37: Hamilton Crossing Trail

trail is moderately rated and suitable for any high-clearance 4WD.

The trail ends on the rim of Clear Creek Canyon. A trail to the left goes approximately 100 yards to a campsite on the rim. A short hiking trail goes 50 yards farther out to the very edge to give an unobstructed view into the canyon, 400 feet below. Take care on the edge when on foot—the surface is very loose and there is little margin for error. Most people stop at this campsite, but vehicles can proceed for 0.2 miles to other viewpoints and to a second, much rockier, campsite. Past this, the trail deteriorates into a serious hiking trail. It quickly descends the side of the cliff to Hamilton Crossing. The trail is very steep, loose, and washed out in places. A view of Hamilton Crossing can be obtained from the first switchback.

Current Road Information

Apache-Sitgreaves National Forest
Black Mesa Ranger District
PO Box 968
Overgaard, AZ 85933
(928) 535-4481

Map References

BLM   Holbrook
USFS Apache-Sitgreaves National Forest: Chevelon Ranger District
USGS 1:24,000 Grama Draw, Hamilton Crossing
        1:100,000 Holbrook
Maptech CD-ROM: East Central Arizona/White Mountains
Arizona Atlas & Gazetteer, p. 43
Arizona Road & Recreation Atlas, pp. 42, 76

Route Directions

▼ 0.0   From FR 34, 6 miles south of the boundary of the Apache-Sitgreaves National Forest, zero trip meter and turn northwest on FR 63. There is a camping area at the intersection.
         GPS: N34°34.51′ W110°53.93′

▼ 0.1 SO Track on left to campsite.
▼ 0.2 SO Cattle guard.
▼ 0.3 BL Track on right.
▼ 0.6 SO Track on right.
▼ 0.9 SO Track on right.
▼ 1.0 BR Track on left over cattle guard is FR 70. Bear right, remaining on FR 63.
         GPS: N34°34.97′ W110°54.74′

▼ 1.3 SO Track on right.
▼ 1.7 SO Track on right.
▼ 1.8 SO Track on left.
▼ 2.4 SO Track on right.
▼ 2.6 SO Track on left.
▼ 3.3 SO Track on right.
▼ 3.5 BL Track on right is FR 63; bear left onto smaller formed trail marked FR 63B and zero trip meter.
         GPS: N34°37.00′ W110°55.85′

▼ 0.0   Continue to the northwest on FR 63B. Trail immediately splits into three, but they all rejoin almost immediately.
▼ 0.2 SO Game water tank on right.
         GPS: N34°37.14′ W110°56.01′

▼ 0.6 SO Track on left.
▼ 3.1 SO Fence line on right; then track on right through wire gate. Continue on and swing away from the fence. Zero trip

View of Hamilton Crossing from the trail

meter.
GPS: N34°38.48′ W110°57.43′

▼ 0.0		Continue to the north.
▼ 0.1	SO	Pass through wire gate; then track on left.
▼ 0.4	BL	Equally used track on right. Keep heading west. **GPS: N34°38.73′ W110°57.67′**

▼ 2.9	BR	Small track on left goes 50 yards to a campsite on the edge of Clear Creek Canyon. Park and hike for 100 yards along the faint hiking trail along the edge for the best, unobstructed view into Clear Creek Canyon. The Coconino National Forest is on the far side, and the San Francisco Peaks can be seen in the distance. **GPS: N34°38.93′ W110°59.58′**

▼ 3.1		Trail ends at second camp spot and another viewpoint into Clear Creek Canyon. Steep, unstable foot trail leaves from this point. Hamilton Crossing can be seen down in the canyon to the northwest. **GPS: N34°39.02′ W110°59.68′**

NORTHEAST REGION TRAIL #38

Chevelon Crossing Road

STARTING POINT: Arizona 260, 1 mile northwest of Heber
FINISHING POINT: Arizona 99 (FR 34), 28 miles south of Winslow
TOTAL MILEAGE: 24 miles
UNPAVED MILEAGE: 24 miles
DRIVING TIME: 1.25 hours
ELEVATION RANGE: 4,600–6,700 feet
USUALLY OPEN: April to October
BEST TIME TO TRAVEL: April to October
DIFFICULTY RATING: 1
SCENIC RATING: 8
REMOTENESS RATING: +0

Special Attractions
- The deep gorge of Chevelon Canyon.
- Access to many backcountry campsites and roads within the Apache-Sitgreaves National Forest.
- Elk may be seen in the area.

Description
This smooth backcountry road winds through pine forests on the Mogollon Plateau in the Apache-Sitgreaves National Forest. The trail is not suitable for vehicles more than 35 feet long because of the winding road and tight curves at Chevelon Crossing. The trail is a well-used, graded gravel road, which can become very washboardy.

Chevelon Crossing is a scenic and historic canyon area. Next to the crossing is a U.S. Forest Service campground that was built originally by the Civilian Conservation Corps in the 1930s. There is water in the canyon year-round.

Current Road Information
Apache-Sitgreaves National Forest
Back Mesa Ranger District
PO Box 968
Overgaard, AZ 85933
(928) 535-4481

Map References
BLM   Show Low, Holbrook
USFS   Apache-Sitgreaves National Forest: Heber Ranger District
USGS   1:24,000   Heber, Hanks Draw, Potato Wash South, Chevelon Crossing, Chevelon Butte
        1:100,000 Show Low, Holbrook
Maptech CD-ROM: East Central Arizona/White Mountains
Arizona Atlas & Gazetteer, pp. 51, 43
Arizona Road & Recreation Atlas, pp. 42, 76
Recreational Map of Arizona

Route Directions

▼ 0.0	From Arizona 260, 1 mile northwest of Heber and 0.4 miles northwest of mile marker 303, zero trip meter and turn

Chevelon Crossing from the trail above

northwest on graded gravel road, FR 504.

5.0 ▲ Trail ends on Arizona 260. Turn left for Heber; turn right for Payson and Winslow.

GPS: N34°26.35' W110°37.09'

▼ 0.1 SO Tracks on left and right along power lines.
4.9 ▲ SO Tracks on left and right along power lines.
▼ 0.2 SO Track on right.
4.8 ▲ SO Track on left.
▼ 0.3 SO Track on left.
4.7 ▲ SO Track on right.
▼ 0.4 SO Cattle guard; then track on right.
4.6 ▲ SO Track on left; then cattle guard.
▼ 0.5 SO Track on left.
4.5 ▲ SO Track on right.
▼ 0.7 SO Track on right.
4.3 ▲ SO Track on left.
▼ 1.2 SO Graded road on right to private property and track on left.

3.8 ▲ SO Graded road on left to private property and track on right.
▼ 1.7 SO Track on left is FR 93.
3.3 ▲ SO Track on right is FR 93.
▼ 1.8 SO Road on right is FR 95.
3.2 ▲ SO Road on left is FR 95.

GPS: N34°27.73' W110°38.04'

▼ 1.9 SO Track on right.
3.1 ▲ SO Track on left.
▼ 2.3 SO Cattle guard; then track on right to corral.
2.7 ▲ SO Track on left to corral; then cattle guard.

GPS: N34°27.99' W110°38.52'

▼ 2.9 SO Crossing through Brookbank Canyon; cross over wash. Track on right down canyon.
2.1 ▲ SO Crossing through Brookbank Canyon; cross

A view of Chevelon Canyon Creek

over wash. Track on left down canyon.

▼ 3.1	SO	Track on right.		4.2 ▲	SO	Track on right.
1.9 ▲	SO	Track on left.		▼ 1.6	SO	Track on right; then cattle guard.
▼ 3.2	SO	Track on right; then track on left.		3.9 ▲	SO	Cattle guard; then track on left.
1.8 ▲	SO	Track on right; then track on left.		▼ 1.9	SO	Track on left.
▼ 3.3	SO	Track on right.		3.6 ▲	SO	Track on right.
1.7 ▲	SO	Track on left.		▼ 2.1	SO	Track on right.
▼ 3.6	SO	Track on right.		3.4 ▲	SO	Track on left.
1.4 ▲	SO	Track on left.		▼ 2.4	SO	Track on left.
▼ 4.2	SO	Track on right; then track on left.		3.1 ▲	SO	Track on right.
0.8 ▲	SO	Track on right; then track on left.		▼ 2.8	SO	Track on left.
▼ 4.5	SO	Track on left is FR 9554B.		2.7 ▲	SO	Track on right.
0.5 ▲	SO	Track on right is FR 9554B.		▼ 2.9	SO	Graded road on right is FR 153.
▼ 4.6	SO	Track on right is FR 228.		2.6 ▲	SO	Graded road on left is FR 153.
0.4 ▲	SO	Track on left is FR 228.				**GPS: N34°31.68′ W110°42.64′**

GPS: N34°29.26′ W110°40.43′

▼ 3.6	SO	Track on right; then cross over Daze Canyon on bridge.
1.9 ▲	SO	Cross over Daze Canyon on bridge; then track on left.

▼ 5.0	SO	Graded road on left is FR 99, Wildcat Road. Zero trip meter.
0.0 ▲		Continue to the southeast on FR 504 toward Heber.

GPS: N34°29.51′ W110°40.73′

▼ 3.9	SO	Track on left; then cattle guard.
1.6 ▲	SO	Cattle guard; then track on right.
▼ 4.3	SO	Cross over Wildcat Canyon on bridge.
1.2 ▲	SO	Cross over Wildcat Canyon on bridge.

GPS: N34°32.40′ W110°43.67′

▼ 0.0		Continue to the northwest on FR 504 toward Chevelon Canyon.
5.5 ▲	SO	Graded road on right is FR 99, Wildcat Road. Zero trip meter.
▼ 1.0	SO	Track on right.
4.5 ▲	SO	Track on left.
▼ 1.3	SO	Track on left.

▼ 4.5	SO	Track on right.
1.0 ▲	SO	Track on left.
▼ 4.6	SO	Track on right.
0.9 ▲	SO	Track on left.
▼ 5.2	SO	Track on right.

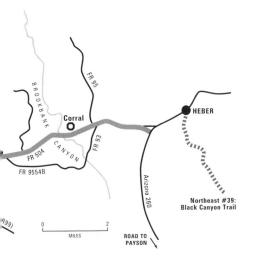

▼ 3.1   SO   Track on left is FR 504H.
3.8 ▲   SO   Track on right is FR 504H.
          GPS: N34°33.91′ W110°46.66′

▼ 3.5   SO   Track on left.
3.4 ▲   SO   Track on right.
▼ 3.7   SO   Track on left is FR 504I.
3.2 ▲   SO   Track on right is FR 504I.
▼ 3.8   SO   Track on left and track on right under power lines.
3.1 ▲   SO   Track on right and track on left under power lines.
▼ 4.1   SO   Track on left.
2.8 ▲   SO   Track on right.
▼ 5.0   SO   Trail starts to drop into Chevelon Canyon.
1.9 ▲   SO   Trail leaves Chevelon Canyon.
▼ 5.4   SO   Chevelon Crossing; cross over Chevelon Canyon on bridge.
1.5 ▲   SO   Chevelon Crossing; cross over Chevelon Canyon on bridge.
          GPS: N34°35.60′ W110°47.23′

▼ 5.5   SO   Chevelon Crossing USFS Campground on left.
1.4 ▲   SO   Chevelon Crossing USFS Campground on right.
          GPS: N34°35.53′ W110°47.26′

▼ 6.1   SO   Two tracks on left.
0.8 ▲   SO   Two tracks on right.
▼ 6.2   SO   Track on left.
0.7 ▲   SO   Track on right.
▼ 6.5   SO   Cattle guard.
0.4 ▲   SO   Cattle guard.
▼ 6.9   BR   Graded road on left is FR 169 to Chevelon Canyon Lake. Zero trip meter and bear right.
0.0 ▲   Continue to the south on FR 504, following the sign to Chevelon Crossing.
          GPS: N34°36.21′ W110°47.49′

▼ 0.0   Continue to the north on FR 504, following the sign to Winslow.
6.6 ▲   BL   Graded road on right is FR 169 to Chevelon Canyon Lake. Zero trip meter and bear left.
▼ 0.9   SO   Cross over West Chevelon Canyon on bridge. This is Mormon Crossing.
5.7 ▲   SO   Cross over West Chevelon Canyon on bridge. This is Mormon Crossing.

0.3 ▲   SO   Track on left.
▼ 5.5   SO   Graded road on left is FR 170, Wagon Draw Road. Zero trip meter.
0.0 ▲   Continue to the east on FR 504.
          GPS: N34°33.20′ W110°44.35′
▼ 0.0   Continue to the west on FR 504.
6.9 ▲   SO   Graded road on right is FR 170, Wagon Draw Road. Zero trip meter.
▼ 0.2   SO   Track on left.
6.7 ▲   SO   Track on right.
▼ 1.2   SO   Track on right is FR 176.
5.7 ▲   SO   Track on left is FR 176.
          GPS: N34°34.04′ W110°44.72′

▼ 1.4   SO   Track on left.
5.5 ▲   SO   Track on right.
▼ 1.6   SO   Track on right.
5.3 ▲   SO   Track on left.
▼ 2.1   SO   Track on left.
4.8 ▲   SO   Track on right.
▼ 2.4   SO   Track on left.
4.5 ▲   SO   Track on right.
▼ 2.5   SO   Track on left.
4.4 ▲   SO   Track on right.
▼ 2.7   SO   Track on left.
4.2 ▲   SO   Track on right.
▼ 2.8   SO   Track on right is FR 504A.
4.1 ▲   SO   Track on left is FR 504A.
          GPS: N34°33.94′ W110°46.43′

Old corral and cattle chute near the trail

▼ 1.4   SO   Cattle guard.
5.2 ▲   SO   Cattle guard.
▼ 1.7   SO   Track on left.
4.9 ▲   SO   Track on right.
▼ 2.2   SO   Two tracks on right.
4.4 ▲   SO   Two tracks on left.
▼ 2.4   SO   Cattle guard; leaving Apache-Sitgreaves National Forest; then graded road on left is FR 191.
4.2 ▲   SO   Graded road on right is FR 191; then cattle guard; entering Apache-Sitgreaves National Forest.
      GPS: N34°38.23′ W110°46.78′

▼ 3.1   SO   Track on right.
3.5 ▲   SO   Track on left.
▼ 4.1   SO   Track on right.
2.5 ▲   SO   Track on left.
▼ 4.4   SO   Track on left and track on right.
2.2 ▲   SO   Track on left and track on right.
      GPS: N34°39.96′ W110°46.23′

▼ 5.3   SO   Track on left.
1.3 ▲   SO   Track on right.
▼ 5.5   SO   Cattle guard.
1.1 ▲   SO   Cattle guard.
▼ 5.9   SO   Track on right.
0.7 ▲   SO   Track on left.
▼ 6.6   Trail ends at the intersection with paved FR 34, 28 miles south of Winslow. Turn right for Winslow.
0.0 ▲   Trail commences on paved FR 34, 28 miles south of Winslow, 5 miles north of the Apache-Sitgreaves National Forest boundary. At the marker for FR 504, zero trip meter and turn south on the graded dirt road, following the sign to Heber.
      GPS: N34°41.70′ W110°46.63′

Black Canyon Trail

STARTING POINT: Arizona 260, 0.1 miles east of mile marker 291
FINISHING POINT: Arizona 260 in Heber
TOTAL MILEAGE: 16.8 miles
UNPAVED MILEAGE: 16.3 miles
DRIVING TIME: 1.5 hours
ELEVATION RANGE: 6,600–7,600 feet
USUALLY OPEN: April to October
BEST TIME TO TRAVEL: April to October
DIFFICULTY RATING: 1
SCENIC RATING: 9
REMOTENESS RATING: +0

Special Attractions
- Black Canyon Lake.
- Graves of three men from the Pleasant Valley Wars and of early settlers.
- Polimana Indian Pictographs and Black Canyon Rock Shelter.

History
The Black Canyon Trail brims with history from start to finish. The route through the canyon was first used by the Mogollon Indians to travel between the Mogollon Rim and settlements in the lower desert. Later, cattle were driven along the road to market, and the trail was a supply route for ranchers in Pleasant Valley and a transportation route served by a biweekly stagecoach.

The Pleasant Valley Wars caused difficulties in the Mogollon Rim and Pleasant Valley for many years in the late 1800s. One small but violent chapter reached its conclusion in Black Canyon. In August 1888, Jamie Stott, a young rancher, and two of his friends, James Scott and Jeff Wilson, were arrested for allegedly shooting Jake Lauffer a few days earlier. The deputy sheriff who made the arrest was J. D. Houck, who had long disliked Jamie and thought him to be on the side of the Grahams and the Hashknife cowboys—the opposing group of a long-running feud.

Jamie and his friends were not worried when they were arrested. They had sound alibis that put them a long way from Jake Lauffer's ranch at the time of the shooting, so they agreed to accompany Houck to the county seat at Prescott.

En route to Prescott, The Committee of Fifty, a group of masked vigilantes, intercepted the posse and made off with the three men. Many believe that Houck had planned the abduction and that by having the masked men "steal" his captives, he would be considered blameless in the following events.

The vigilantes took the three men to a small clearing in the woods and began to play a cruel game. Jamie was made to watch as the vigilantes at first only pretended to hang his friends by tying ropes around their necks, which were tossed over the limb of a large ponderosa. When Scott and Wilson refused to beg for their lives, their horses were driven out from under them and the men hung.

The vigilantes' attention then turned to Jamie. They dragged him off his horse and pretended to hang him too, repeatedly stringing him up on the same tree limb as his friends and then lowering him. Finally, they left him up too long and when they brought him down, he was dead. The three bodies were found a few days later and were buried in the clearing.

A happier story associated with Black Canyon is that of the Baca family, which started ranching the area in 1889. There were seven daughters in the family, and with young, eligible women in short supply, there was a steady trail of suitors to the Baca Ranch. One suitor went so far as to build a road from Brookbank to the Black Canyon wagon trail so that he could more easily visit his beloved.

In the 1880s, Mormons reached Black Canyon and the settlement of Wilford was founded in 1883 by John Bushman and others unable to sustain a living in Brigham City, Joseph City, and Sunset. Named after President Wilford Woodruff of the Church of Jesus Christ of Latter-day Saints, the small settlement had its share of problems. Local cowboys and thieves made things difficult for the settlers. With the passing of a law that made polygamy illegal, many of Wilford's families moved to Mexico. Most of the remaining families moved to Heber after only a couple of years when their water supply dried up.

Graves of three victims lynched during the Pleasant Valley Wars lie near the trail

Description

The Black Canyon region encompasses much in the way of historical interest: Indian pictographs, early settlements, and a violent chapter of the Pleasant Valley Wars. Throw in an easy, graded trail, a plethora of backcountry campsites, and a secluded lake for trout fishing and there is truly something for everyone.

The Black Canyon Trail leaves Arizona 260 near Forest Lakes and initially follows FR 300, the continuation of Northeast #36: The Mogollon Rim Road, and a section of the General Crook Trail. Passing by the Black Canyon Rim Campground, the trail follows the dirt road through ponderosa pine forests along Black Canyon.

The first historical feature of the trail is the site of the graves of Jamie Stott, James Scott, and Jeff Wilson. To reach the site, turn down a small formed trail marked with auto tour number 7. Take the side trail, which immediately forks; follow the right-hand fork for 1 mile. When you reach two "Closed Road" signs at the end of the vehicle trail, you are there. The graves are just past the second sign on the right, hidden in the trees and surrounded by a wooden fence. The coordinates of the graves are—GPS: N34º18.34' W110º44.00'.

Black Canyon Lake, a long narrow lake ringed by tall pine trees, is located just off the main trail. The Three Oak Hiking Trail leaves from the parking area. The lake is stocked with trout and is a popular fishing spot. No camping is allowed at the lake, but there are two large informal camping areas nearby: the West Camping Area and the South Camping Area. There are no facilities, but there are plenty of large sites set among the trees on the edge of a large, open area.

The next stop along the trail is the Baca Ranch and graves. Nothing remains of the ranch, but the graves—in a small stand of aspens—can easily be seen. The historic Black Canyon Ranch and the site of the township of Wilford are passed before the short hiking trail to the Black Canyon Rock Shelter is reached. The shelter is on the far side of the canyon and can be seen without hiking up to it. There are a few pictographs at the shelter. The final stop on the trail is the Polimana Pic-

tographs. They are located right beside the main trail, but you will need to hike up a short, steep climb to view them closely. The pictographs were painted by the Mogollon Indians.

The Chevelon-Heber Ranger Districts publish a free auto tour guide for this trail; in the guide, the auto tour marker posts refer to points of interest discussed.

Current Road Information

Apache-Sitgreaves National Forest
Back Mesa Ranger District
PO Box 968
Overgaard, AZ 85933
(928) 535-4481

Map References

BLM   Show Low
USFS Apache-Sitgreaves National Forest:
      Heber Ranger District
USGS 1:24,000   O W Point, Brookbank
      Point, Hanks Draw, Heber
      1:100,000 Show Low
Maptech CD-ROM: East Central
      Arizona/White Mountains
Arizona Atlas & Gazetteer, p. 51
Arizona Road & Recreation Atlas, p. 42 & p. 76
Recreational Map of Arizona

Route Directions

▼ 0.0		From Arizona 260, 7 miles east of the intersection with Arizona 288, 0.1 miles east of mile marker 291, zero trip meter and turn south over cattle guard on graded dirt road marked FR 300. Immediately past the turn, the road is marked to Rim Road and Black Canyon Lake. There is a message board on the right.
2.3 ▲		Trail ends at the T-intersection with Arizona 260. Turn right for Heber; turn left for Payson.
		GPS: N34º20.02' W110º45.13'

▼ 0.1	SO	Track on left.
2.2 ▲	SO	Track on right.
▼ 0.3	SO	Track on left.
2.0 ▲	SO	Track on right.
▼ 0.6	SO	Track on left through camp area; then two tracks on right; then track on left.

Northeast Trail #39: Black Canyon Trail

1.7 ▲   SO   Track on right; then two tracks on left; then track on right through camp area.

▼ 0.7   SO   Graded road on left is FR 9555Y; track on right.

1.6 ▲   SO   Track on left; graded road on right is FR 9555Y.
        GPS: N34°19.35' W110°45.00'

▼ 0.9   SO   Track on left.
1.4 ▲   SO   Track on right.
▼ 1.0   SO   Track on right.
1.3 ▲   SO   Track on left.
▼ 1.4   SO   Track on right.
0.9 ▲   SO   Track on left.
▼ 1.8   BL   Track on right is FR 196.
0.5 ▲   BR   Track on left is FR 196.
        GPS: N34°18.45' W110°45.27'

▼ 1.9   SO   Track on left.
0.4 ▲   SO   Track on right.
▼ 2.2   SO   Track on right is FR 168.
0.1 ▲   SO   Track on left is FR 168.
        GPS: N34°18.24' W110°44.88'

▼ 2.3   TL   Turn onto graded road FR 86, following the sign to Black Canyon Lake. FR 300 continues ahead. Black Canyon Rim USFS Campground at intersection. Zero trip meter.
0.0 ▲   Continue to the west.
        GPS: N34°18.23' W110°44.74'

▼ 0.0   Continue to the north.
1.7 ▲   TR   T-intersection; turn right onto FR 300 following the sign to Arizona 260. Black Canyon Rim USFS Campground at intersection. Zero trip meter.

▼ 0.1   SO   Campground entrance on right. Closure gate.

1.6 ▲   SO   Closure gate. Campground entrance on left.

▼ 0.8   SO   Track on left.
0.9 ▲   SO   Track on right.
▼ 0.9   SO   Track on left.
0.8 ▲   SO   Track on right.
▼ 1.5   SO   Track on left.
0.2 ▲   SO   Track on right.
▼ 1.7   SO   Track on right is FR 9559U, which goes to the graves of Stott, Scott, and Wilson. Track is marked by auto tour stop 7 sign. Zero trip meter.
0.0 ▲   Continue to the west.
        GPS: N34°18.98' W110°43.26'

▼ 0.0   Continue to the east.
1.1 ▲   SO   Track on left is FR 9559U, which goes to the graves of Stott, Scott, and Wilson. Track is marked by auto tour stop 7 sign. Zero trip meter.
▼ 0.1   SO   Track on right; then track on left. Area is marked as West Camping Area. Many tracks right and left for next 0.3

		miles, mainly to campsites.
1.0 ▲	SO	Track on right; then track on left.
▼ 0.4	SO	End of main camping area.
0.7 ▲	SO	Many tracks on right and left for next 0.3 miles, mainly to campsites. Area is marked as West Camping Area.
▼ 0.6	SO	Track on right.
0.5 ▲	SO	Track on left.
		GPS: N34°19.30′ W110°42.75′

▼ 0.8	SO	Track on right.
0.3 ▲	SO	Track on left.
▼ 0.9	SO	Track on right is FR 9561R.
0.2 ▲	SO	Track on left is FR 9561R.
		GPS: N34°19.37′ W110°42.42′

▼ 1.1	BR	Track on left is FR 86B, which goes to Black Canyon Lake (0.25 miles). Zero trip meter.
0.0 ▲		Continue to the west on FR 86.
		GPS: N34°19.38′ W110°42.23′
▼ 0.0		Continue to the east toward Heber.
4.1 ▲	BL	Track on right is FR 86B, which goes to Black Canyon Lake (0.25 miles). Zero trip meter.
▼ 0.2	SO	South Camping Area on right; FR 9561S.

3.9 ▲	SO	South Camping Area on left; FR 9561S.
▼ 0.3	SO	Track on right to camping area.
3.8 ▲	SO	Track on left to camping area.
▼ 0.4	SO	Track on right to camping area.
3.7 ▲	SO	Track on left to camping area.
▼ 0.7	SO	Closure gate; then track on left is FR 9562.
3.4 ▲	SO	Track on right is FR 9562; then closure gate.
		GPS: N34°18.77′ W110°42.28′

▼ 0.8	SO	Track on right.
3.3 ▲	SO	Track on left.
▼ 1.6	SO	Track on left.
2.5 ▲	SO	Track on right.
▼ 1.7	SO	Track on right is FR 9562F.
2.4 ▲	SO	Track on left is FR 9562F.
		GPS: N34°19.28′ W110°41.62′

▼ 1.9	SO	Track on left.
2.2 ▲	SO	Track on right.
▼ 2.0	SO	Two tracks on left.
2.1 ▲	SO	Two tracks on right.
▼ 2.2	SO	The Baca graves are on the right surrounded by a fence; also track on right.
1.9 ▲	SO	The Baca graves are on the left sur-

The Polimana Pictographs near the east end of the trail

rounded by a fence; also track on left.
GPS: N34°19.35' W110°41.13'

▼ 2.3   SO   Cross through wash; then Baca Meadow on right. Track on right is FR 9562P.

1.8 ▲   SO   Track on left is FR 9562P. Baca Meadow on left; cross through wash.
GPS: N34°19.38' W110°40.98'

▼ 2.7   SO   Track on right.

1.4 ▲   SO   Track on left.

▼ 3.2   SO   Cattle guard; then track on right.

0.9 ▲   SO   Track on left; then cattle guard.

▼ 3.5   SO   Track on left. Road becomes paved.

0.6 ▲   SO   Track on right. Road turns to graded dirt.
GPS: N34°20.04' W110°40.04'

▼ 3.7   SO   Black Canyon Ranch on left (private property).

0.4 ▲   SO   Black Canyon Ranch on right (private property).
GPS: N34°20.07' W110°39.88'

▼ 4.0   SO   Road turns to graded dirt.

0.1 ▲   SO   Road turns to paved.

▼ 4.1   TL   Graded road on right is FR 87. Turn left on FR 86 and zero trip meter.

0.0 ▲   Turn onto FR 86 and continue to the west.
GPS: N34°20.23' W110°39.46'

▼ 0.0   Continue to the north and cross over creek on bridge.

3.2 ▲   TR   Cross over creek on bridge; then graded road on left is FR 87. Zero trip meter.

▼ 0.2   SO   Cattle guard.

3.0 ▲   SO   Cattle guard.

▼ 0.8   SO   Track on right.

2.4 ▲   SO   Track on left.

▼ 1.7   SO   Track on right.

1.5 ▲   SO   Track on left.

▼ 1.8   SO   Cattle guard.

1.4 ▲   SO   Cattle guard.

▼ 1.9   SO   Cross over Black Canyon on bridge. Open grassy area immediately west of the bridge was the site of Wilford. Nothing remains. The site is marked by marker post 6 on the auto tour.

1.3 ▲   SO   Open grassy area immediately west of the bridge was the site of Wilford.

Nothing remains. The site is marked by marker post 6 on the auto tour. Cross over Black Canyon on bridge.
GPS: N34°21.87' W110°38.68'

▼ 2.0   SO   Track on right.

1.2 ▲   SO   Track on left.

▼ 2.4   SO   Track on left is FR 9596F.

0.8 ▲   SO   Track on right is FR 9596F.
GPS: N34°22.25' W110°38.65'

▼ 2.6   SO   Track on right.

0.6 ▲   SO   Track on left.

▼ 3.2   SO   Track on right at auto tour marker 3 goes a short distance to a parking area. Follow the blue diamond markers a short distance on foot to Black Canyon Creek and the rock shelter. Zero trip meter.

0.0 ▲   Continue to the west.
GPS: N34°22.83' W110°38.18'

▼ 0.0   Continue to the east.

4.4 ▲   SO   Track on left at auto tour marker 3 goes a short distance to a parking area. Follow the blue diamond markers on foot a short distance to Black Canyon Creek and the rock shelter. Zero trip meter.

▼ 0.5   SO   Track on left to corral.

3.9 ▲   SO   Track on right to corral.

▼ 0.6   SO   Cattle guard.

3.8 ▲   SO   Cattle guard.

▼ 0.9   SO   Track on left.

3.5 ▲   SO   Track on right.

▼ 1.2   SO   Polimana Pictographs on the left. Park close to auto tour marker 2 and take the short, steep hiking trail for approximately 100 yards up the cliff to the pictographs. They can be seen from the road immediately after the marker by looking up underneath the rock overhang.

3.2 ▲   SO   Polimana Pictographs on the right. Park close to auto tour marker 2 and take the short, steep hiking trail for approximately 100 yards up the cliff to the pictographs. They can be seen from the road immediately after the marker by looking up underneath the rock

THE PLEASANT VALLEY WAR—1883 TO 1892

The Pleasant Valley War raged between the Tewksbury and Graham families. The Tewksburys lived on the Mogollon Rim in Pleasant Valley. For four years they lived a tranquil life raising horses, but things changed when the Grahams moved in nearby and started raising cattle. A strange thing about the Grahams' cattle was that the population grew incredibly fast. The Tewksburys soon learned that the Grahams were cattle rustlers. Pleasant Valley divided itself into two factions when the Tewksburys complained: those for the Grahams and those for the Tewksburys. The foundations for the feud were laid.

In 1883, John Gilliand and his nephew (both Graham supporters) were wounded by gunfire after a violent argument with Ed Tewksbury. After that incident, expectations of open war loomed. Instead, the situation cooled until 1887 when the Tewksburys started to raise sheep and let them graze over the valley. Feuds between cattle ranchers and sheepherders are infamous; the presence of the sheep riled up the Grahams. The boiling point had been reached. The Grahams and Blevins (who were solid Graham supporters) hired a gunman. The Tewksbury sheepherder was later drilled by gunfire. In August 1887, a Blevins brother lay dead and his companions were wounded after a meeting with Ed and Jim Tewksbury. William Graham was the next to fall when an avenging bullet fired by the brother-in-law of the murdered sheepherder struck him down. Two weeks later, the Tewksbury ranch house was attacked by a man identified as Andy Cooper, accompanied by John Blevins and a mob of Graham supporters. When the smoke cleared, John Tewksbury and William Jacobs were found dead. The war raged between the two factions and eventually the law noticed the blood and murder.

Sheriff Commodore Perry Owens rode up to the house of Eva Blevins on September 4, 1887, looking for Andy Cooper. Owens was a dead shot with the Winchester he had cradled in his arms. His sharp eyes spotted Cooper by the front door. Cooper drew his six-gun, Owens swung his rifle, and the two fired. Owens burst through the door and Cooper fell bleeding into the arms of his mother. John Blevins appeared and fired at the sheriff, but missed. Owens felled him with a shot to the shoulder. The steely-eyed sheriff shot Mose Roberts and sent him crashing through the rear window. Sam Houston was the next to exit the house. The 16-year-old boy was armed with a six-gun, but before he could fire the sheriff killed him with a clean shot to the head. John Blevins was the only one to survive Owens's wrath and precise shooting.

The feud ended finally in 1892 when Ed Tewksbury, the last of the Tewksburys, was found guilty of murdering Tom Graham. Today the conflict is long past, but on a drive through the area it is interesting to think about the violent turmoil that once engulfed these quiet surroundings.

overhang.

GPS: N34°23.82' W110°37.81'

▼ 1.4   SO   Track on right.
3.0 ▲   SO   Track on left.
▼ 1.7   SO   Track on right.
2.7 ▲   SO   Track on left.
▼ 2.2   SO   Track on left is FR 160.
2.2 ▲   SO   Track on right is FR 160.

GPS: N34°24.46' W110°37.14'

▼ 2.6   SO   Track on right.
1.8 ▲   SO   Track on left.
▼ 2.8   SO   Track on right goes to site of old Heber Ranger Station. Road is marked by auto tour post 1.
1.6 ▲   SO   Track on left goes to site of old Heber Ranger Station. Road is marked by

auto tour post 1.

GPS: N34°24.88' W110°36.71'

▼ 2.9   SO   Cattle guard; leaving Apache-
                Sitgreaves National Forest.
1.5 ▲   SO   Cattle guard; entering Apache-
                Sitgreaves National Forest.

GPS: N34°24.93' W110°36.69'

▼ 3.5   SO   Road on left is Hill Road.
0.9 ▲   SO   Road on right is Hill Road.
▼ 4.3   TL   Turn left onto Black Canyon Lane
                immediately before wash crossing.
0.1 ▲   TR   Turn right onto Black Canyon Road and
                proceed west.
▼ 4.4   Trail ends at the intersection with
                Arizona 260 in Heber. Turn left for
                Payson; turn right for Overgaard.
0.0 ▲   Trail commences from Arizona 260 in
                Heber. Zero trip meter and turn south
                on graded dirt road at the sign for FR
                86, Black Canyon Lane.

GPS: N34°25.90' W110°36.02'

NORTHEAST REGION TRAIL #40

Defiance Plateau Trail

STARTING POINT: I-40, exit 343 (Querino
Road)
FINISHING POINT: Arizona 264, 5.1 miles west
of St. Michaels
TOTAL MILEAGE: 32.3 miles
UNPAVED MILEAGE: 32.2 miles
DRIVING TIME: 1.5 hours
ELEVATION RANGE: 6,100–7,800 feet
USUALLY OPEN: Year-round
BEST TIME TO TRAVEL: Dry weather
DIFFICULTY RATING: 2
SCENIC RATING: 7
REMOTENESS RATING: +0

Special Attractions

■ Oak Ridge Fire Lookout Tower.
■ Long trail through open forest along
Defiance Plateau.
■ Alternative route to Window Rock from
the south.

Description

Most people who enter the Navajo Nation
from the south travel via Indian Road 12,
from I-40 to Window Rock. However, a lit-
tle-known dirt road parallels this paved
route to the west, traveling through open
forest on Defiance Plateau.

The trail is used as a main access to the
settlement of Pine Springs and by many
Navajo who live on the plateau. Consequently, the route stays open year-round but
may be snow-covered in winter and impassable after summer monsoons. In dry weather, it is suitable for high-clearance 2WDs.

From I-40 to Pine Springs the road is
wide and well graded, although there are a
few sand traps and rutted sections that might
be uncomfortable for those traveling in a
passenger vehicle. The remains of the old
Pine Springs Trading Post are on the west
side of the road; only the walls still stand.

Past Pine Springs, the trail continues to
be wide but is only roughly graded with a
loose surface and deep, powder-fine sand
traps. Take care: The edges of the road are
very soft and sandy and it would be easy to
get bogged down. The vegetation on Defiance Plateau is mainly pinyon-juniper at the
lower elevations; as the trail gradually
climbs, there are dense stands of ponderosa
pines. There are many side tracks leading
from the main one, most of which lead to
dwellings. Only the major ones and ones
that do not immediately lead to houses are
mentioned in the route directions. The side
trails are mentioned for navigation purposes
only; most are not open to public travel.

The fire lookout tower on Oak Ridge is
manned during daylight hours in the fire
season. Visitors are usually welcome to
climb the tower when it is manned but must
ask permission from the lookout first. From
the top, there is a good view of Defiance
Plateau, an unbroken flat expanse of vegetation. Other fire lookout towers can be seen
to the north.

The trail ends at Arizona 264, a paved
road a short distance to the west of St.
Michaels and Window Rock. St. Michaels
Mission and Museum warrant a visit.

Northeast Trail #40: Defiance Plateau Trail

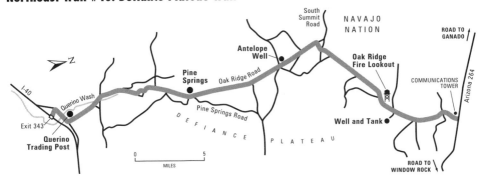

Current Road Information

Navajo Nation Parks and Recreation
PO Box 2520
Window Rock, AZ 86515
(928) 871-6647

Map References

BLM   Sanders, Ganado
USGS 1:24,000 Burntwater Wash, Pine
        Springs, Antelope Lake, Joe Woody
        Well, West of Window Rock
        1:100,000 Sanders, Ganado
Maptech CD-ROM: Northeast
        Arizona/Navajo County
Arizona Atlas & Gazetteer, pp. 45, 35
Arizona Road & Recreation Atlas, pp. 37, 71
Recreational Map of Arizona

Route Directions

▼ 0.0		From exit 343 on I-40, Querino Road, proceed to the north side of the freeway exit. Zero trip meter at cattle guard and continue northwest on paved road.
1.7 ▲		Trail ends at exit 343 on I-40.

GPS: N35°15.58′ W109°16.72′

▼ 0.1	SO	Road is now graded dirt. Track on left and right.
1.6 ▲	SO	Track on left and right. Road is now paved.
▼ 0.6	TR	Turn right at T-intersection onto Big Arrow Road (unmarked); track ahead into private property.
1.1 ▲	TL	Turn left on unmarked graded road;

track on right into private property.

GPS: N35°15.83′ W109°17.24′

▼ 0.7	SO	Two graded roads on left.
1.0 ▲	SO	Two graded roads on right.
▼ 0.8	SO	Graded road on right and many tracks on right and left into private property.
0.9 ▲	SO	Graded road on left and many tracks on right and left into private property.
▼ 1.3	SO	Track on right; then cross over Querino Wash on bridge.
0.4 ▲	SO	Cross over Querino Wash on bridge; then track on left.

GPS: N35°16.30′ W109°16.54′

▼ 1.7	TL	Turn left onto graded dirt road. The Querino Trading Post is at the intersection and there is a wooden sign for Pine Lake and Burnt Water. Zero trip meter.
0.0 ▲		Continue to the southwest.

GPS: N35°16.43′ W109°16.24′

▼ 0.0		Continue to the northwest.
2.9 ▲	TR	T-intersection at the Querino Trading Post; turn right onto graded dirt road and zero trip meter.
▼ 0.1	SO	Track on right.
2.8 ▲	SO	Track on left.
▼ 0.6	SO	Two tracks on right.
2.3 ▲	SO	Two tracks on left.
▼ 0.7	SO	Track on right.
2.2 ▲	SO	Track on left.
▼ 1.3	SO	Two tracks on right.
1.6 ▲	SO	Two tracks on left.
▼ 1.8	SO	Track on right.

St. Michaels Mission

1.1 ▲ SO Track on left.

▼ 2.0 SO Track on right.

0.9 ▲ SO Track on left.

▼ 2.9 SO Graded road on right; graded road on left and track on left. Continue straight on, following the sign for Pine Springs. Zero trip meter.

0.0 ▲ Continue to the southeast.
GPS: N35°18.72' W109°17.66'

▼ 0.0 Continue to the north.

6.4 ▲ SO Graded road on left; graded road on right and track on right. Zero trip meter.

▼ 0.1 SO Track on left.

6.3 ▲ SO Track on right.

▼ 0.2 SO Track on left.

6.2 ▲ SO Track on right.

▼ 0.9 SO Track on left and track on right.

5.5 ▲ SO Track on left and track on right.

▼ 1.2 SO Graded road on right and track on left.

5.2 ▲ SO Graded road on left and track on right.

▼ 1.5 SO Track on left.

4.9 ▲ SO Track on right.

▼ 2.7 BL Graded road on right.

3.7 ▲ SO Graded road on left.
GPS: N35°21.15' W109°17.52'

▼ 3.1 SO Track on right.

3.3 ▲ SO Track on left.

▼ 4.0 SO Major graded road on left.

2.4 ▲ BL Major graded road on right.
GPS: N35°22.31' W109°17.79'

▼ 4.3 SO Track on left.

2.1 ▲ SO Track on right.

▼ 4.6 SO Track on right.

1.8 ▲ SO Track on left.

▼ 4.8 SO Track on right and track on left.

1.6 ▲ SO Track on left and track on right.

▼ 5.2 SO Track on left.

1.2 ▲ SO Track on right.

▼ 5.8 SO Track on right.

0.6 ▲ SO Track on left.

▼ 6.3 SO Pine Springs. Water tower on left; track on left and track on right.

0.1 ▲ SO Water tower on right; track on left and track on right. Leaving Pine Springs.
GPS: N35°24.24' W109°16.80'

▼ 6.4 BL Bear left at fork onto Oak Ridge Road. Pine Springs Road continues ahead. Zero trip meter.

0.0 ▲ Continue to the south.
GPS: N35°24.37' W109°16.73'

▼ 0.0 Continue to the north.

9.3 ▲ BR Bear right onto Pine Springs Road and enter Pine Springs. Zero trip meter.

▼ 0.2 SO Track on right.

9.1 ▲ SO Track on left.

▼ 0.6 SO Track on right.

8.7 ▲ SO Track on left.

▼ 0.9 SO Track on left.

8.4 ▲ SO Track on right.

▼ 1.0 SO Track on left and track on right.

8.3 ▲ SO Track on right and track on left.

▼ 1.6 SO Track on right.

7.7 ▲ SO Track on left.

▼ 1.7 SO Graded road on right.

7.6 ▲ SO Graded road on left.

▼ 3.6 SO Two tracks on right; then track on left.

5.7 ▲ SO Track on right; then two tracks on left.

▼ 4.1 SO Track on right.

5.2 ▲ SO Track on left.

▼ 5.2 SO Track on right.

4.1 ▲ SO Track on left.

▼ 5.9 SO Track on right.

3.4 ▲ SO Track on left.

▼ 6.4 SO Two tracks on right and track on left; then cross through wash.

2.9 ▲ SO Cross through wash; then track on right and two tracks on left.
GPS: N35°30.02' W109°18.06'

▼ 6.5 SO Track on left to Antelope Well.

2.8 ▲ SO Track on right to Antelope Well.

▼ 6.6 SO Track on left.

2.7 ▲ SO Track on right.

▼ 7.1 SO Track on left.

2.2 ▲ SO Track on right.

▼ 7.6 SO Track on left to well and tank.

1.7 ▲ SO Track on right to well and tank.
GPS: N35°31.18' W109°18.66'

▼ 7.8 SO Track on right.

1.5 ▲ SO Track on left.

▼ 7.9 SO Track on left and track on right.

1.4 ▲ SO Track on right and track on left.

Oak Ridge Fire Lookout is staffed during the day in fire season

▼ 8.0   SO Two tracks on left.
1.3 ▲   SO Two tracks on right.
▼ 8.2   SO Two tracks on right.
1.1 ▲   SO Two tracks on left.
▼ 8.7   SO Track on left.
0.6 ▲   SO Track on right.
▼ 9.2   SO Track on right.
0.1 ▲   SO Track on left.
▼ 9.3   TR Major staggered intersection. Turn
             right at the sign for Banana Wash
             Road at major graded road intersec-
             tion. Graded road straight on is South
             Summit Road; bear right, remaining on
             the major graded road. Zero trip meter.
0.0 ▲   Continue to the southeast.
             GPS: N35°32.48' W109°19.34'

▼ 0.0   Continue to the northeast; second
             track on left.
6.0 ▲   TL Track on right; then South Summit
             Road goes to the right. Bear left; then
             turn left on Oak Ridge Road. Banana
             Wash Road signed to Antelope is
             straight on at this point. Zero trip
             meter.
▼ 0.1   SO Track on right.
5.9 ▲   SO Track on left.
▼ 0.2   SO Track on right.
5.8 ▲   SO Track on left.
▼ 0.5   SO Track on right and track on left.
5.5 ▲   SO Track on left and track on right.
▼ 1.0   SO Track on right.
5.0 ▲   SO Track on left.
▼ 1.6   SO Track on left.
4.4 ▲   SO Track on right.
▼ 1.9   SO Track on left.
4.1 ▲   SO Track on right.
▼ 2.0   SO Track on right.
4.0 ▲   SO Track on left.
▼ 2.2   SO Track on left.
3.8 ▲   SO Track on right.
▼ 2.4   SO Track on right.
3.6 ▲   SO Track on left.
▼ 2.7   SO Track on left.
3.3 ▲   SO Track on right.
▼ 2.8   SO Track on left.
3.2 ▲   SO Track on right.
▼ 2.9   SO Two tracks on right and track on left.
3.1 ▲   SO Track on right and two tracks on left.
▼ 3.5   SO Track on right.

2.5 ▲   SO Track on left.
▼ 3.6   SO Two tracks on right and track on left.
2.4 ▲   SO Two tracks on left and track on right.
▼ 3.8   SO Track on right; then cross over gas
             pipeline.
2.2 ▲   SO Cross over gas pipeline; then track
             on left.
             GPS: N35°34.89' W109°16.36'

▼ 4.3   SO Track on left.
1.7 ▲   SO Track on right.
▼ 5.3   SO Track on left.
0.7 ▲   SO Track on right.
▼ 5.7   SO Track on left.
0.3 ▲   SO Track on right.
▼ 6.0   SO Track on right; then track on left signed
             to Oak Ridge Lookout. Zero trip meter.
0.0 ▲   Continue to the southwest.
             GPS: N35°36.07' W109°14.48'

▼ 0.0   Continue to the northeast.
6.0 ▲   SO Track on right signed to Oak Ridge
             Lookout; then track on left. Zero trip
             meter.
▼ 0.1   SO Track on right.
5.9 ▲   SO Track on left.
▼ 0.3   SO Track on right.
5.7 ▲   SO Track on left.
▼ 0.5   SO Pass under power lines; then track on
             right and track on left alongside gas
             pipeline.
5.5 ▲   SO Track on right and track on left along-
             side gas pipeline; then pass under
             power lines.
             GPS: N35°36.27' W109°13.97'

▼ 1.3   SO Track on right to well and tank and
             track on left.
4.7 ▲   SO Track on left to well and tank and track
             on right.
             GPS: N35°36.79' W109°13.41'

▼ 1.8   SO Track on left.
4.2 ▲   SO Track on right.
▼ 1.9   SO Track on right.
4.1 ▲   SO Track on left.
▼ 2.2   SO Track on right.
3.8 ▲   SO Track on left.
▼ 2.6   SO Two tracks on right.
3.4 ▲   SO Two tracks on left.

Crossing through mature pines on the quiet Defiance Plateau

▼ 2.9	SO	Two tracks on right.
3.1 ▲	SO	Two tracks on left.
▼ 3.1	SO	Track on right.
2.9 ▲	SO	Track on left.
▼ 3.2	SO	Track on right and track on left.
2.8 ▲	SO	Track on right and track on left.
▼ 3.4	SO	Track on left.
2.6 ▲	SO	Track on right.
▼ 3.8	SO	Track on left.
2.2 ▲	SO	Track on right.
▼ 4.1	SO	Track on right.
1.9 ▲	SO	Track on left.
▼ 4.3	SO	Track on right and track on left.
1.7 ▲	SO	Track on right and track on left.
▼ 4.7	SO	Track on left and track on right.
1.3 ▲	SO	Track on left and track on right.
▼ 4.8	SO	Track on left.
1.2 ▲	SO	Track on right.
▼ 5.0	SO	Track on left.
1.0 ▲	SO	Track on right.
▼ 5.3	SO	Track on left and track on right.
0.7 ▲	SO	Track on left and track on right.
▼ 5.4	SO	Track on right to communications tower.
0.6 ▲	SO	Track on left to communications tower.

GPS: N35°40.33′ W109°12.48′

▼ 5.5	SO	Track on right and track on left to communications tower.
0.5 ▲	SO	Track on left and track on right to communications tower.
▼ 5.6	SO	Track on right and track on left.
0.4 ▲	SO	Track on left and track on right.
▼ 6.0		Trail ends at the T-intersection with paved Arizona 264. Turn right for St. Michaels and Window Rock; turn left for Ganado.
0.0 ▲		From Arizona 264, 5.1 miles west of St. Michaels and 1.5 miles west of mile marker 468, zero trip meter and turn south over cattle guard on graded dirt road toward communications towers.

GPS: N35°40.72′ W109°12.25′

Black Creek Trail

STARTING POINT: Intersection of IR 112 and IR 7
FINISHING POINT: IR 12 near Red Lake
TOTAL MILEAGE: 11.6 miles
UNPAVED MILEAGE: 11.2 miles
DRIVING TIME: 45 minutes
ELEVATION RANGE: 7,000–7,200 feet
USUALLY OPEN: Year-round
BEST TIME TO TRAVEL: Dry weather
DIFFICULTY RATING: 1
SCENIC RATING: 8
REMOTENESS RATING: +0

Special Attractions

■ Easy trail running along a wide, scenic valley.
■ Camping and fishing at Red Lake.

Description

This graded road runs along Black Creek Valley, parallel to paved Indian Road 12. It is a well-used road because it accesses several houses. The valley is wide and shallow, and the meandering, often dry Black Creek is to the east. The Chuska Mountains are to the east of the valley, just across the state line in New Mexico.

The trail ends on Indian Road 12 a short distance into New Mexico, at the entrance to Red Lake, a popular fishing and camping place. For more information on Red Lake, refer to Northeast #42: Red Valley Trail.

Current Road Information

Navajo Nation Parks and Recreation
PO Box 2520
Window Rock, AZ 86515
(928) 871-6647

Map References

BLM   Ganado
USGS   1:24,000   Fort Defiance, Buell Park
        1:100,000 Ganado
Maptech CD-ROM: Northeast
        Arizona/Navajo County

Arizona Atlas & Gazetteer, p. 35
New Mexico Atlas & Gazetteer, p. 20
Arizona Road & Recreation Atlas, pp. 37, 71
New Mexico Road & Recreation Atlas,
pp. 10, 34

Route Directions

▼ 0.0   From IR 12, 1.7 miles north of Fort Defiance, turn west at the stop light onto IR 7 and proceed west for 1.5 miles. Zero trip meter and turn north on IR 112, which is a short distance west of Black Creek. Road is initially paved; cross cattle guard.

10.6 ▲   Trail ends at the 4-way intersection with IR 7. Cross cattle guard and then turn left onto IR 7; proceed for 1.5 miles to stoplight. Turn right at stoplight for Fort Defiance.

GPS: N35°45.62′ W109°04.30′

▼ 0.3   SO   Road is now graded dirt. Many tracks on right and left to houses. Remain on main road.

10.3 ▲   Road is now paved.

▼ 1.7   SO   Track on right to well and tank.

8.9 ▲   SO   Track on left to well and tank.

GPS: N35°46.98′ W109°03.35′

▼ 2.4   SO   Well-used track on left and small track on right.

8.2 ▲   SO   Well-used track on right and small track on left.

▼ 2.9   SO   Track on left.
7.7 ▲   SO   Track on right.
▼ 4.6   SO   Track on right.
6.0 ▲   SO   Track on left.
▼ 4.9   SO   Two tracks on right and track on left.
5.7 ▲   SO   Two tracks on left and track on right.
▼ 5.5   SO   Track on right.
5.1 ▲   SO   Track on left.
▼ 5.7   SO   Track on right.
4.9 ▲   SO   Track on left.
▼ 6.9   SO   Track on right.
3.7 ▲   SO   Track on left.

GPS: N35°51.40′ W109°02.97′

▼ 7.0   SO   Graded road on right.

3.6 ▲   SO   Graded road on left.

GPS: N35°51.50′ W109°03.05′

Black Creek Valley with the Chuska Mountains in the distance

Northeast Trail #41: Black Creek Trail

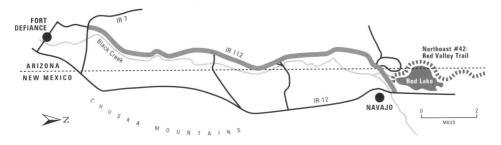

▼ 7.8	SO	Track on right.
2.8 ▲	SO	Track on left.
▼ 8.1	SO	Cross over irrigation ditch; tracks on left and right along ditch.
2.5 ▲	SO	Cross over irrigation ditch; tracks on left and right along ditch.
▼ 9.1	SO	Track on left.
1.5 ▲	SO	Track on right.
▼ 9.6	SO	Cross over irrigation ditch.
1.0 ▲	SO	Cross over irrigation ditch.
▼ 10.6	TR	Trail intersection with large graded dirt road. Also road ahead. Zero trip meter and turn right toward the town of Navajo.
0.0 ▲		Continue to the south.

GPS: N35°54.51′ W109°02.79′

▼ 0.0		Continue to the northeast.
1.0 ▲	TL	Turn left onto graded dirt road at unmarked intersection. Also track on right over cattle guard. Zero trip meter.
▼ 0.1	SO	Track on right; then cross over Black Creek.
0.9 ▲	SO	Cross over Black Creek; then track on left.
▼ 0.4	SO	Track on right.
0.6 ▲	SO	Track on left.
▼ 0.5	SO	Cross over drainage ditch.
0.5 ▲	SO	Cross over drainage ditch.

Eye-catching red sandstone walls of the Chuska Mountains on the east side of the valley

LOST ADAMS DIGGINGS

Near Fort Defiance, by the Arizona–New Mexico state line, and just a bit north of Window Rock, the fabled Adams Mine is said to exist. The story begins with Henry Adams (sometimes called Jim Adams). He established a small trading post at Fort Defiance and was making a tidy profit by catering to Indians, particularly the Navajo. One day, three Navajo entered the general store and bought a large amount of goods. They paid for their purchases with a glittering mound of gold nuggets. Adams was astonished. Every time the three came into the store, they'd pay for their goods in gold dust or gold nuggets. Adams was determined to find out the source of their wealth.

Slowly, he gained the Indians' confidence and after some time Adams was able to discuss the location of the gold. In fact, the Navajo trusted Adams so much that they agreed to show him where the gold was coming from. There was one catch—Adams had to be blindfolded during the trip. Adams agreed and the four rode off to the mouth of a canyon. When the blindfold came off he was in a cavernous room and the floor was glittering with gold. The sight was breathtaking, but it was also brief as the blindfold quickly came back on. A blast of cool air hit him in the face, which made him think that the cave had more than one entrance. He asked the Indians if he could take some gold with him. Politely, the Indians refused and led him out of the cave. Curiosity, and probably greed, overtook Adams and he slid the blindfold away from his eyes. He saw three similar peaks in a triangular formation. The Indians realized he had peeked, and feeling betrayed, they re-covered his eyes and hustled him away. That was the last time they ever met.

The sight of so much gold possessed Adams, and upon his return he immediately sold his shop and spent his days, and his money, looking for the Navajo gold. Each expedition proved futile. He arrived in Tucson broken-hearted, but his stories captured the attention of Judge Griscom. Griscom financed further searches but Adams continually came up empty-handed. The financing was cut and Adams was left bankrupt. The search for the fortune consumed Adams and left him broken and despondent. When no one else would finance his search, Adams shot himself in the head, and he died in Tucson.

▼ 0.9   SO   Track on left goes across the dam wall of Red Lake and is the start of Northeast #42: Red Valley Trail.

0.1 ▲   SO   Track on right goes across the dam wall of Red Lake and is the start of Northeast #42: Red Valley Trail.
GPS: N35°54.99′ W109°01.95′

▼ 1.0   Trail ends at the intersection with IR 12. Turn right for Fort Defiance.

0.0 ▲   The trail starts on IR 12, 13.3 miles north of Fort Defiance. The trail begins in New Mexico but crosses into Arizona almost immediately. The state line is unmarked. Zero trip meter.
GPS: N35°55.05′ W109°01.90′

Red Valley Trail

STARTING POINT: Northeast #41: Black Creek Trail, IR 112, near Red Lake

FINISHING POINT: Intersection with Northeast #43: Sawmill Navajo Trail, IR 72

TOTAL MILEAGE: 7.5 miles

UNPAVED MILEAGE: 7.5 miles

DRIVING TIME: 1 hour

ELEVATION RANGE: 7,100–7,300 feet

USUALLY OPEN: Year-round

BEST TIME TO TRAVEL: Dry weather

DIFFICULTY RATING: 3

SCENIC RATING: 8

REMOTENESS RATING: +0

Northeast Trail #42: Red Valley Trail

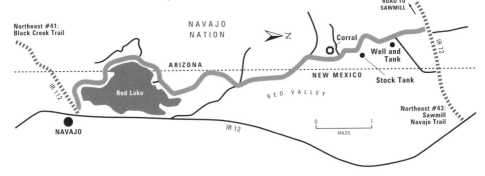

Special Attractions
- Fishing for catfish at Red Lake.
- Camping opportunities near Red Lake.

Description

Red Lake is very popular with fishermen. It is one of the best places to catch catfish in the Navajo Nation. The lake, set in a wide valley under the shadow of the Chuska Mountains to the east in New Mexico, has several miles of grassy shoreline interspersed with marshy banks and some rocky outcrops. This trail commences by crossing the rutted track that leads across the top of the dam at the south end of the lake. The deep ruts show that this area is extremely muddy and best avoided in wet weather—a good policy for the entire trail.

Once on the west side of the dam wall, the trail runs northward around the lakeshore. There are numerous pull-ins for fishermen and campers. A tribal fishing permit is essential if you are planning to fish; for night fishing, a camping permit is required as well.

The north end of the lake is quieter than the south. The trail, which gradually travels along Red Valley, is unmarked once it leaves the lake; a plethora of small trails crisscross the main trail. For the most part, the best-used trail is the correct one, but there are a couple of turns that will keep navigators on their toes. In particular the 4-way intersection at the zero trip meter point approximately halfway along the trail is easily missed, especially in the reverse direction.

The trail continues up Red Valley, giving views over the Chuska Mountains to the east and Sonsela Buttes to the north. It finishes at the intersection with Northeast #43: Sawmill Navajo Trail, Indian Road 72. From here, Indian Road 12, a paved road, is 1.8 miles to the east.

Current Road Information

Navajo Nation Parks and Recreation
PO Box 2520
Window Rock, AZ 86515
(928) 871-6647

Map References

BLM   Ganado
USGS 1:24,000   Buell Park, Sonsela Buttes
         1:100,000 Ganado
Maptech CD-ROM: Northeast
         Arizona/Navajo County
Arizona Atlas & Gazetteer, p. 35;
New Mexico Altas & Gazetteer, p. 20

Route Directions

▼ 0.0   0.1 miles from the western end of
         Northeast #41: Black Creek Trail at
         Red Lake, zero trip meter and turn
         west across the cattle guard and start
         to cross the dam wall at the south end
         of Red Lake.

4.0 ▲   Cattle guard; then trail ends at the
         intersection with Northeast #41:
         Black Creek Trail. Turn right to follow
         Black Creek Trail to Fort Defiance. Turn
         left and travel 0.1 miles to join IR 12,
         the paved road to Fort Defiance.

GPS: N35°54.99′ W109°01.95′

▼ 0.5   BR   Bear right off dam wall and wrap north along the lakeshore.

3.5 ▲   BL   Bear left and start to cross the dam wall.

▼ 1.0   BL   Track on right stays close to lakeshore and goes to pull-ins and fishing spots. Bear left up hill.

3.0 ▲   BR   Track on left stays close to lakeshore and goes to pull-ins and fishing spots. Bear right and continue along the lakeshore.

GPS: N35°55.46′ W109°02.60′

▼ 1.1   SO   Track on left and track on right on crest of hill.

2.9 ▲   SO   Track on left and track on right on crest of hill.

▼ 1.2   SO   Track on right.

2.8 ▲   SO   Track on left.

▼ 1.7   BR   Track on left through gate; bear right, remaining along lakeshore.

2.3 ▲   SO   Track on right through gate; continue on around the lakeshore.

GPS: N35°55.88′ W109°02.96′

▼ 1.8   BR   Track on left.

2.2 ▲   BL   Track on right.

▼ 2.1   SO   Track on right.

1.9 ▲   SO   Track on left.

GPS: N35°56.20′ W109°02.76′

▼ 2.3   SO   Track on right on slight rise.

1.7 ▲   SO   Track on left on slight rise.

▼ 2.4   SO   Track on right.

1.6 ▲   SO   Track on left.

GPS: N35°56.33′ W109°02.51′

▼ 2.7   BL   Two tracks on right; bear left across cattle guard; then track on right.

1.3 ▲   BR   Track on left; then cattle guard; then bear right past two tracks on left.

GPS: N35°56.47′ W109°02.31′

▼ 2.9   SO   Track on right.

1.1 ▲   SO   Track on left.

▼ 3.3   SO   Track on right.

0.7 ▲   BR   Track on left.

▼ 3.4   SO   Cattle guard.

0.6 ▲   SO   Cattle guard.

▼ 3.9   BL   Track on right.

0.1 ▲   SO   Track on left.

Red Lake, noted for its catfish

The trail heads toward the Chuska Mountains

▼ 4.0   TL   4-way intersection. Turn left onto slightly larger trail. Zero trip meter. Intersection is unmarked.

0.0 ▲   Continue to the southwest.
      GPS: N35°57.49' W109°02.42'

▼ 0.0   Continue to the north; track on right.

2.9 ▲   BR   Bear right onto well-used trail; track on left; then turn immediately right onto well-used, smaller trail heading southwest. Zero trip meter.

▼ 0.1   BR   Track on left.
2.8 ▲   SO   Track on right.

▼ 0.4   SO   Track on right and track on left.
2.5 ▲   SO   Track on left and track on right.

▼ 0.7   SO   Faint track on right.
2.2 ▲   SO   Faint track on left.

▼ 0.9   SO   Faint track on right.
2.0 ▲   SO   Faint track on left.

▼ 1.3   BR   Track on left; bear right and cross cattle guard.

1.6 ▲   BL   Cross cattle guard; then bear left past track on right.
      GPS: N35°58.62' W109°02.94'

▼ 1.7   BR   Track on left to corral and sheds.
1.2 ▲   SO   Track on right to corral and sheds.

▼ 1.9   SO   Track on left and track on right.
1.0 ▲   SO   Track on right and track on left.
      GPS: N35°59.09' W109°02.74'

▼ 2.2   SO   Track on right; then cattle guard.
0.7 ▲   SO   Cattle guard; then track on left.

▼ 2.3   SO   Stock tank on right.
0.6 ▲   SO   Stock tank on left.

▼ 2.4   SO   Track on right and track on left.
0.5 ▲   SO   Track on left and track on right.

▼ 2.7   SO   Track on left.
0.2 ▲   BL   Track on right.

▼ 2.9   SO   Well and tank on right; track on right and track on left. Zero trip meter.

0.0 ▲   Continue to the south.
      GPS: N35°59.93' W109°03.31'

▼ 0.0   Continue to the north.
0.6 ▲   SO   Well and tank on left; track on right and track on left. Zero trip meter.

▼ 0.2   SO   Track on right.
0.4 ▲   SO   Track on left.

▼ 0.4   SO   Track on left.
0.2 ▲   SO   Track on right.

▼ 0.6   SO   Trail ends at the intersection with Northeast #43: Sawmill Navajo Trail (IR 72). Turn right to exit to IR 12; turn left to continue along the trail to Sawmill. There is also a track straight ahead.

0.0 ▲   Trail starts on Northeast #43: Sawmill Navajo Trail (IR 72), 1.8 miles from the intersection with IR 12 (the eastern end of the trail). Zero trip meter and turn south on the unmarked, formed trail. A well and tank can be seen a short distance down the trail. There is also a track to the north.

GPS: N36°00.40′ W109°03.58′

Sawmill Navajo Trail

STARTING POINT: IR 12, 0.2 miles north of mile marker 49
FINISHING POINT: IR 7 at Sawmill
TOTAL MILEAGE: 12.3 miles
UNPAVED MILEAGE: 12.3 miles
DRIVING TIME: 1 hour
ELEVATION RANGE: 7,200–8,000 feet
USUALLY OPEN: YEAR-ROUND
BEST TIME TO TRAVEL: Dry weather
DIFFICULTY RATING: 2
SCENIC RATING: 8
REMOTENESS RATING: +1

Special Attractions

■ Great views traveling along a ridge top in the Navajo Nation.

Description

This trail travels through some of the forest areas of the Navajo Nation. The trail leaves Indian Road 12, 7 miles north of the small settlement of Navajo, New Mexico, which is just to the south of Red Lake. The well-used, single-track trail crests a rise and then runs across open Red Valley before entering the forest. Much of the trail travels along a ridge top, giving views east over red rock buttes and the Chuska Mountains. The surface is very rutted and eroded and only suitable for travel in dry weather. The final section of the trail follows a graded dirt road as it emerges from the forest at the settlement of Sawmill.

Current Road Information

Navajo Nation Parks and Recreation
PO Box 2520
Window Rock, AZ 86515
(928) 871-6647

Map References

BLM   Canyon de Chelly, Ganado
USGS 1:24,000 Sonsela Buttes, Buell Park, Sawmill
     1:100,000 Canyon de Chelly, Ganado
Maptech CD-ROM: Northeast Arizona/Navajo County
Arizona Atlas & Gazetteer, p. 35
New Mexico Atlas & Gazetteer, p. 20
Recreational Map of Arizona

Route Directions

▼ 0.0   Trail commences on IR 12, 7.3 miles north of Navajo, New Mexico. Zero trip meter and turn southwest across cattle guard. Intersection is unmarked but is 0.2 miles north of mile marker 49. Small track opposite.

1.8 ▲   Cattle guard; then trail ends at T-intersection with IR 12. Turn right for Window Rock; turn left for Tsaile.

    GPS: N36°01.02′ W109°01.71′

▼ 0.1 SO Track on right to house.
1.7 ▲ SO Track on left to house.
▼ 0.2 SO Track on right and track on left on top of rise.
1.6 ▲ SO Track on right and track on left on top of rise.

    GPS: N36°00.88′ W109°01.88′

▼ 0.3 SO Track on left.
1.5 ▲ SO Track on right.
▼ 0.5 SO Track on left.
1.3 ▲ SO Track on right.
▼ 0.7 SO Track on left.
1.1 ▲ SO Track on right.
▼ 0.9 SO Track on right.
0.9 ▲ SO Track on left.
▼ 1.0 SO Faint track on left; then track on right.
0.8 ▲ SO Track on left; then faint track on right.
▼ 1.3 SO Track on left.

Ruts created by drivers unwisely attempting the trail in wet conditions

Crossing Defiance Plateau on Sawmill Navajo Trail

0.5 ▲ SO Track on right.
▼ 1.4 SO Track on right.
0.4 ▲ SO Track on left.
▼ 1.6 SO Track on right; then cross through wash.
0.2 ▲ SO Cross through wash; then track on left.
▼ 1.7 SO Track on left.
0.1 ▲ SO Track on right.
▼ 1.8 Track on left is Northeast #42: Red Valley Trail. Zero trip meter.
0.0 ▲ Continue to the northeast.
GPS: N36°00.40' W109°03.58'

▼ 0.0 Continue to the southwest.
2.7 ▲ Track on right is Northeast #42: Red Valley Trail. Zero trip meter.

▼ 0.7 BL 4-way intersection. Bear left, leaving two tracks on the right.
2.0 ▲ BR 4-way intersection. Bear right, leaving two tracks on the left.
GPS: N36°00.03' W109°04.16'

▼ 0.8 SO Track on left and track on right.
1.9 ▲ SO Track on left and track on right.
GPS: N35°59.95' W109°04.19'

▼ 1.5 SO Track on right.
1.2 ▲ SO Track on left.
▼ 2.1 BL Track on right.
0.6 ▲ SO Track on left.
GPS: N35°59.37' W109°05.42'

▼ 2.6 SO Track on right.
0.1 ▲ SO Track on left.
▼ 2.7 SO Well-used track on left and track on right in small clearing. Zero trip meter.
0.0 ▲ Continue to the north.
GPS: N35°58.97' W109°05.77'

▼ 0.0 Continue to the south.
4.7 ▲ SO Well-used track on right and track on left in small clearing. Zero trip meter.
▼ 0.3 SO Track on right.
4.4 ▲ SO Track on left.
▼ 1.0 SO Track on right.
3.7 ▲ SO Track on left.
▼ 1.2 SO Track on left.
3.5 ▲ SO Track on right.
▼ 1.9 SO Track on left; then well-used track on right.
2.8 ▲ SO Well-used track on left; then track on right.

![map]

ROAD TO TSAILE

R E D V A L L E Y

IR 12

ROAD TO WINDOW ROCK

NEW MEXICO
ARIZONA

Northeast #42: Red Valley Trail

NAVAJO NATION

CR 445

N

0   2
MILES

CR 313

SAWMILL

IR 7

ROAD TO GANADO

ROAD TO FORT DEFIANCE

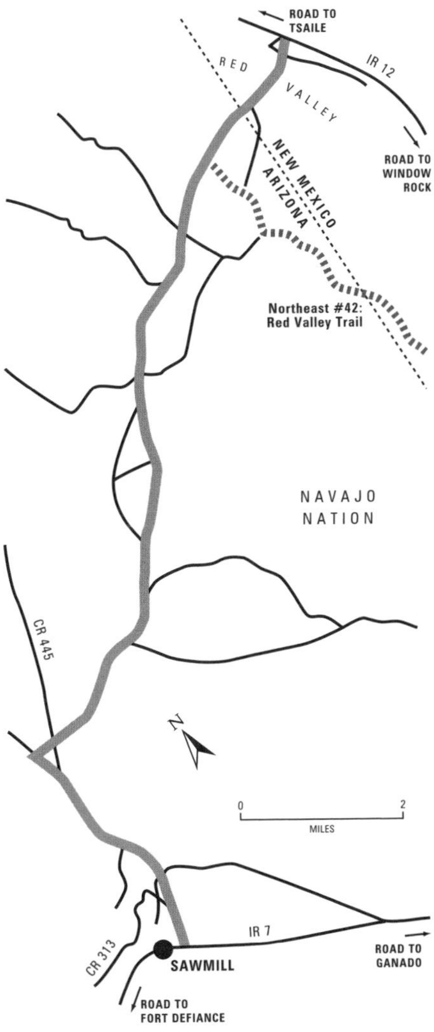

GPS: N35°57.52' W109°06.88'

▼ 2.1 SO Track on right.
2.6 ▲ SO Track on left.
▼ 2.2 SO Track on right.
2.5 ▲ BR Track on left.
▼ 2.3 SO Track on left.
2.4 ▲ SO Track on right.
▼ 2.6 SO Track on left.
2.1 ▲ BL Track on right.
GPS: N35°57.04' W109°07.26'

▼ 3.0 SO Track on left.
1.7 ▲ SO Track on right.

▼ 3.2	SO	Well-used track on left and small track on right.
1.5 ▲	SO	Small track on left and well-used track on right.

GPS: N35°56.77′ W109°07.81′

▼ 3.8	SO	Track on left.
0.9 ▲	BL	Track on right.
▼ 4.5	SO	Two tracks on left.
0.2 ▲	SO	Two tracks on right.
▼ 4.7	BL	Join larger graded dirt road. Graded dirt road on right is marked CR 445. Zero trip meter.
0.0 ▲		Continue to the east.

GPS: N35°56.31′ W109°09.35′

▼ 0.0		Continue to the west.
0.2 ▲	BR	Bear right onto smaller graded dirt road. Larger graded dirt road, CR 445, continues around to the left. Zero trip meter.
▼ 0.2	TL	T-intersection with large, graded gravel road. Zero trip meter.
0.0 ▲		Continue to the east.

GPS: N35°56.31′ W109°09.61′

▼ 0.0		Continue to the south toward Sawmill.
2.9 ▲	TR	Turn right onto graded gravel road and zero trip meter. Intersection is unmarked.
▼ 0.1	SO	Track on right.
2.8 ▲	SO	Track on left.
▼ 0.3	SO	Track on left.
2.6 ▲	SO	Track on right.
▼ 0.4	SO	Track on left.
2.5 ▲	SO	Track on right.
▼ 0.8	SO	Track on right.
2.1 ▲	SO	Track on left.
▼ 1.2	SO	Track on right and track on left.
1.7 ▲	SO	Track on right and track on left.
▼ 1.5	SO	Graded road on right.
1.4 ▲	SO	Graded road on left.
▼ 2.0	SO	Well-used track on left and graded road on right.
0.9 ▲	SO	Graded road on left and well-used track on right.

GPS: N35°54.59′ W109°09.11′

▼ 2.4	SO	Graded road on right is CR 313.
0.5 ▲	SO	Graded road on left is CR 313.

GPS: N35°54.26′ W109°09.21′

▼ 2.9		Cattle guard; then trail finishes on IR 7 at Sawmill. Turn left for Fort Defiance; turn right for Ganado.
0.0 ▲		Trail commences on IR 7 at Sawmill. Zero trip meter and turn north on wide, graded dirt White Clay Road marked with a road sign. Also sign to White Clay. Immediately cross cattle guard. Turn is 0.2 miles east of mile marker 14.

GPS: N35°53.81′ W109°09.35′

NORTHEAST REGION TRAIL #44

Fluted Rock Road

STARTING POINT: IR 7, 2.5 miles southwest of Sawmill
FINISHING POINT: Canyon de Chelly Visitor Center
TOTAL MILEAGE: 31.1 miles
UNPAVED MILEAGE: 20.6 miles
DRIVING TIME: 3 hours
ELEVATION RANGE: 5,500–8,100 feet
USUALLY OPEN: Year-round
BEST TIME TO TRAVEL: Dry weather
DIFFICULTY RATING: 2
SCENIC RATING: 9
REMOTENESS RATING: +0

Special Attractions
- South Rim Drive of Canyon de Chelly National Monument.
- Shady forest drive.
- Excellent photo opportunities from many overlooks into Canyon de Chelly.
- Optional 4-rated climb up to Fluted Rock Fire Lookout.

Description
Canyon de Chelly National Monument is one of the biggest attractions within the Navajo Nation and deservedly so. The paved South Rim Drive takes visitors past many overlooks into the canyon, where they can peer down into the red-walled chasm and see farmland and the vehicle trail far below. It al-

so offers glimpses of some of the famous rock formations and ruins, such as Spider Woman Rock and White House Ruin. The rim drive does not equal the trail along the floor of the canyon for a real feel of the nature and life in the canyon, but it complements it well. For those with limited time, it makes a stunning introduction to Canyon de Chelly.

The trail starts on Indian Road 7, a short distance west of the settlement of Sawmill. Most of the road early on is wide graded dirt. It is very rutted, and in wet weather the clay quickly becomes impassable, even to 4WD vehicles. The section from Sawmill to the South Rim Drive runs mainly through a shady pine forest.

One highlight along this section is the accurately named Fluted Rock. The folds of the rock resemble organ pipes or the fluted edge of a pie crust; hence the name. A short side trail rewards drivers of high-clearance 4WDs with a spectacular view from the top of the rock. The 4-rated trail climbs the north face of Fluted Rock, crossing a loose rocky surface and expanses of the rock itself to the fire lookout perched on the top. When the lookout is manned in fire season, you are usually welcome to climb into the tower. Do be sure that you have the lookout's permission first. As the tower is small, only two visitors at any one time can climb up. The view from the tower is one of the best in the region. The red rock face of the Chuska Mountains can be seen stretching from north to south. Fluted Rock Lake, a small body of water, can be seen to the north in a clearing in the trees, and there are expansive views over the forest toward Canyon de Chelly, although the canyon itself is not distinguishable.

The trail joins the paved South Rim Drive of Canyon de Chelly close to its final point—the overlook of Spider Woman Rock. There are many turns along the trail to overlooks into the canyon. The overlook of White House Ruin is also the trailhead for White House Ruin Trail (1.5 miles each way) and a strenuous hike that descends to the floor of the canyon to the ruin. This is the only trail into the canyon that visitors may take unaccompanied by a Navajo guide.

The trail finishes at Canyon de Chelly National Monument Visitor Center, where you can arrange guide services for journeys into the canyon. There are also interpretive displays. The rangers are active in organizing walks and excellent interpretive talks, many of which are by local Navajo.

Current Road Information

Navajo Nation Parks and Recreation
PO Box 2520
Window Rock, AZ 86515
(928) 871-6647

Map References

BLM   Ganado, Canyon de Chelly
USGS 1:24,000   Sawmill, White Rock
        Wash, Spider Rock, Three Turkey
        Canyon, Del Muerto, Chinle
        1:100,000 Ganado, Canyon de
        Chelly
Maptech CD-ROM: Northeast
        Arizona/Navajo County
Arizona Atlas & Gazetteer, p. 35
Arizona Road & Recreation Atlas, pp. 37,
        31, 71, 65
Recreational Map of Arizona

Route Directions

▼ 0.0   From IR 7, 2.5 miles southwest of
         Sawmill, at a major fork in the road,
         zero trip meter and turn west on wide
         graded dirt road. The wide graded road
         to the south goes to Ganado. The inter-
         section is unmarked. There are some
         picnic tables under the trees on the
         right at the intersection.

3.3 ▲   Trail ends at major intersection with
         graded dirt road on the right that goes
         to Ganado. Turn right for Ganado; bear
         left to continue to Sawmill.
         GPS: N35°52.52′ W109°12.14′

▼ 0.6   SO Track on right.
2.7 ▲   SO Track on left.
▼ 1.0   SO Track on right.
2.3 ▲   SO Track on left.
▼ 1.2   SO Track on right.
2.1 ▲   SO Track on left.

View from Tsegi Overlook into Canyon de Chelly

▼ 1.6   SO Track on left.

1.7 ▲   SO Track on right.

      GPS: N35°52.73′ W109°13.79′

▼ 2.1   SO Track on right; then track on left.

1.2 ▲   SO Track on right; then track on left.

      GPS: N35°53.00′ W109°14.25′

▼ 2.3   SO Track on left and track on right.

1.0 ▲   SO Track on left and track on right.

▼ 2.8   SO Track on right; then track on left. Fluted Rock on right.

0.5 ▲   SO Track on right; then track on left. Fluted Rock on left.

▼ 3.1   SO Track on left.

0.2 ▲   SO Track on right.

▼ 3.3   SO Track on left and graded road on right goes to Fluted Rock Fire Lookout. An old sign marks the turn. Small track on left. Zero trip meter.

0.0 ▲   Continue to the east.

      GPS: N35°52.92′ W109°15.49′

▼ 0.0   Continue to the west.

0.7 ▲   SO Graded road on left goes to Fluted Rock Fire Lookout. An old sign marks

the turn. Track on right; small track on right. Zero trip meter.

▼ 0.2   SO Track on left.

0.5 ▲   SO Track on right.

▼ 0.6   SO Track on right and track on left under power lines.

0.1 ▲   SO Track on left and track on right under power lines.

▼ 0.7   SO Graded dirt road on left is IR 9450. Smaller track on right. Zero trip meter.

0.0 ▲   Continue to the south.

      GPS: N35°53.51′ W109°15.82′

▼ 0.0   Continue to the north.

12.1 ▲   SO Graded road on right is IR 9450. Smaller track on left; continue straight on. Zero trip meter.

▼ 0.2   SO Track on left.

11.9 ▲   SO Track on right.

▼ 0.7   SO Track on left.

11.4 ▲   SO Track on right.

▼ 1.3   SO Small track on right.

10.8 ▲   SO Small track on left.

▼ 1.6   SO Track on left.

10.5 ▲   SO Track on right.

▼ 2.4   SO Track on left.

Fluted Rock

9.7 ▲ SO Track on right.

▼ 2.6 SO Track on right.

9.5 ▲ SO Track on left.

▼ 2.7 SO Track on right.

9.4 ▲ SO Track on left.

▼ 3.3 SO Track on left.

8.8 ▲ SO Track on right.

▼ 4.0 SO Track on left and track on right.

8.1 ▲ SO Track on left and track on right.
      GPS: N35°57.08′ W109°15.41′

▼ 4.1 SO Track on right.

8.0 ▲ SO Track on left.

▼ 4.2 SO Track on right.

7.9 ▲ SO Track on left.

▼ 4.3 SO Track on right.

7.8 ▲ SO Track on left.

▼ 4.6 SO Track on left.

7.5 ▲ SO Track on right.

▼ 4.8 SO Track on right.

7.3 ▲ SO Track on left.

▼ 5.1 SO Track on right.

7.0 ▲ SO Track on left.

▼ 5.4 SO Track on left; then track on right.

6.7 ▲ SO Track on left; then track on right.

▼ 5.5 SO Track on right and track on left.

6.6 ▲ SO Track on right and track on left.
      GPS: N35°57.66′ W109°16.84′

▼ 6.0 SO Track on left.

6.1 ▲ SO Track on right.

▼ 6.2 SO Track on right.

5.9 ▲ SO Track on left.

▼ 6.3 SO Track on left.

5.8 ▲ SO Track on right.

▼ 6.4 SO Track on right.

5.7 ▲ SO Track on left.

▼ 6.7 SO Track on left and track on right.

5.4 ▲ SO Track on left and track on right.

▼ 6.9 SO Track on right; then track on left.

5.2 ▲ SO Track on right; then track on left.

▼ 7.1 SO Track on right.

5.0 ▲ SO Track on left.

▼ 7.2 SO Track on right.

4.9 ▲ SO Track on left.

▼ 7.4 SO Track on left.

4.7 ▲ SO Track on right.

▼ 7.6 SO Track on right.

4.5 ▲ SO Track on left.

▼ 7.7 SO Track on right and track on left.

Northeast Trail #44: Fluted Rock Road

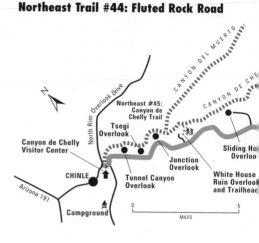

4.4 ▲ SO Track on right and track on left.

▼ 7.9 SO Track on right and track on left.

4.2 ▲ SO Track on right and track on left.

▼ 8.0 SO Track on left and track on right.

4.1 ▲ SO Track on left and track on right.

▼ 8.2 SO Track on right.

3.9 ▲ SO Track on left.

▼ 8.5 SO Three tracks on right.

3.6 ▲ SO Three tracks on left.

▼ 8.7 SO Track on left.

3.4 ▲ SO Track on right.

▼ 8.9 SO Two tracks on right and two tracks on left; road starts to descend.

3.2 ▲ SO Two tracks on right and two tracks on left.
      GPS: N35°59.49′ W109°19.30′

▼ 9.5 SO Track on right.

2.6 ▲ SO Track on left.

▼ 10.6 SO Track on left; then track on right.

1.5 ▲ SO Track on left; then track on right.

▼ 11.0 SO Track on right.

1.1 ▲ SO Track on left.

▼ 11.2 SO Track on left.

0.9 ▲ SO Track on right.

▼ 11.3 SO Track on right.

0.8 ▲ SO Track on left.

▼ 11.9 SO Track on left.

0.2 ▲ SO Track on right.

▼ 12.1 SO Major graded road on right and major graded road on left. The intersection is unmarked. Zero trip meter.

0.0 ▲   Continue to the southeast.
      GPS: N36°01.70′ W109°20.77′

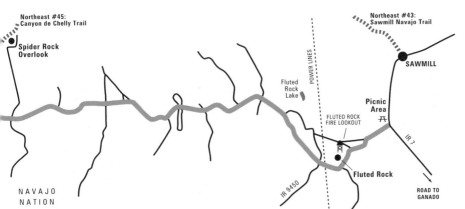

▼ 0.0   Continue to the northwest.

4.5 ▲   SO   Major graded road on right and major graded road on left. The intersection is unmarked. Zero trip meter.

▼ 0.4   SO   Track on right and track on left.

4.1 ▲   SO   Track on right and track on left.

▼ 0.7   SO   Track on right.

3.8 ▲   SO   Track on left.

▼ 0.9   SO   Track on left and track on right.

3.6 ▲   SO   Track on left and track on right.

▼ 1.0   SO   Two tracks on right.

3.5 ▲   SO   Two tracks on left.

▼ 1.1   SO   Track on right.

3.4 ▲   SO   Track on left.

▼ 1.8   SO   Track on left and two tracks on right.

2.7 ▲   SO   Track on right and two tracks on left.

▼ 2.2   SO   Track on right.

2.3 ▲   SO   Track on left.

       GPS: N36°02.94′ W109°22.48′

▼ 2.3   SO   Track on right.

2.2 ▲   SO   Track on left.

▼ 2.5   SO   Track on right.

2.0 ▲   SO   Track on left.

▼ 2.7   SO   Track on right.

1.8 ▲   SO   Track on left.

▼ 2.8   SO   Track on left and track on right.

1.7 ▲   SO   Track on right and track on left.

▼ 3.1   SO   Graded road on right; road on left to private property.

1.4 ▲   SO   Graded road on left; road on right to private property.

       GPS: N36°03.59′ W109°22.98′

▼ 3.3   SO   Track on left.

1.2 ▲   SO   Track on right.

▼ 3.6   SO   Track on left.

0.9 ▲   SO   Track on right.

▼ 4.5   SO   Paved road on right goes to Spider Rock Overlook (4.3 miles). Join paved road and continue straight on. Zero trip meter.

0.0 ▲   Continue to the southeast, following the sign to Fort Defiance.

       GPS: N36°04.22′ W109°24.41′

▼ 0.0   Continue to the northwest; graded road on left. Remain on paved road, ignoring turns to right and left, most of which go to private property.

2.3 ▲   SO   Graded road on right; then paved road on left goes to Spider Rock Overlook (4.3 miles). Continue straight on graded dirt road. Zero trip meter.

▼ 2.3   SO   Paved road on right goes to Sliding House Overlook (1.6 miles). Zero trip meter.

0.0 ▲   Continue to the southeast.

       GPS: N36°05.78′ W109°25.93′

▼ 0.0   Continue to the northwest.

3.4 ▲   SO   Paved road on left goes to Sliding House Overlook (1.6 miles). Zero trip meter.

▼ 3.4   SO   Paved road on right goes to White House Ruin Overlook and to hiking trailhead (0.7 miles). Zero trip meter.

A view into Canyon de Chelly where it joins Canyon del Muerto, with Dog Rock in the foreground

0.0 ▲   Continue to the east.
     GPS: N36°07.31′ W109°28.73′

▼ 0.0   Continue to the west.
1.4 ▲   SO Paved road on left goes to White House Ruin Overlook and to hiking trailhead (0.7 miles). Zero trip meter.

▼ 1.4   SO Paved road on right goes to Junction Overlook (0.1 miles), which overlooks the junction of Canyon de Chelly and Canyon del Muerto. Zero trip meter.
0.0 ▲   Continue to the east.
     GPS: N36°08.22′ W109°29.60′

▼ 0.0   Continue to the west.
3.4 ▲   SO Paved road on left goes to Junction Overlook (0.1 miles), which overlooks the junction of Canyon de Chelly and Canyon del Muerto. Zero trip meter.

▼ 1.2   SO Tsegi Overlook on right.
2.2 ▲   SO Tsegi Overlook on left.
     GPS: N36°08.32′ W109°30.68′

▼ 1.6   SO Tunnel Canyon Overlook on right.
1.8 ▲   SO Tunnel Canyon Overlook on left.

     GPS: N36°08.57′ W109°30.97′

▼ 3.1   SO Entrance to Canyon de Chelly on right. Road on left goes to free campground.
0.3 ▲   SO Entrance to Canyon de Chelly on left. Road on right goes to free campground.
     GPS: N36°08.57′ W109°30.97′

▼ 3.3   SO Paved road on right is North Rim Overlook Drive.
0.1 ▲   SO Paved road on left is North Rim Overlook Drive.

▼ 3.4   Trail ends at the entrance to the Canyon de Chelly Visitor Center on the left. Continue on to Chinle.
0.0 ▲   Trail commences at the entrance to the Canyon de Chelly Visitor Center, which is on the right. Zero trip meter and proceed northeast on the paved road toward the entrance to Canyon de Chelly.
     GPS: N36°09.20′ W109°32.35′

Antelope House Ruin

NAVAJO

The Navajo and their relatives the Apache are descendants of the Athapascan peoples who wandered from western Canada into the Southwest about a millennium ago. Like the Apache, the Navajo call themselves Diné, meaning "the People." They established their homeland between the Colorado, Rio Grande, and San Juan Rivers, in the Four Corners region of the modern United States. At first, the Navajo survived in the area by hunting and gathering, occasionally raiding Pueblo and Spanish settlements. However, the Navajo later adopted many Pueblo customs and crafts, such as farming and pottery making. Sheep and goats stolen from the Spanish were bred into large herds. These herds, combined with horses, gave the Navajo greater mobility.

Art and religion play key roles in tribal culture, and the two were often intertwined. Unique sand paintings were used to invoke spirits and relate to ancestors. In the absence of written records, oral chants related Navajo history and mythology from generation to generation. They brought to life fantastical images of the tribe's gods—creatures like the wily Coyote, the life-giving Earth Mother, and the far-seeing Spider Man. The Navajo also believed in malevolent ghosts, dead tribesmen who wander the land, bringing misfortune to the living.

Navajo rituals were lengthy and intricate. They varied from the Night Way Ceremony, used to cure illness, to the Enemy Way Ceremony, which freed a warrior from the ghosts of slain enemies. Most important was perhaps the *kinaaldá*, a significant event marking a girl's coming of age. This ceremony was essential before a female Navajo could be married.

The Navajo lived in conical or 8-sided structures known as hogans. The houses consisted of log frames covered in bark and earth with a single, east-facing doorway. The Navajo organized themselves into small groups, usually made up of a large extended family. For most of their history, no nationwide leader existed. Only in its struggles with the U.S. Army did the Navajo Nation unite.

The Navajo had a long history of aggression, often retributive, against white settlers. Spaniards in the area often kidnapped Indian children for use as slaves. The Navajo would respond by stealing settlers' livestock. Attempts to curtail the raiding tribe usually proved futile, although in 1805 the Spanish killed 115 Navajo who were fortified in Canyon del Muerto. The site is now known as Massacre Cave.

The United States took control of Navajo land in 1848. By the 1860s, conflicts between the settlers and Indians had climaxed. The disputes arose around grazing rights in the area near Canyon de Chelly, a sacred place to the Navajo. In 1860, the Indians, led by Manuelito, raided and almost conquered nearby Fort Defiance. Two years later, having driven Confederate troops from the area, the Union army focused its efforts on the belligerent tribe. Using the harsh tactics of the Civil War, United States forces, led in the field by Colonel Christopher "Kit" Carson burned their way through Navajo farmlands and orchards, destroying livestock and homes. By 1866 at least 8,500 Indians had surrendered, the largest capitulation in Native American history.

The unfortunate captives were forced on a terrible 300-mile trek to Bosque Redondo in eastern New Mexico, a journey now known as the "Long Walk." More than 2,000 Navajo perished before they were allowed to return to their homeland two years later. The Navajo Nation now covers 16 million acres, mostly in northeastern Arizona. Almost 250,000 Native Indians call the reservation home. Navajo land is open to the public, and tourism and recreation help sustain the tribe's economy. Also important are the oil and mineral resources that are rich in this area. However, many Navajo make a living producing traditional crafts. Their jewelry and rug weaving are especially renowned.

The Navajo are a proud people, and have also proved to be most patriotic. During World War II, 450 Navajos volunteered to serve in six Marine battalions. Their language was an unbreakable code, and the messages sent in that tongue were vital in the U.S. defeat of Japan.

Canyon de Chelly Trail

STARTING POINT: Canyon de Chelly Visitor Center
FINISHING POINT: Canyon de Chelly/Canyon del Muerto
TOTAL MILEAGE: Approximately 18 miles (one-way) for Canyon de Chelly, add approximately 12 miles (one-way) for Canyon del Muerto
UNPAVED MILEAGE: All unpaved
DRIVING TIME: 3 hours minimum for both canyons
ELEVATION RANGE: 5,500–6,200 feet
USUALLY OPEN: May to October
BEST TIME TO TRAVEL: May to October
DIFFICULTY RATING: 5
SCENIC RATING: 10
REMOTENESS RATING: +0

Special Attractions

- A rare chance to explore a beautiful canyon in the company of a Navajo guide.
- Many cliff dwellings, pictographs, and petroglyphs.
- Personal guided tour of the canyon in your own vehicle.

History

Canyon de Chelly is best known for its strikingly red, sheer cliffs streaked by desert varnish. Two forces—stream cutting and land uplifting—created the cliff walls of this marvelous canyon. The canyon walls are made of sandstone from the de Chelly Formation, which is more than 200 million years old. The canyon depth ranges from 30 feet to 1,000 feet. Canyon del Muerto, the principal tributary of Canyon de Chelly, received its name when James Stevenson, with a Smithsonian Institution expedition, found the re-

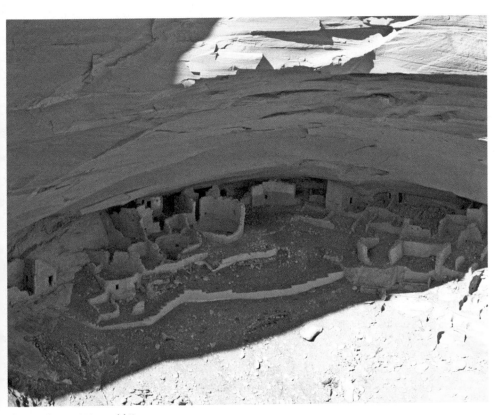

Mummy Cave ruins in Canyon del Muerto

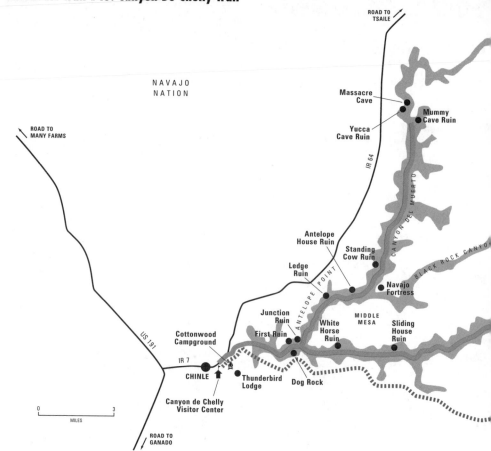

mains of prehistoric Indian burials. The name means "canyon of the dead."

Canyon de Chelly is actually a Spanish corruption of the Navajo word *tsegi* (or *tseyi*), which means "rock canyon" or "in the rock." Over time the pronunciation of the word "de Chelly" has changed from "day shay-yee" to "d'SHAY." Chinle, the name of the town just west of the canyon, comes from another Navajo word, *ch'inli*, which simply refers to the mouth of the canyon. In 1882, this town began as a trading post but over the years has grown into a larger town, currently serving as the gateway to Canyon de Chelly.

Canyon de Chelly is as rich in history as it is in beauty. The ruins and rock art of a people referred to as Basketmakers can be found there. These people lived here from about 200 B.C. to about A.D. 750. The Basketmak-

er people made way for the cliff-dwelling Pueblo people, who lived between A.D. 750 and 1300. Drought then ravaged the land, and it is possible that this drought drove the Pueblo people to abandon their cliff dwellings. A myriad of other conjectures have been offered to explain their disappearance, including overcrowding, disease, and war. They scattered across the Southwest, becoming the ancestors for some of Arizona's and New Mexico's Pueblo Indians. The Navajo (see page 226), the next people to inhabit this colorful canyon, arrived around A.D. 1700. Their tranquility was destroyed first by other Indians, then by encroaching Spanish settlers, and finally by the U.S. Army. A year after their defeat in 1863, the Navajo were forced out of their homeland in a bitter march known as "The Long Walk." On June

1, 1868, a peace treaty signed between the Navajo and the United States permitted them to return to their homeland, including the beautiful Canyon de Chelly.

Description

Canyon de Chelly is one of the most spectacular and awe-inspiring settings in Arizona. Part of its magic arises from the towering red sandstone walls and spires, the ancient ruins, and a sandy, winding trail; but Canyon de Chelly is more than just scenery. The Diné, as the Navajo people call themselves, continue to live in the canyon and the surrounding area, and the glimpse that we are allowed into their lives enhances an already special experience.

This trail is different from all the others in this book in that you are not permitted to enter the canyon unless a Navajo guide accompanies you. This requirement includes vehicle touring, hiking, and horseback riding. The only exception to this rule is the White House Ruin Hiking Trail, accessed from the South Rim Drive.

There are a variety of tours available. It is possible to sign up for a vehicle tour run by one of the hotels or to hire horses or hike for an hour or several days. For people wishing to enter the canyon via vehicle, the best way is

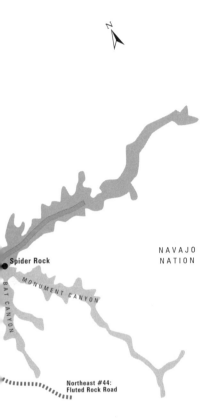

NAVAJO
NATION

Spider Rock

MONUMENT CANYON

BAT CANYON

Northeast #44:
Fluted Rock Road

Mummy Cave Ruin in Canyon del Muerto

White House ruin in Canyon de Chelly

undoubtedly to hire a guide to accompany you in your own 4WD vehicle. The advantages of this arrangement over the hotel-run tours are obvious: flexibility, a more personalized experience, and the fun of driving your own vehicle. The cost is reasonable, and for a family it is generally less than the hotel tours. Note that pets are not allowed within the canyon, even if confined to a vehicle.

You can arrange for a Navajo guide at the Canyon de Chelly Visitor Center, where you can also see displays on life within the canyon and its history. Usually you do not need to book ahead. The guides are waiting at the center; but if you are visiting on a long weekend or have limited time, it is possible to call ahead. Visitors wanting to take multiday hiking trips must call ahead.

The minimum amount of time required is three hours, which is barely enough to scratch the surface of what the canyon offers. Six hours allows for a leisurely tour to the end of Canyon del Muerto and back and partway up Canyon de Chelly. Both canyons have a lot to offer.

Mile-by-mile details of the trails within both canyons are not given here; they would be redundant because the Navajo guide directs you along the route and explains the features that you will see. Only an overview is given here.

The trail commences a short distance past the visitor center, turning off the paved road into the sandy mouth of the canyon. This first section is what gives the trail its difficulty rating of 5. The sand is very loose and extremely deep and limits this trail to high-clearance 4WD vehicles only. Lower tire pressures are recommended. At this stage the canyon is shallow, but it quickly deepens as you progress.

The intersection of Canyon de Chelly and Canyon del Muerto is reached after 4 miles and you have the choice of continuing in Canyon de Chelly or taking the Canyon del Muerto trail.

In Canyon del Muerto the track becomes easier and the sand less deep. The trail turns to a formed dirt trail that winds through the deepening canyon, past many cliff dwellings, rock formations, petroglyphs, and pictographs. Your guide will direct you to the best ones. At many of the larger ruins, such as Antelope House Ruin, people (often children) sell jewelry and souvenirs. If you buy from the people in the canyon, all the profits go directly to the Navajo themselves. However, quality can vary widely. The vehicle trail in Canyon del Muerto ends at Mummy Cave, one of the largest ancient Pueblo ruins in the canyon.

Canyon de Chelly is still used by the Navajo for farming, and the trail passes alongside many of the small traditional fields, most planted with corn. Many plots have either a traditional hogan or a smaller, summer shade shelter. The farms in the canyon, which are often only occupied during the summer months, are passed down through the daughters of the family. Farms have to be actively worked if the owner is to retain the holding; another person who has a traditional claim to the area can take possession of any unworked plot. Flocks of sheep and goats and other livestock roam the canyons.

The spur that travels up Canyon de Chelly passes the famous White House Ruin as well as the base of Spider Woman Rock. In either case, you return the way you came in.

Guides charge $15 per hour, with a minimum of three hours. A gratuity is appropriate. One guide can escort multiple vehicles, although for maximum benefit it helps if they are equipped with CB radios to share the commentary.

Current Road Information
Canyon de Chelly National Monument
PO Box 588
Chinle, AZ 86503-0588
(928) 674-5500

Maps References
BLM   Canyon de Chelly
USGS 1:24,000   Chinle, Del Muerto,
       Three Turkey Canyon, Mummy
       Cave Ruins, Spider Rock
       1:100,000 Canyon de Chelly
Maptech CD-ROM: Northeast
       Arizona/Navajo County
Arizona Atlas & Gazetteer, p. 35

Pictographs near the trail

Arizona Road & Recreation Atlas, pp. 31, 65
Recreational Map of Arizona
Other: Canyon de Chelly National
Monument Park Map

NORTHEAST REGION TRAIL #46

Tunitcha Mountains Trail

STARTING POINT: IR 13, 12.1 miles northeast
of the intersection with IR 12
FINISHING POINT: IR 12, 8 miles south of
intersection of IR 12 and IR 64
TOTAL MILEAGE: 18 miles
UNPAVED MILEAGE: 18 miles
DRIVING TIME: 2 hours
ELEVATION RANGE: 7,400–9,000 feet
USUALLY OPEN: Year-round
BEST TIME TO TRAVEL: Dry weather
DIFFICULTY RATING: 2
SCENIC RATING: 9
REMOTENESS RATING: +0

Special Attractions

- Optional 3-rated spur to Roof Butte Fire
  Lookout.
- Easy trail that travels along the pictur-
  esque Tsaile Creek.
- Tsaile Butte and the Tunitcha Mountains.
- Views of Shiprock from the north end of
  the trail.
- View golden aspen on the north end of
  the trail in early fall.

Description

This roughly graded road takes you through
the green Tunitcha Mountains, part of the
larger north-south Chuska Mountains.
Along the way, the trail passes through the
peaceful rural landscape of the Navajo Nation, offers views of Shiprock and Tsaile
Butte, and has an optional 3-rated climb to
the fire lookout at Roof Butte.

The trail commences by leaving Indian
Road 13 and climbing around the north face
of Roof Butte, easily picked out by the communications masts on its summit. As it
climbs, the distinctive shape of isolated

The trail weaves through ponderosa pine below Roof Butte

A lush meadow fed by Tsaile Creek

Shiprock, with its resemblance to a ship under full sail, can be seen just over the border in New Mexico. This section also passes through many stands of aspen; in fall their golden leaves contrast with the green pines to form a tapestry of color.

After 2 miles, a well-used unmarked trail leads north and swiftly climbs to the top of Roof Butte and the communications masts and fire lookout there. This rocky, 3-rated spur trail stops at the end of a ridge (1.6 miles); but on the way you will have a clear view of the main trail ahead, winding its way along the valley close to Tsaile Creek. When the fire tower is manned you are usually welcome to climb the tower with the lookout's permission. This tower is only a few feet above the ground; the height and aspect of Roof Butte obviate the need for a tall structure.

Back on the main trail, the track follows the Tsaile Creek Valley, crossing the creek on occasion. Along the way you are likely to see flocks of grazing sheep and goats, either accompanied by mounted shepherds or, more likely, guarded only by shaggy sheepdogs. Small side trails that lead to private property are noted in the route directions only for navigational purposes. Those that lead only to private property have been omitted. Many Navajo live in the peaceful areas off this trail, and you can see their traditional hogans, corrals, and other buildings along the way. Don't be surprised if people stop to see if you are all right or if you need directions along the way. This lightly traveled road sees few visitors.

The trail turns toward prominent Tsaile Butte and travels on a smooth gravel road for the last few miles before rejoining Indian Road 12 a few miles south of Tsaile Lake. Campers may take advantage of the campground at Tsaile Lake, and fishermen may fish for trout. Tsaile means "water entering the rock." The town of Tsaile is close to the head of the canyon.

One advantage of this trail is the section of paved road that approaches the north end. If you approach from Chinle, the 12 miles of road that run from Indian Road 12 at

The end of the spur trail on Roof Butte overlooking Tsaile Creek

Lukachukai (which means "field of reeds") to the start of the trail is one of the most dramatic and picturesque stretches in Arizona. This road climbs through a gap in the red rock face of the Chuska Mountains, passing pillars and cliffs of red sandstone—a landscape more commonly associated with the Sedona region. This stretch used to be a rough, narrow dirt road, but when the trail was surveyed, it was in the middle of extensive works to widen and pave the road. Some of the quiet, intimate character will be lost, but this stretch of road will still rate highly for scenic value in anyone's eyes.

Current Road Information
Navajo Nation Parks and Recreation
PO Box 2520
Window Rock, AZ 86515
(928) 871-6647

Map References
BLM   Canyon de Chelly
USGS 1:24,000   Roof Butte, Tsaile Butte,
         Tsaile, Lower Wheatfields
         1:100,000 Canyon de Chelly
Maptech CD-ROM: Northeast
         Arizona/Navajo County
Arizona Atlas & Gazetteer, p. 27
Arizona Road & Recreation Atlas, pp. 31, 65
Recreational Map of Arizona

Route Directions

▼ 0.0   From IR 13, 12.1 miles northeast of the
            intersection with IR 12, zero trip meter
            and turn north across cattle guard on
            graded dirt road. IR 7500 is painted
            on a tree at the intersection.
2.0 ▲   Trail ends at the T-intersection with
            paved IR 13. Turn left for Lukachukai
            and Tsaile; turn right for Red Rocks.
            GPS: N36°28.40′ W109°05.92′

▼ 1.1   SO Spring on left; then track on right.
0.9 ▲   SO Track on left; then spring on right.
▼ 1.2   SO Track on left.
0.8 ▲   SO Track on right.
▼ 1.3   SO Track on left is #7174.
0.7 ▲   SO Track on right is #7174.

Northeast Trail #46:
Tunitcha Mountains Trail

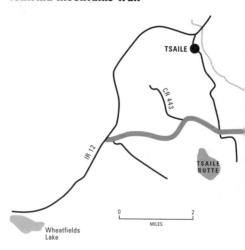

GPS: N36°27.65′ W109°04.98′

▼ 1.4   SO Track on left.
0.6 ▲   SO Track on right.
▼ 1.6   SO Track on right; then track on left.
0.4 ▲   SO Track on right; then track on left.
▼ 1.7   SO Track on left.
0.3 ▲   SO Track on right.
▼ 2.0   BL Track on right goes to Roof Butte Fire
            Lookout (1.6 miles). Zero trip meter.
            There is no sign, but the turn is well
            used and in a small clearing. There is a
            wooden post at the intersection.
0.0 ▲   Continue to the northeast.
            GPS: N36°27.19′ W109°05.29′

Spur to Roof Butte Fire Lookout

▼ 0.0   Turn north on the unmarked well-used
            trail and zero trip meter. Immediately
            small track on left.
            GPS: N36°27.19′ W109°05.29′

▼ 0.1   BR Track on left.
▼ 0.8   SO Track on left.
            GPS: N36°27.56′ W109°05.85′

▼ 1.2   SO Closure gate; open when the tower
            is manned.
            GPS: N36°27.59′ W109°05.63′

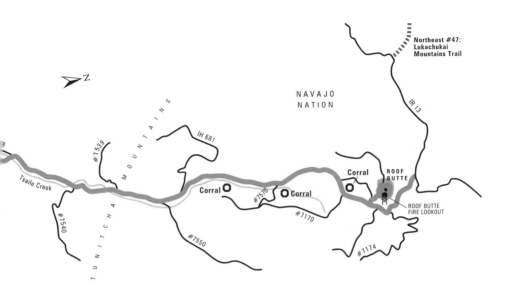

▼ 1.4   SO   Communications towers on right. The fire lookout is on the right.

▼ 1.6   UT   Spur ends at farther towers. Retrace your steps back to the main trail.
         GPS: N36°27.61' W109°05.55'

Continuation of Main Trail

▼ 0.0   Continue to the southwest.

5.7 ▲   BR   Track on left goes to Roof Butte Fire Lookout (1.6 miles). Zero trip meter. There is no sign but the turn is well used and in a small clearing. There is a wooden post at the intersection.

▼ 0.6   SO   Graded dirt road on left is #7170; corral on right.

5.1 ▲   SO   Graded dirt road on right is #7170; corral on left.
         GPS: N36°26.66' W109°05.63'

▼ 0.8   SO   Track on right and track on left.

4.9 ▲   SO   Track on right and track on left.

▼ 1.0   SO   Track on right.

4.7 ▲   SO   Track on left.

▼ 1.1   SO   Track on right.

4.6 ▲   SO   Track on left.

▼ 1.2   SO   Track on right is #7500-N.

4.5 ▲   SO   Track on left is #7500-N.
         GPS: N36°26.48' W109°06.18'

▼ 1.4   SO   Track on left.

4.3 ▲   SO   Track on right.

▼ 1.5   SO   Track on left and track on right.

4.2 ▲   SO   Track on left and track on right.

▼ 2.3   SO   Cross over creek.

3.4 ▲   SO   Cross over creek.
         GPS: N36°25.57' W109°06.33'

▼ 2.4   SO   Track on left; then cross over creek.

3.3 ▲   SO   Cross over creek; then track on right.

▼ 2.7   SO   Corral on left.

3.0 ▲   SO   Corral on right.

▼ 2.9   SO   Track on left is #7570.

2.8 ▲   SO   Track on right is #7570.
         GPS: N36°25.09' W109°06.15'

▼ 4.2   SO   Corral on left.

1.5 ▲   SO   Corral on right.

▼ 4.6   SO   Track on right.

1.1 ▲   SO   Track on left.

▼ 5.7   SO   Major graded road on the right is IH 681. A small sign points right to Geese Nest Pond. Zero trip meter. The highway sign is faded and very difficult to read.

0.0 ▲   Continue to the northwest.
         GPS: N36°22.76' W109°06.12'

▼ 0.0   Continue to the southeast; track on left.

4.8 ▲   BR   Track on right and major graded road

The trail with Tsaile Butte in the distance

on the left is IH 681. A small sign points right to Roof Butte. Zero trip meter.

▼ 0.4   SO   Track on left.
4.4 ▲   SO   Track on right.
▼ 0.5   SO   Well-used track on left is #7550.
4.3 ▲   BL   Well-used track on right is #7550.
      GPS: N36°22.30' W109°05.99'

▼ 0.8   SO   Track on right.
4.0 ▲   SO   Track on left.
▼ 1.3   SO   Track on right.
3.5 ▲   SO   Track on left.
▼ 1.6   SO   Track on left; then track on right is #7539.
3.2 ▲   SO   Track on left is #7539; then track on right.
      GPS: N36°21.35' W109°06.48'

▼ 1.9   SO   Cross over Tsaile Creek.
2.9 ▲   SO   Cross over Tsaile Creek.
      GPS: N36°21.12' W109°06.55'

▼ 2.1   SO   Track on left.
2.7 ▲   SO   Track on right.
▼ 2.2   SO   Track on right.
2.6 ▲   SO   Track on left.
▼ 3.0   SO   Track on left is #7540.
1.8 ▲   SO   Track on right is #7540.
      GPS: N36°20.34' W109°06.77'

▼ 3.1   SO   Cross over Tsaile Creek.
1.7 ▲   SO   Cross over Tsaile Creek.
▼ 3.2   SO   Track on left.
1.6 ▲   SO   Track on right.
▼ 3.9   SO   Track on right.
0.9 ▲   SO   Track on left.
▼ 4.2   SO   Track on left.
0.6 ▲   SO   Track on right.
▼ 4.4   SO   Track on right; then track on left.
0.4 ▲   SO   Track on right; then track on left.
▼ 4.5   SO   Track on left.
0.3 ▲   SO   Track on right.
▼ 4.8   TL   Track on left; then graded road on left is IR 68. Turn left down the graded road and zero trip meter. View directly ahead to Tsaile Butte.
0.0 ▲   Continue to the northeast.
      GPS: N36°18.90' W109°07.81'

▼ 0.0   Continue to the southeast and cross over Tsaile Creek.
3.1 ▲   TR   Cross over creek; then T-intersection with graded road. Turn right and zero trip meter. Immediately track on right.
▼ 0.8   SO   Track on left.
2.3 ▲   SO   Track on right.
▼ 1.1   SO   Track on left; then track on right.
2.0 ▲   SO   Track on left; then track on right.
▼ 1.8   SO   Track on left.
1.3 ▲   SO   Track on right.
▼ 1.9   SO   Two tracks on right.
1.2 ▲   SO   Two tracks on left.
▼ 2.1   SO   Track on left and track on right. Tsaile Butte is on the left.
1.0 ▲   SO   Track on left and track on right. Tsaile Butte is on the right.
      GPS: N36°17.14' W109°07.64'

▼ 2.8   SO   Track on left; then track on right.
0.3 ▲   SO   Track on left; then track on right.
▼ 3.0   SO   Track on right.
0.1 ▲   SO   Track on left.
▼ 3.1   BL   Graded road on right is CR 443. Zero trip meter.
0.0 ▲   Continue to the northwest.
      GPS: N36°16.34' W109°08.05'

▼ 0.0   Continue to the southeast.
2.4 ▲   BR   Graded road on left is CR 443. Zero trip meter.
▼ 0.3   SO   Track on left.
2.1 ▲   SO   Track on right.
▼ 0.5   SO   Track on left.
1.9 ▲   SO   Track on right.
▼ 1.0   SO   Track on left.
1.4 ▲   SO   Track on right.
▼ 1.6   SO   Pinnache Lake on right (dry).
0.8 ▲   SO   Pinnache Lake on left (dry).
      GPS: N36°15.09' W109°07.80'

▼ 2.2   SO   Graded road on left.
0.2 ▲   BL   Graded road on right; bear left, remaining on IR 19. There is a faded route marker past the junction.
▼ 2.3   SO   Cross over wash; then track on left.
0.1 ▲   SO   Track on right; then cross over wash.
▼ 2.4   Trail ends at the intersection with paved IR 12. Turn right for Tsaile; turn left for Wheatfields Lake.

0.0 ▲ Trail starts on IR 12. Zero trip meter and turn north on graded dirt road marked #7500. The dirt road has been realigned and the turn is now 0.2 miles north of the original marker to Roof Butte, 0.2 miles north of Wheatfields Chapter house and approximately 3 miles north of Wheatfields Lake.
GPS: N36°14.43' W109°07.72'

NORTHEAST REGION TRAIL #47

Lukachukai Mountains Trail

STARTING POINT: IR 13, 8.5 miles northeast of the intersection with IR 12
FINISHING POINT: IR 33, in Cove
TOTAL MILEAGE: 11.2 miles
UNPAVED MILEAGE: 11.2 miles
DRIVING TIME: 1.5 hours
ELEVATION RANGE: 6,400–9,000 feet
USUALLY OPEN: Year-round
BEST TIME TO TRAVEL: Dry weather
DIFFICULTY RATING: 3
SCENIC RATING: 10
REMOTENESS RATING: +1

Special Attractions
■ The red rock of the Lukachukai Mountains.
■ Aspen viewing in the fall.
■ Extremely scenic smaller trail.

Description
This lightly traveled trail is smaller and rougher than many in the Navajo Nation. It also travels through some of the most breathtaking scenery in the Navajo Nation—the red sandstone cliffs and buttes of the Lukachukai Mountains.

The trail leaves Indian Road 13 just south of Buffalo Pass and for the first 1.6 miles travels through the pine and aspen forest. The shallow pan of Big Lake is passed, and briefly the trail passes through an open area in the forest that has many small natural ponds, some of which are carpeted with water lilies.

The trail drops in standard from a roughly graded road to a smaller, formed, single-track. It starts to descend through more aspens and pines, twisting its way through the red rock canyons on the north side of the Lukachukai Mountains along a shelf road that is only wide enough for one vehicle. The trail surface is definitely suitable for dry weather only, and the route should not be attempted in wet weather. Navigation can be a little tricky as the trail descends; none of the tracks are marked and there are many side trails. Pay close attention to the route description to avoid going the wrong way.

As the road descends, the view to the northwest opens up to reveal a glorious panorama of contrasting colors: the red sandstone of the mountains, the dark green of the oaks and junipers, and the muted yellow of the plain below. Far below, the settlement of Cove sits cradled in the natural bowl formed by the mountains. To reach it, the trail descends steeply along a series of switchbacks and through a gap in the bowl, the roughest and most uneven part of the trail. Black Rock, to the north, is easily recognizable by its dark color among all the red pinnacles that surround it. Shiprock, visible to the east, stands alone on the plains in New Mexico.

The trail ends at paved Indian Road 33 in Cove. From this point, the road is paved all the way back to the main highway to Shiprock.

Current Road Information
Navajo Nation Parks and Recreation
PO Box 2520
Window Rock, AZ 86515
(928) 871-6647

Map References
BLM   Canyon de Chelly, Rock Point
USGS 1:24,000 Lukachukai, Cove
            1:100,000 Canyon de Chelly,
            Rock Point
Maptech CD-ROM: Northeast
            Arizona/Navajo County
Arizona Atlas & Gazetteer, p. 27
Arizona Road & Recreation Atlas, pp. 31, 65

The shelf road provides some fabulous views of the Carrizo Mountains

This natural bowl is the location of the settlement of Cove

Route Directions:

▼ 0.0   From IR 13, 8.5 miles from the intersection with IR 12, zero trip meter and
turn northwest on graded dirt road,
just south of Buffalo Pass Picnic
Ground. Road is unmarked.

3.3 ▲   Trail ends on IR 13. Turn left for Red
Rocks; turn right for Lukachukai and
Tsaile.

     GPS: N36°28.06′ W109°09.27′

▼ 0.1   SO Track on right along power lines.

3.2 ▲   SO Track on left along power lines.

▼ 0.2   SO Track on right; then track on left.

3.1 ▲   SO Track on left; then track on right.

▼ 0.5   SO Well-used track on right and small
track on left.

2.8 ▲   SO Small track on right and well-used
track on left. Continue straight on,
following the homemade sign on the
tree to Lukachukai.

     GPS: N36°28.42′ W109°09.64′

▼ 0.8   SO Track on left.

2.5 ▲   SO Track on right.

▼ 0.9   SO Track on right; then track on left is
#7565.

2.4 ▲   SO Track on right is #7565; then track
on left.

     GPS: N36°28.43′ W109°10.06′

▼ 1.1   SO Track on left.

2.2 ▲   SO Track on right.

▼ 1.6   SO Track on left.

1.7 ▲   SO Track on right.

▼ 1.7   SO Track on right.

1.6 ▲   SO Track on left.

▼ 1.8   SO Track on left.

1.5 ▲   SO Track on right.

▼ 1.9   SO The depression on the left is Big Lake
(often dry).

1.4 ▲   SO The depression on the right is Big Lake
(often dry).

     GPS: N36°28.68′ W109°10.73′

▼ 2.1   SO Cross over creek.

1.2 ▲   SO Cross over creek.

▼ 2.2   SO Track on right past corral.

1.1 ▲   SO Track on left past corral.

▼ 2.3   SO Track on right and track on left.

1.0 ▲   SO Track on left and track on right.

▼ 2.4	SO	Pond on right.
0.9 ▲	SO	Pond on left.
▼ 2.5	SO	Pond on left.
0.8 ▲	SO	Pond on right.
▼ 2.7	SO	Track on right is #N4.
0.6 ▲	SO	Track on left is #N4.
▼ 2.8	SO	Corral on right.
0.5 ▲	SO	Corral on left.
▼ 3.3	SO	4-way intersection. Small track on left; well-used tracks straight on and to the right. A homemade sign is affixed to

an aspen at the intersection. Zero trip meter and continue straight up the hill, following the sign to Cove and Boundary Butte.

| 0.0 ▲ | | Continue to the east. |

GPS: N36°29.51′ W109°11.47′

| ▼ 0.0 | | Continue to the west. |
| 3.4 ▲ | SO | 4-way intersection. Small track on right; well-used tracks straight on and to the left. Continue straight uphill and |

The trail snakes down a roughly cut shelf road towards Cove

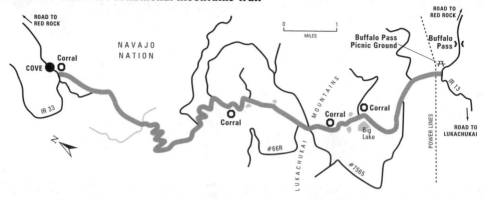

▼ 0.1	SO	Track on left.
3.3 ▲	SO	Track on right.
▼ 0.2	SO	Track on left is #66-R.
3.2 ▲	SO	Track on right is #66-R.
▼ 0.3	SO	Track on right.
3.1 ▲	SO	Track on left.
▼ 0.7	SO	Track on right.
2.7 ▲	SO	Track on left.
▼ 0.8	SO	Pond on right.
2.6 ▲	SO	Pond on left.
▼ 0.9	SO	Track on right.
2.5 ▲	SO	Track on left.
▼ 1.2	SO	Pond on left; then track on right.
2.2 ▲	SO	Track on left; then pond on right.
▼ 1.4	SO	Two tracks on right; trail starts to head downhill.
2.0 ▲	SO	Two tracks on left; top of hill.
▼ 1.8	SO	Track on right and corral on left.
1.6 ▲	SO	Track on left and corral on right.

GPS: N36°30.77′ W109°11.85′

▼ 2.3	SO	Track on right.
1.1 ▲	SO	Track on left.
▼ 3.4	SO	Well-used roughly graded narrow trail to the right. Intersection is unmarked. Zero trip meter and continue straight on.
0.0 ▲		Continue to the east.

GPS: N36°31.09′ W109°12.48′

▼ 0.0		Continue to the west.
4.5 ▲	SO	Well-used roughly graded narrow trail to the left. Intersection is unmarked. Zero trip meter and continue straight on.
▼ 0.3	SO	Track on left.
4.2 ▲	SO	Track on right.

▼ 0.5	SO	Track on right.
4.0 ▲	SO	Track on left.
▼ 1.1	SO	Track on left.
3.4 ▲	SO	Track on right.

GPS: N36°31.53′ W109°13.31′

▼ 2.5	SO	Cross through wash.
2.0 ▲	SO	Cross through wash.

GPS: N36°31.89′ W109°13.05′

▼ 2.8	SO	Track on left and track on right.
1.7 ▲	SO	Track on left and track on right.
▼ 3.1	SO	Track on right.
1.4 ▲	SO	Track on left.
▼ 3.3	SO	Track on right.
1.2 ▲	SO	Track on left.
▼ 3.4	SO	Track on right.
1.1 ▲	SO	Track on left.
▼ 3.7	SO	Track on right; then track on left.
0.8 ▲	SO	Track on left; then track on right.
▼ 3.9	SO	Track on right.
0.6 ▲	SO	Track on left.
▼ 4.4	SO	Corral and track on right.
0.1 ▲	SO	Corral and track on left.
▼ 4.5	TR	Trail ends at the T-intersection with the paved road in Cove. A very large arch is ahead and slightly to the south. Turn right to exit to Red Rock and IR 63.
0.0 ▲		From IR 33 in Cove, zero trip meter and turn southeast over cattle guard onto graded dirt road, marked IH N336. The sign is clear and easy to read.

GPS: N36°33.48′ W109°13.04′

Selected Further Reading

Alden, Peter, and Peter Friederici. *National Audubon Society: Field Guide to the Southwestern States.* New York: Alfred A. Knopf, 1999.

Anderson, Dorothy Daniels. *Arizona Legends and Lore.* Phoenix: Golden West Publishers, 1991.

Annerino, John. *Adventuring in Arizona: The Sierra Club Travel Guide to the Grand Canyon State.* San Francisco: Sierra Club Books, 1991.

Arizona: A State Guide. New York: Hastings House, 1940.

Arizona: The Grand Canyon State. 2 Vols. N.p.: Western States Historical Publishers, Inc., 1975.

Bahti, Tom, and Mark Bahti. *Southwestern Indian Tribes.* Las Vegas: KC Publications, 1997.

Barker, Scott. *Arizona off the Beaten Path.* Old Saybrook, Conn.: The Globe Pequot Press, 1996.

Barnes, Will C. *Arizona Place Names.* Tucson, Ariz.: The University of Arizona Press, 1988.

Billingsley, George H., Spamer, Earle E., and Menkes, Don. *Quest for the Pillar of Gold: The Mines and Miners of the Grand Canyon.* N.p.: Grand Canyon Association, 1997.

Bischoff, Mike. *Touring Arizona Hot Springs.* Helena, Mont.: Falcon Publishing, Inc., 1999.

Brant, Keith L. Jr. *History of the Atchison, Topeka and Santa Fe Railway.* London: University of Nebraska Press, 1974.

Burke, Larry. *Arizona Boonies: The Arizona Even the Zonies Don't Know About.* Phoenix: Niche Publishing, 1998.

Canyon De Chelly National Monument: Motoring Guide to the South and North Rims. N.p.: Southwest Parks and Monument Association, 1999.

Canyon De Chelly Official Map and Guide. N.p.: U.S. Department of the Interior, n.d.

Canyon Overlook: A Visitor's Guide to Canyon de Chelly National Monument. N.p.: N.p., n.d.

Chronic, Halka. *Roadside Geology of Arizona.* Missoula, Mont.: Mountain Press Publishing Company, 1983.

Cook, James E., Sam Negri, and Marshall Trimble. *Travel Arizona: The Back Roads.* 3rd ed. Edited by Dean Smith and Wesley Holden. Phoenix: Book Division of Arizona Highways Magazine, 1994.

Cowgill, Pete. *Back Roads and Beyond.* 2nd ed. Tucson, Ariz.: Broken Toe Press, 1997.

Cross, Jack L., Elizabeth H. Shaw, and Kathleen Scheifele, eds. *Arizona: Its People and Resources.* Tucson, Ariz.: the University of Arizona Press, 1960.

Crutchfield, James A. *It Happened in Arizona.* Helena, Mont.: Falcon Press Publishing Co., 1994.

Dale, Edward Everett. *The Indians of the Southwest.* London: University of Oklahoma Press, 1949.

Dunning, Charles H. *Rocks to Riches.* N.p.: Southwest Publishing Company, Inc., 1959.

Eastep, Alan, and Ron Locke. *Bradshaw Mountains Back Roads.* Litchfield Park, Ariz.: Back Road Press, 1996.

Etter, Patricia A. *To California on the Southern Route 1849: A History and Annotated Bibliography.* Spokane, Wash.: The Arthur H. Clark Company, 1998.

Farrell, Robert J., and Bob Albano, eds. *Wild West Collections.* 4 vols. Phoenix: Book Division of Arizona Highways Magazine, 1997–99.

Fireman, Bert M. *Arizona: Historic Land.* New York: Alfred A. Knof, 1982.

Florin, Lambert. *Ghost Towns of the West.* New York: Promontory Press, 1993.

Granger, Byrd Howell, *Arizona's Names: X Marks the Place.* N.p.: Falconer Publishing Company, 1983.

Grubbs, Bruce. *Camping Arizona.* Helena, Mont.: Falcon Publishing, Inc., 1999.

Hait, Pam. *Shifra Stein's Day Trips from Phoenix, Tucson, and Flagstaff.* Old Saybrook, Conn.: The Globe Pequot Press, 1986.

Heatwole, Thelma. *Arizona off the Beaten Path!.* Phoenix: Golden West Publishers, 1982.

————. *Ghost Towns and Historical Haunts in Arizona*. Phoenix: Golden West Publishers, 1981.

Hernandez, Luis F. Aztlan: *The Southwest and Its Peoples*. Rochelle Park, N.J.: Hayden Book Company, Inc., 1975.

Hinton, Richard J. *The Handbook to Arizona: Its Resources, History, Towns, Mines, Ruins and Scenery*. Tucson, Ariz.: Arizona Silhouettes, 1954.

Hirschfelder, Arlene. *Native Americans: A History in Pictures*. New York: Dorling Kindersley Publishing, Inc., 2000.

Hoxie, Frederick E., ed. *Encyclopedia of North American Indians*. Boston: Houghton Mifflin Company, 1996.

Jaeger, Edmund C. *Desert Wildlife*. Stanford, Calif.: Stanford University Press, 1950.

Kosik, Fran. *Native Roads*. Tucson, Ariz.: Treasure Chest Books, 1996.

Leland, Hanchett L., Jr. *Catch the Stage to Phoenix*. Phoenix: Pine Rim Publishing, 1998.

Lockwood, Frank C. *Pioneer Days in Arizona*. New York: The Macmillan Company, 1932.

————. *Thumbnail Sketches of Famous Arizona Desert Riders 1538–1946*. Tucson, Ariz.: University of Arizona, 1946.

Love, Frank. *Mining Camps and Ghost Towns*. N.p.: Westernlore Press, 1974.

Marks, Paula Mitchell. *And Die in the West*. New York: Simon and Schuster Inc., 1989.

Martin, Douglas D. *Tombstone's "Epitaph."* London: University of Oklahoma Press, 1958.

Maurer, Stephen G. *Visitors Guide: Mogollon Rim*. Albuquerque, N.Mex.: Southwest Natural and Cultural Heritage Association, 1991.

————. *Visitors Guide: Coconino National Forest*. Albuquerque, N.Mex: Southwest Natural and Cultural Heritage Association, 1990.

McCarty, Kieran, ed. *A Frontier Documentary: Sonora and Tucson, 1821–1848*. Tucson, Ariz.: The University of Arizona Press, 1997.

Miller, Donald C. *Ghost Towns of the Southwest*. Boulder, Colo.: Pruett Publishing Company, 1980.

Mitchell, James R. *Gem Trails of Arizona*. Baldwin Park, Calif.: Gem Guides Book Co., 1995.

Mitchell, John D. *Lost Mines of the Great Southwest*. Glorieta, N. Mex.: The Rio Grande Press, Inc., 1933.

Morris, Eleanor, and Steve Cohen. *Adventure Guide to Arizona*. Edison, N. Jer.: Hunter Publishing, 1996.

Murbarger, Nell. *Ghost of the Adobe*. Tucson, Ariz.: Treasure Chest Publications, Inc., 1964.

Noble, David Grant. *Ancient Ruins of the Southwest*. Flagstaff, Ariz.: Northland Publishing, 1991.

Officer, James E. *Hispanic Arizona, 1536–1856*. Tucson, Ariz.: The University of Arizona Press, 1987.

Paher, Stanley W. *Western Arizona Ghost Towns*. Las Vegas: Nevada Publications, 1990.

Palatki Red Cliffs. N.p.: U.S. Forest Service, n.d.

Palatki Red Cliffs Tour Guide. N.p.: The Friends of the Forest, n.d.

Penfield, Thomas. *Dig Here!* San Antonio, Tex.: The Naylor Company, 1962.

Recreation Sites in Southwestern National Forests and Grasslands. N.p.: United States Department of Agriculture, n.d.

Ruland-Thorne, Kate. *Experience Sedona Legends and Legacies*. Sacramento, Calif.: Thorne Enterprises Publications, Inc., 1999.

Searchy, Paula. *Travel Arizona: The Scenic Byways*. Edited by Bob Albano, Evelyn Howell, and Laura A. Lawrie. Phoenix: Book Division of Arizona Highways Magazine, 1997.

Sheridan, Thomas E. *Arizona: A History*. London: The University of Arizona Press, 1995.

Sherman, James E., and Barbara H. Sherman. *Ghost Towns of Arizona*. Norman, Okla.: University of Oklahoma Press, 1969.

Snyder, Ernest E. *Prehistoric Arizona*. Phoenix: Golden West Publishers, 1987.

Taylor, Colin F. *The Native Americans: The Indigenous People of North America*. London: Thunder Bay Press, 1991.

Trimble, Marshall. *Arizona: A Cavalcade of History*. Tucson, Ariz.: Treasure Chest Publications, 1989.

————. *Arizona Adventure!*. Phoenix: Golden

West Publishers, 1982.

———. *Roadside History of Arizona.* Missoula, Mont.: Mountain Press Publishing Company, 1986.

Tweit, Susan J. *The Great Southwest Nature Factbook.* Anchorage: Alaska Northwest Books, 1992.

Varney, Philip. *Arizona Ghost Towns and Mining Camps.* Phoenix: Book Division of Arizona Highways Magazine, 1994.

———. *Arizona's Best Ghost Town.* Flagstaff, Ariz.: Northland Press, 1980.

Walker, Henry P., and Don Bufkin. *Historical Atlas of Arizona.* 2nd ed. London: University of Oklahoma Press, 1979.

Wagoner, Jay J. *Arizona's Heritage.* Salt Lake City: Peregrine Smith, Inc., 1977.

———. *Early Arizona: Prehistory to Civil War.* Tucson, Ariz.: The University of Arizona Press, 1975.

Wahmann, Russell. *Auto Road Log.* Cottonwood, Ariz.: Starlight Publishing, 1982.

Waldman, Carl. *Atlas of the North American Indian.* New York: Checkmark Books, 2000.

———. *Encyclopedia of Native American Tribes.* New York: Facts on File, 1988.

Ward, Geoffrey C. *The West: an Illustrated History.* Boston: Little, Brown and Company, 1996.

Warren, Scott S. *Exploring Arizona's Wild Areas.* Seattle: Mountaineers Books, 1996.

Weight, Harold O. *Lost Mines of Old Arizona.* Ridgecrest, Calif.: Hubbard Printing, 1959.

Wilderness and Primitive Areas in Southwestern National Forests. N.p.: United States Department of Agriculture, n.d.

Zauner, Phyllis. *Those Legendary Men of the Wild West.* Sacramento, Calif.: Zanel Publications, 1991.

Selected Web sources

Desert USA: http://www.desertusa.com

Flagstaff, Arizona, http://www.flagstaff.az.us/

Ghosttowns.com: http://www.ghosttowns.com

GORP.com, http://gorp.away.com

Jerome, Arizona: http://www.azjerome.com

National Center for Disease Control: Hantavirus Pulmonary Syndrome, http://www.cdc.gov/ncidad/diseases/hanta/hps/

Navajo Nation: http://www.navajo.org

Sedona, Arizona: http://www.experiencesedona.com

U.S. Bureau of Land Management, Arizona: http://www.blm.gov/az/

U.S. Forest Service, Southwestern Region (Arizona): http://www.fs.fed.us/r3

Photo Credits

Unless otherwise indicated in the following acknowledgments, all photographs were taken by Bushducks—Maggie Pindar and Donald McGann.

98 Arizona State Library, Archives & Public Records, Phoenix; **160** Corel.

Cover photography: Bushducks—Maggie Pinder and Donald McGann

About the Authors

Peter Massey grew up in the outback of Australia, where he acquired a life-long love of the backcountry. After retiring from a career in investment banking in 1986 at the age of thirty-five, he served as a director for a number of companies in the United States, the United Kingdom, and Australia. He moved to Colorado in 1993.

Jeanne Wilson was born and grew up in Maryland. After moving to New York City in 1980, she worked in advertising and public relations before moving to Colorado in 1993.

After traveling extensively in Australia, Europe, Asia, and Africa, the authors covered more than 80,000 miles touring the United States and the Australian outback between 1993 and 1997. This experience became the basis for creating the Backcountry Adventures and Trails guidebook series.

As the research team grew, a newcomer became a dedicated member of the Swagman team.

Angela Titus was born in Missouri and grew up in Virginia, where she attended the University of Virginia. She traveled extensively throughout the western states pursuing her interests in four-wheeling, hiking, and mountain biking. She moved to Alabama and worked for *Southern Living Magazine* traveling, photographing, and writing about the southeastern U.S. She moved to Colorado in 2002.

Since research for the Backcountry Adventures and Trails books began, Peter, Jeanne, and Angela have traveled more than 75,000 miles throughout the western states.

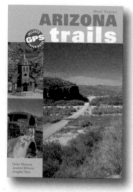
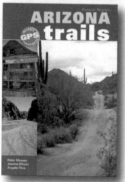

california trails
backroad guides

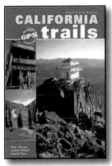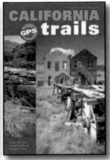

California Trails–Northern Sierra This book outlines detailed trail information for 55 off-road routes located near the towns of Sacramento (east), Red Bluff (east), Truckee, South Lake Tahoe, Sonora, Susanville, Chico, Oroville, Yuba City, Placerville, Stockton (east), Jackson, and Sonora. ISBN-10, 1-930193-23-8; ISBN-13, 978-1-930193-23-9; Price $19.95

California Trails–High Sierra This guidebook navigates and describes 50 trails located near the towns of Fresno (north), Oakhurst, Lone Pine, Bishop, Bridgeport, Coulterville, Mariposa, and Mammoth Lakes. ISBN-10, 1-930193-21-1; ISBN-13, 978-1-930193-21-5; Price $19.95

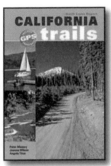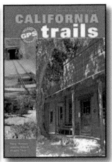

California Trails–North Coast This guide meticulously describes and rates 47 off-road routes located near the towns of Sacramento, Redding (west), Red Bluff, Clear Lake, McCloud, Mount Shasta, Yreka, Crescent City, and Fort Bidwell. ISBN-10, 1-930193-22-X; ISBN-13, 978-1-930193-22-2; Price $19.95

California Trails–Central Mountains This guide is comprised of painstaking detail and descriptions for 52 trails located near the towns of Big Sur, Fresno, San Luis Obispo, Santa Barbara, Bakersfield, Mojave, and Maricopa. ISBN-10, 1-930193-19-X; ISBN-13, 978-1-930193-19-2; Price $19.95

California Trails–South Coast This field guide includes meticulous trail details for 50 trails located near the towns of Los Angeles, San Bernardino, San Diego, Salton Sea, Indio, Borrego Springs, Ocotillo and Palo Verde. ISBN-10, 1-930193-24-6; ISBN-13, 978-1-930193-24-6; Price $19.95

California Trails–Desert This edition of our Trails series contains detailed trail information for 51 off-road routes located near the towns of Lone Pine (east), Panamint Springs, Death Valley area, Ridgecrest, Barstow, Baker and Blythe. ISBN-10, 1-930193-20-3; ISBN-13, 978-1-930193-20-8; Price $19.95

to order
call 800-660-5107 or
visit 4WDbooks.com

colorado trails
backroad guides

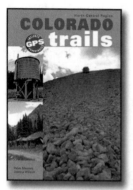

Colorado Trails—North-Central

This guidebook is composed of comprehensive statistics and descriptions of 28 trails, including 8 trails additional to those profiled in the Adventures Colorado book, around Breckenridge, Central City, Fraser, Dillon, Vail, Leadville, Georgetown, and Aspen. **ISBN-10, 1-930193-11-4; ISBN-13, 978-1-930193-11-6; Price $16.95**

Colorado Trails—South-Central

This edition of our Trails series includes meticulous trail details for 30 off-road routes located near the towns of Gunnison, Salida, Crested Butte, Buena Vista, Aspen, and the Sand Dunes National Monument. **ISBN-10, 1-930193-29-7; ISBN-13, 978-1-930193-29-1; Price $16.95**

Colorado Trails—Southwest

This field guide is comprised of painstaking details and descriptions for 31 trails, including 15 trails additional to those described in the Adventures Colorado book. Routes are located around Silverton, Ouray, Telluride, Durango, Lake City, and Montrose. **ISBN-10, 1-930193-32-7; ISBN-13, 978-1-930193-32-1; Price $19.95**

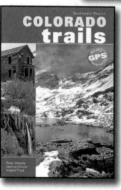

to order

call 800-660-5107 or
visit 4WDbooks.com

4WDBOOKS.COM

utah trails
backroad guides

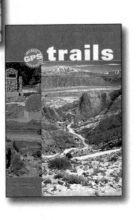

Utah Trails–Northern
This field guide includes meticulous trail details for 35 off-road routes near the towns of Vernal, Logan, Salt Lake City, Price, Wendover, Beaver, and Milford. **ISBN-10, 1-930139-30-0; ISBN-13, 978-1-930193-30-7; Price $16.95**

Utah Trails–Central
This volume is composed of comprehensive trail statistics for 34 trails near the towns of Green River, Richfield, Hanksville, Crescent Junction, and Castle Dale. **ISBN-10, 1-930193-31-9; ISBN-13, 978-1-930193-31-4; Price $16.95**

Utah Trails–Moab
This guidebook contains detailed trail information for 57 trails in and around Moab, Monticello, Canyonlands National Park, Arches National Park, Green River, Mexican Hat, Bluff, and Blanding. **ISBN-10, 1-930193-09-2; ISBN-13, 978-1-930193-09-3; Price $19.95**

Utah Trails–Southwest
This travel guide outlines detailed trail information for 49 off-road routes in the Four Corners region and around the towns of Escalante, St. George, Kanab, Boulder, Bryce Canyon, Hurricane, and Ticaboo. **ISBN-10, 1-930193-10-6; ISBN-13, 978-1-930193-10-9; Price $19.95**

to order
call 800-660-5107 or
visit 4WDbooks.com

4WDBOOKS.COM

backcountry adventures
guides

Each book in the award-winning *Adventures* series listed below is a beautifully crafted, high-quality, sewn, 4-color guidebook. In addition to meticulously detailed backcountry trail directions and maps of every trail and region, extensive information on the history of towns, ghost towns, and regional history is included. The guides provide wildlife information and photographs to help readers identify the great variety of native birds, plants, and animals they are likely to see. This series appeals to everyone who enjoys the backcountry: campers, anglers, four-wheelers, hikers, mountain bikers, snowmobilers, amateur prospectors, sightseers, and more...

Backcountry Adventures Northern California

Backcountry Adventures Northern California takes readers along 2,653 miles of back roads from the rugged peaks of the Sierra Nevada, through volcanic regions of the Modoc Plateau, to majestic coastal redwood forests. Trail history comes to life through accounts of outlaws like Black Bart; explorers like Ewing Young and James Beckwourth; and the biggest mass migration in America's history—the Gold Rush. Contains 152 trails, 640 pages, and 679 photos.
ISBN-10, 1-930193-25-4; ISBN-13, 978-1-930193-25-3
Price, $39.95.

Backcountry Adventures Southern California

Backcountry Adventures Southern California provides 2,970 miles of routes that travel through the beautiful mountain regions of Big Sur, across the arid Mojave Desert, and straight into the heart of the aptly named Death Valley. Trail history comes alive through the accounts of Spanish missionaries; eager prospectors looking to cash in during California's gold rush; and legends of lost mines. Contains 153 trails, 640 pages, and 645 photos.
ISBN-10, 1-930193-26-2; ISBN-13, 978-1-930193-26-0
Price, $39.95.

to order
call 800-660-5107 or
visit 4WDbooks.com

backcountry adventures
guides

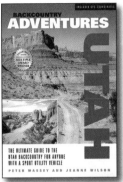

Backcountry Adventures Utah

Backcountry Adventures Utah navigates 3,721 miles through the spectacular Canyonlands region, to the top of the Uinta Range, across vast salt flats, and along trails unchanged since the riders of the Pony Express sped from station to station and daring young outlaws wreaked havoc on newly established stage lines, railroads, and frontier towns. Trail history comes to life through the accounts of outlaws like Butch Cassidy; explorers and mountain men; and early Mormon settlers. Contains 175 trails, 544 pages, and 532 photos.
ISBN-10, 1-930193-27-0; ISBN-13, 978-1-930193-27-7
Price, $39.95.

Backcountry Adventures Arizona

Backcountry Adventures Arizona guides readers along 2,671 miles of the state's most remote and scenic back roads, from the lowlands of the Yuma Desert to the high plains of the Kaibab Plateau. Trail history is colorized through the accounts of Indian warriors like Cochise and Geronimo; trailblazers; and the famous lawman Wyatt Earp. Contains 157 trails, 576 pages, and 524 photos.
ISBN-10, 1-930193-28-9; ISBN-13, 978-1-930193-28-4
Price, $39.95.

4WD Adventures Colorado

4WD Adventures Colorado takes readers to the Crystal River or over America's highest pass road, Mosquito Pass. This book identifies numerous lost ghost towns that speckle Colorado's mountains. Trail history is brought to life through the accounts of sheriffs and gunslingers like Bat Masterson and Doc Holliday; millionaires like Horace Tabor; and American Indian warriors like Chief Ouray. ains 71 trails, 232 pages, and 209 photos.
ISBN 0-9665675-5-2.
Price, $29.95.

to order
call 800-660-5107 or
visit 4WDbooks.com

4WD BOOKS.COM

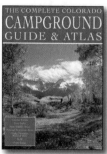

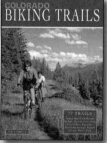

other
colorado outdoors
guides

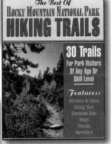

Colorado's Guide to Hunting

Colorado's backcountry is habitat for all sorts of game animals. The guide contains land regulations, permits needed, detailed directions and maps for the best places to hunt. **ISBN 0-930657-42-X; Price $14.95**

Best of Northern Colorado Hiking Trails

Contains 77 trails from short, easy day hikes to difficult backpacking adventures. The book covers Arapaho, Roosevelt, White River, and Routt National Forests. It includes directions, maps, trail length, elevation gains, and difficulty. **ISBN 0-930657-18-7; Price $12.95**

Best of Western Colorado Hiking Trails

Contains 50 trails from short, easy day hikes to difficult backpacking adventures. The book covers White River and Gunnison National Forests. It includes directions, maps, trail length, elevation gains, and difficulty. **ISBN 0-930657-17-9; Price $9.95**

Best of Rocky Mountain National Park Hiking Trails

Contains 30 trails for hikers of all skill levels from short, easy hikes to more difficult trails. It includes camping information, estimated hiking time, trail narratives, directions, maps, trail length, elevation gains, and difficulty. **ISBN 0-930657-39-X; Price $9.95**

Colorado Lakes & Reservoirs: Fishing and Boating Guide

Colorado is home to hundreds of natural and man-made lakes. This book provides information about 150 of them. Included are driving directions, maps, fishing regulations, lake size, fish species, boating ramps, camping facilities, and contact information. **ISBN 0-930657-00-4; Price $14.95**

to order
call 800-660-5107 or
visit 4WDbooks.com